Popular Culture
and Social Relations

Popular Culture and Social Relations

Edited by

TONY BENNETT,
School of Humanities, Griffith University

COLIN MERCER
School of Humanities, Griffith University

and

JANET WOOLLACOTT
Faculty of Social Sciences, Open University

Open University Press
Milton Keynes · Philadelphia

Open University Press
Open University Educational Enterprises Limited
12 Cofferidge Close
Stony Stratford
Milton Keynes MK11 1BY, England
and
242 Cherry Street
Philadelphia, PA 19106, USA

First Published 1986

British Library Cataloguing in Publication Data

Popular culture and social relations.
    1. Great Britain—Popular culture
    I. Bennett, Tony   II. Mercer, Colin
    III. Woollacott, Janet
    306'.1   DA589.4

    ISBN 0-335-15108-6

    ISBN 0-335-15107-8 PbK

Library of Congress Cataloging in Publication Data

Popular culture and social relations
    1. Popular culture—History—Addresses, essays, lectures. 2. Popular culture—Great Britain—History—Addresses, essays, lectures. I. Bennett, Tony. II. Mercer, Colin. III. Woollacott, Janet.
    HM101.P645 1986   306   85-28449
    ISBN 0-335-15108-6
    ISBN 0-335-15107-8 (pbk.)

Typeset by Colset Private Ltd, Singapore
Printed in Great Britain at the Alden Press Ltd, Oxford

Contents

Contents

Preface

If the train of events which made this book possible were traceable to a single originating source, they would ultimately be tracked down to the initiative of Arnold Kettle during his period as founding Professor of Literature at the Open University. With characteristic breadth of vision, Professor Kettle urged the University, during the early years of its history, to reserve a space within its undergraduate degree profile for the production of interdisciplinary courses. It was envisaged that such courses, drawing on the expertise of staff from different Faculties, would enable the University's students to become acquainted with new and developing areas of knowledge, particularly those emerging outside the frameworks of conventional disciplines or those requiring the contributions of a range of different disciplines for their conception and development. After several years vigorous campaigning on behalf of this concept, Professor Kettle was instrumental in securing the establishment of the Open University's U-Area, a small clutch of courses specifically earmarked for interdisciplinary course initiatives.

Shortly after this, toward the end of 1976, a small group of staff from the Arts and Social Science Faculties proposed a course on *Popular Culture* as suitable for inclusion in the U-Area. It seemed, to those of us involved, a 'natural' topic both in terms of the considerable array of disciplinary inputs such a course would require (history, sociology, literary studies, technology, musicology and the newly emerging discipline of cultural studies, to name but a few) as well as being ideally suited to take full advantage of the facility for teaching via television provided by the Open University's connection with the BBC. While the idea that popular culture might be regarded as worthy of serious academic study was viewed with a bemused scepticism in certain quarters, the proposal was widely enough supported to secure, two years later, its eventual approval. The work of detailed course planning and production began in 1979 and was completed in 1982 when, in the first year of its presentation, the course, code-named U203, attracted an enrolment of over a thousand students.

Popular Culture and Social Relations is not, in any direct or immediately evident way, an adaptation of the *Popular Culture* course, upon which we all worked for the best part of four years. Although envisaged as a project derived from this experience, it soon became clear to us that the course was too large and diverse for its concerns to be intelligibly addressed within the limits of a single anthology. Nor would it have been appropriate to attempt to do so. Rather than repeating work already done, and publicly available, our intention was to produce a collection of essays that would address and, hopefully, make a worthwhile and independent contribution to some of the main theoretical and political debates which currently characterise the study of popular culture. In short: an anthology that would stand, or fall, on its own merits rather than leaning unduly on the course which had served as its initial spawning ground.

None the less, the book does bear the impress of its origins, and in a number of important and interacting ways. Firstly, and most obviously, all of the contributors, except for one, helped in the making of U203, either as members of the Open University working on the course team or, if working elsewhere, as consultants. The one exception, Catherine Hall, is really no exception at all since, although not directly contributing to the Open University *Popular Culture* course, her historical and theoretical work on the relations between women and popular culture was widely and freely drawn on in many parts of the course. In all cases, however, the contributors, while addressing issues related to those that concerned them in the Open University context, have revised and extended their work to take account of more recent intellectual developments or, in some cases, have used their essays as springboards from which to open up new concerns.

Secondly, the essays collected in this volume reflect the broadly based interdisciplinary orientation of U203. So much so that it would be difficult to place any of the contributions neatly within a single disciplinary pigeon-hole. Stuart Hall's survey of the changing relations between popular culture and the state, for example, combines historical scholarship with a probing examination of some of the key intersections between cultural and political theory. Or, to take another example, Richard Middleton's approach to the study of popular music brings the combined contributions of semiology, musicology and psychoanalysis to bear on the vexed question of musical pleasure.

Most of all, though, the book reflects, and has been greatly enriched by, the collaborative conditions of working which the Open University has so effectively developed. Although this collection bears our names, as editors, and the names of the individual contributors, the work presented here is — and more so than usually — the product of a collective process. We owe our thanks, and freely give them, to all those associated with U203 — whether as members of the University, consultants, the part-time staff who teach the course or take part in its Summer School and last, although by no means least, its students. Far too many people to thank them all individually. However, particular thanks are due, first and foremost, to Jane Bailey, now Jane Clegg, for her unparalleled zeal and dedicated competence throughout all stages of U203's production, and to Lynn

Troughton for her patient help in preparing the early drafts of our sections of this book. Thanks, also, to Graham Martin for his unfailing friendship and sound advice on matters too many to mention; to Ken Thompson, whose idea it was in the first place; and to James Donald for selflessly assisting in many stages in the preparation of this book. To our colleagues at the BBC, especially Susan Boyd-Bowman and Vic Lockwood, thanks for their part in making the production of the television and radio components of U203 such an invigorating experience. And our thanks to the general staff in the School of Humanities of Griffith University for their help in preparing the final typescript, and to the School's Research Committee for assisting financially in the completion of the project.

Finally, to return to our starting point, our thanks, once again, to Arnold Kettle and our commiserations at the fact that, at the time of writing, his pioneering work is in danger of being undone. Apart from providing a home for the study of popular culture, the U-Area he helped to found has supported many other equally innovative forms of curriculum development: courses in the areas of women's studies and Third World studies, for example. Subjected to the astringent financial discipline of Thatcherism, the Open University has been forced to cut back on its activities to the degree that the long-term future of the U-area is now, to say the least, exceedingly uncertain. Our dedication of this book to U203 staff and students is meant as a gesture of solidarity with a concept, and with those struggling to defend it, which we hope, against the odds, will survive the glacial ministrations which currently masquerade as an education policy.

Tony Bennett
Colin Mercer
Janet Woollacott
Brisbane and New York
January 1985

Tony Bennett

Introduction: popular culture and 'the turn to Gramsci'

Why study popular culture? It's tempting to answer: why not? To do so, however, would merely be to lend hostage to fortune, for many reasons have been advanced as to why popular culture should not, or at least need not, be studied — on the grounds that it is too slight and ephemeral to be worthy of any sustained inquiry, for example — and, for the greater part of this century, such arguments have largely carried the day. Moreover, even where they have not prevailed, the grounds upon which the study of popular culture has been justified have been mainly negative: to expose its morally corrupting influences and aesthetic poverty, for example, or, in Marxist approaches, to reveal its role as a purveyor of dominant ideology. In the context of such assumptions, to study popular culture has also meant to adopt a position against and opposed to it, to view it as in need of replacement by a culture of another kind, usually 'high culture' — the view not only of reformist critics, such as F.R. Leavis, but, oddly enough, equally influential in Marxist circles too, especially in the work of Theodor Adorno, Herbert Marcuse and the other members of the Frankfurt School.

It is one of the quirks of history that these arguments, which once nowhere had quite so much sedimented cultural weight as in Britain, have been overturned perhaps more decisively in Britain than anywhere else over the course of the last 20 to 30 years. The study of cinema, popular music, sport, youth sub-cultures and of much else besides has now developed to the point where these are well established fields of inquiry, with considerably developed bodies of theory and highly elaborated methodologies, in which debate is no longer stalked by the ghost of Leavis — or by the gloomy prognostications of the Frankfurt School, for that matter. Equally important, significant advances have been made in theorising the sphere of popular culture as a whole. The term had previously been used quite loosely to refer to a miscellaneous collection of cultural forms and practices having little in common beyond the fact of their exclusion from the accepted canon of 'high culture'. In more recent debates, by contrast, the many and diverse practices which are typically grouped under the heading of popular culture are more usually regarded as being systematically interconnected by virtue of the parts they play in relation to broader social and political processes, particularly those bearing on the production of consent to the prevailing social order in both its patriarchial and capitalist dimensions. These theoretical developments, finally, have been accompanied by a sureness of political purpose as the study of popular culture has been defined as a site of *positive* political engagement by both socialists and feminists in their concern to identify both those aspects of popular culture which serve to secure consent to existing social arrangements as well as those which, in embodying alternative values, supply a source of opposition to those arrangements.

Having said this, many problems, of both theory and politics, remain. Albeit in different ways, the essays collected in this anthology seek to consolidate the advances of recent years by engaging with these problems and outlining the directions in which their resolution might most productively be sought. In particular, they reflect an attempt to confront and go beyond the terms in which problems in the field were posed in the late 1970s. Debates in the area, at that time, were often deadlocked around the polar opposites of structuralism and culturalism represented, respectively, as the 'imported' and 'home-grown' varieties of cultural studies.[1] In the perspective of structuralism, popular culture was often regarded as an 'ideological machine' which dictated the thoughts of the people just as rigidly and with the same law-like regularity as, in Saussure's conspectus — which provided the originating paradigm for structuralism — the system of *langue* dictated the events of *parole*. Focusing particularly on the analysis of textual forms, structuralist analysis was concerned to reveal the ways in which textual structures might be said to organise reading or spectating practices, often with scant regard to the conditions regulating either the production or the reception of those textual forms.[2] Culturalism, by contrast, was often uncritically romantic in its celebration of popular culture as expressing the authentic interests and values of subordinate social groups and classes. This conception, moreover, resulted in an essentialist view of culture: that is, as the embodiment of specific class or gender essences. In the logic of this approach, as Roszika Parker and Griselda Pollock put it, many feminists were led to look for an authentically female culture as if this could 'exist isolated like some deep frozen essence in the freezer of male culture',[3] just as many socialists rummaged through popular culture in search of the authentic voice of the working class, as if this could exist in some pure form, preserved and nurtured in a recess immune to the socially preponderant forms of cultural production in a capitalist society.[4]

These theoretical divergences were accentuated by their association with different disciplinary perspectives, structuralism being most strongly present in the study of cinema, television and popular writings while culturalism tended to predominate within history and sociology, particularly in studies concerned with working class 'lived cultures' or 'ways of life'. Given this division of the field — a division that was sometimes provocatively and needlessly deepened, particularly by E.P.

Thompson's *The Poverty of Theory*[5] — there seemed little alternative but to pay one's money and take one's choice. Worse, it seemed as though, depending on one's area of interest, one was constrained to be either a structuralist or a culturalist — the former if one studied cinema, television or popular writing, and the latter if one's interests were in sport, say, or youth sub-cultures. It was almost as if the cultural sphere were divided into two hermetically separate regions, each exhibiting a different logic. While this was unsatisfactory, it was equally clear that the two traditions could not be forced into a shot-gun marriage either. The only way out of this impasse, therefore, seemed to be to shift the debate on to a new terrain which would displace the structuralist-culturalist opposition, a project which inclined many working in the field at the time to draw increasingly on the writings of Antonio Gramsci, particularly those on the subject of hegemony.[6]

This is not the place for a detailed exposition of the whys and wherefores of this strategy, or for an appraisal of its productivity. These are matters the reader will be in a better position to assess having read the essays collected here since, with few exceptions, Gramsci's work, especially when viewed in the light of recent developments in discourse theory,[7] provides the organising framework within which the studies are located. However, some brief remarks are in order so as to give some general sense of the new kinds of emphasis which the 'turn to Gramsci' has helped to inaugurate.

Put in the most general terms, the critical spirit of Gramsci's work, totally shunning the intolerable condescension of the mass culture critic while simultaneously avoiding any tendency toward a celebratory populism, both avoids and disqualifies the bipolar alternatives of structuralism and culturalism. However, this is less a question of style or of Gramsci's mode of address — although these are important considerations in Gramsci's writing — than one of theory. In Gramsci's conspectus, popular culture is viewed neither as the site of the people's cultural deformation nor as that of their cultural self-affirmation or, in any simple Thompsonian sense, of their own self-making; rather, it is viewed as a force field of relations shaped, precisely, by these contradictory pressures and tendencies — a perspective which enables a significant reformulation of both the theoretical and the political issues at stake in the study of popular culture.

Politically speaking, both the structuralist and culturalist paradigms subscribe to a rather similar conception of the structure and organisation of the cultural and ideological spheres viewed in relation to the antagonistic economic and political relationships between social classes. Although importantly different in other respects, both paradigms regard the sphere of cultural and ideological practices as being governed by a dominant ideology, essentially and monolithically bourgeois in its characteristics, which, albeit with varying degrees of success, is imposed from without, as an alien force, on the subordinate classes. Viewed from this perspective, the main differences between the two perspectives are largely nominal or ones of orientation. In structuralism, 'popular culture', 'mass culture' and 'dominant ideology' are usually equated through a series of sliding definitions. In consequence, the chief political task assigned to the study of popular culture is that of reading through popular cultural forms and practices to reveal the obfuscating mechanisms of the dominant ideology at work within them, thus arming the reader against the occurrence of similar mechanisms in related practices. In culturalism, by contrast, popular culture, in being equated with the 'autochthonous' culture of subordinate classes, is explicitly distinguished from and opposed to dominant ideology in the form of mass culture. Where this conception prevails, analysis is dominated by a positive political hermeneutic: that of, having found the people's authentic voice, interpreting its meaning and amplifying its cultural volume. To be sure, the consequences of these contrasting orientations are by no means negligible. In spite of these, however, the two approaches share a conception of the cultural and ideological field as being divided between two opposing cultural and ideological camps — bourgeois and working class — locked in a zero-sum game in which one side gains only at the expense of the other and in which the ultimate objective is the liquidation of one by the other so that the victor might then stand in the place of the vanquished.

For Gramsci too, of course, cultural and ideological practices are to be understood and assessed in terms of their functioning within the antagonistic relations between the bourgeoisie and the working class as the two fundamental classes of capitalist society. Indeed, Gramsci's insistence that these antagonistic class relations form the ultimately determining horizon within which cultural and ideological analysis must be located constitutes the outer limit to the programme of theoretical revision he inaugurated in relation to classical Marxist theories of ideology.[8] Where Gramsci departed from the earlier Marxist tradition was in arguing that the cultural and ideological relations between ruling and subordinate classes in capitalist societies consist less in the *domination* of the latter by the former than in the struggle for *hegemony* — that is, for moral, cultural, intellectual and, thereby, political leadership over the whole of society — between the ruling class and, as the principal subordinate class, the working class.

This substitution of the concept of hegemony for that of domination is not, as some commentators have suggested, merely terminological; it brings in tow an entirely different conception of the means by which cultural and ideological struggles are conducted.[9] Whereas, according to the dominant ideology thesis, bourgeois culture and ideology seek to take the place of working class culture and ideology and thus to become directly operative in framing working class experience, Gramsci argues that the bourgeoisie can become a hegemonic, leading class only to the degree that bourgeois ideology is able to accommodate, to find some space for, opposing class cultures and values. A bourgeois hegemony is secured not via the obliteration of working class culture, but via its *articulation to* bourgeois culture and ideology so that, in being associated with and expressed in the forms of the latter, its political affiliations are altered in the process.

As a consequence of its accommodating elements of opposing class cultures, 'bourgeois culture' ceases to be purely or entirely bourgeois. It becomes, instead, a mobile combination of cultural and ideological elements derived from different class locations which are, but only provisionally and for the duration of a specific historical conjuncture, affiliated to bourgeois values, interests and objectives. By the same token, of course, the members of subordinate classes never encounter or are oppressed by a dominant ideology in some pure or class essentialist form; bourgeois ideology is encountered only in the compromised forms it must take in order to provide some accommodation for opposing class values. As Robert Gray remarks, if the Gramscian concept of hegemony refers to the processes through which the ruling class seeks to negotiate opposing class cultures onto a cultural and ideological terrain which wins for it a position of leadership, it is also true that what is thereby consented to is a *negotiated version* of ruling class culture and ideology:

> Class hegemony is a dynamic and shifting relationship of social subordination, which operates in two directions. Certain aspects of the behaviour and consciousness of the subordinate classes may reproduce a version of the values of the ruling class. But in the process value systems are modified, through their necessary adaptation to diverse conditions of existence; the subordinate classes thus follow a 'negotiated version' of ruling-class values. On the other hand, structures of ideological hegemony transform and incorporate dissident values, so as effectively to prevent the working through of their full implications.[10]

Although an over-rapid and somewhat abstract summary of a complex body of theory, the main point is, perhaps, clear enough: that the spheres of culture and ideology cannot be conceived as being divided into two hermetically separate and entirely opposing class cultures and ideologies. The effect of this is to disqualify the bipolar options of the structuralist and culturalist perspectives on popular culture, viewed as either the carrier of an undiluted bourgeois ideology or as the site of the people's authentic culture and potential self-awakening, as unmitigated villain or unsullied hero. To the contrary, to the degree that it is implicated in the struggle for hegemony — and, for Gramsci, the part played by the most taken-for-granted, sedimented cultural aspects of everday life are crucially implicated in the processes whereby hegemony is fought for, won, lost, resisted — the field of popular culture is structured by the attempt of the ruling class to win hegemony and by the forms of opposition to this endeavour. As such, it consists not simply of an imposed mass culture that is coincident with dominant ideology, nor simply of spontaneously oppositional cultures, but is rather an area of negotiation between the two within which — in different particular types of popular culture — dominant, subordinate and oppositional cultural and ideological values and elements are 'mixed' in different permutations.

In sum, then, the 'turn to Gramsci' has been influential in both disputing the assumption that cultural forms can be assigned an essential class-belongingness and contesting a simply 'bourgeois versus working class' conception of the organisation of the cultural and ideological relationships. These reorientations have resulted in two decisive shifts of political emphasis within the study of popular culture. First, they have produced a perspective, within Marxism, from which it is possible to analyse popular culture without adopting a position that is either opposed to it or uncritically for it. The forms of political assessment of cultural practices which the theory of hegemony calls for are much more conjunctural and pliable than that. A cultural practice does not carry its politics with it, as if written upon its brow for ever and a day; rather, its political functioning depends on the network of social and ideological relations in which it is inscribed as a consequence of the ways in which, in a particular conjuncture, it is articulated to other practices. In brief, in suggesting that the political and ideological articulations of cultural practices are *movable* — that a practice which is articulated to bourgeois values today may be disconnected from those values and connected to socialist ones tomorrow — the theory of hegemony opens up the field of popular culture as one of enormous political possibilities. It is thus, for example, that in many recent debates, the call has been made that nationalism, and the forms in which it is constructed and celebrated, should be given a socialist articulation rather than be dismissed as essentially and irredeemably bourgeois.[11]

Equally important, the Gramscian critique of class essentialist conceptions of culture and ideology and the associated principles of class reductionism enables due account to be taken of the relative separation of different regions of cultural struggle (class, race, gender) as well as of the complex and changing ways in which these may be overlapped on to one another in different historical circumstances. Apart from being an important advance on classical Marxism, this has also served as an important check on the Foucauldian tendency to view power and the struggle against it as equally diffuse and unrelated. Most important, though, it has offered a framework within which the relations between the cultural politics of socialist movements and those of, say, feminist or national liberation struggles can be productively debated without their respective specifications threatening either to engulf or be engulfed by the others.

This is not to suggest that Gramsci's writings contain the seeds of an answer to all problems in the field of popular culture analysis. There are specific and detailed technical and theoretical problems peculiar to television and film analysis, popular music, the study of lived cultures and the field of popular writings which no amount of general theorising might resolve. Likewise, questions concerning the relations between culture and class, culture and gender and culture and nation remained vexed and complex, requiring separate and detailed attention if progress is to be made. The value of the Gramscian theory of hegemony is that of providing an integrating framework within which both sets of issues might be addressed and worked through in relation to each other. By the same token, of course, it is liable to the criticism that it is too accommodating and expansive a framework, over-totalising in its analytical claims and ambit. The charge has certainly been made often enough, and it seems one likely to be pressed with increased vigour, particularly in the area of cultural studies.

For the moment, however, Gramsci's work constitutes a critical point of engagement for anyone interested in popular culture; certainly, it has been the most important single influence conditioning the organisation of this anthology and its main orientations. Viewed collectively, the various essays collected here examine a range of popular cultural forms and practices in the context of the varying social relations — principally those of class, gender and nation — which constitute the interacting fields of struggle within which such forms and practices are operative and have effects. The essays comprising the first section, in offering an overview of the main theoretical and political issues at stake in the study of popular culture, outline in greater detail the relevance of Gramsci's thought to work in the area: to theorising the changing nexus of relations between the state and popular culture in the case of Stuart Hall's essay or, in Colin Mercer's case, to examining the little-explored question of the relations between the mechanisms of pleasure and those of consent.

In the second section, the level of attention shifts toward an examination of more localised and specific cultural forms and practices in the context of the social and historical relations within which they were shaped and which, in turn, they helped to shape. In some cases, the main focus is on the practices of a particular cultural institution, as in David Cardiff's and Paddy Scannell's examination of the BBC's radio policies during the war and their part in reorganising the basis of consent in British society. In others, the analysis concentrates on a particular cultural form, as in Colin McArthur's study of national exhibitions and their functioning, in the Scottish context, within relations of colonial domination. In their different ways, Catherine Hall and Tony Bennett's essays in this section are concerned with the interactive relations between a range of popular cultural practices in the context of a wider cultural formation. Catherine Hall thus focuses on the position of women in the predominantly masculinist culture of early nineteenth-century radicalism while Tony Bennett examines the place of Blackpool, and its organisation as a pleasure complex, in relation to the more general patterns of class cultural relations in late nineteenth- and early twentieth-century Lancashire.

In the third section, finally, the contributors focus either upon specific textual practices, as in Janet Woollacott's examination of situation comedy and Alan Clarke's discussion of the television police series, or on the more general theoretical and political questions implicated in the study of textual practices. The questions of realism and pleasure thus supply the starting points for the explorations of textual politics offered by Colin Mercer and Richard Middleton respectively.

It's perhaps worth adding, in conclusion, that this collection avoids, and deliberately so, any attempt at apologetics. There are countless books which seek to justify, even dignify, the study of popular culture by claiming that popular culture is just as complex, as richly rewarding, historically exciting, and so on, as 'high culture'. It is not that the argument is wrong but that the constant *making* of it merely confirms the existing hierarchy of the arts in accepting the claim that 'high culture' constitutes a pre-given standard to which popular culture must measure up or be found wanting. Brecht gently satirised the logic of such comparisons in his story *A Question of Taste*. A German, dining with a group of French artists and intellectuals who guy their visitor for the German penchant for idealist philosophies in contrast to the almost gastronomic materialism of the French, hesitates before praising the meal:

> The joint was excellent, a work of art. I was on the brink of saying so but feared they would ask me straight away if I could name one single German work of art that deserved to be called a joint of roast beef. Better stick to politics . . .[12]

Quite so.

Notes

1. While the term 'structuralism' has a more general currency, the concept of culturalism and the structuralism/culturalism polarity are mainly attributable to the collective work of the Centre for Contemporary Cultural Studies at the University of Birmingham. For the classic statement of this position, see S. Hall, 'Cultural studies: two paradigms', *Media, Culture and Society*, vol. 2, no. 1, 1980 (shortened version in T. Bennett *et al.* (eds), *Culture, Ideology and Social Process*, Batsford, London, 1981.)

2. The heyday of structuralism, in this respect, is probably best represented by Umberto Eco's *The Role of the Reader*, Hutchinson, London, 1981 (first published in Italian in 1979). In addition to providing rigorous structuralist analyses of the ideological encoding of a range of popular texts (*Superman*, the James Bond novels, etc.), Eco's approach to the processes of reading is one in which such processes are conceived as entirely regulated by textual structures. For critical discussions of this aspect of Eco's work, see chapter 6 of T. de Lauretis, *Alice Doesn't: Feminism, Semiotics, Cinema*, Macmillan, London, 1984 and chapter 3 of T. Bennett and J. Woollacott, *Bond and Beyond: The political career of a popular hero*, Macmillan, London, 1986.

3. R. Parker and G. Pollock, *Old Mistresses: Women, Art and Ideology*, Pantheon Books, New York, 1982, p. 136.
4. The most pronounced recent example of this approach is David Harker's *One for the Money: Politics and Popular Song*, Hutchinson, London, 1980.
5. E.P. Thompson, *The Poverty of Theory, and Other Essays*, Merlin Press, London, 1978.
6. See, especially, A. Gramsci, *Selections from the Prison Notebooks*, Lawrence and Wishart, London, 1971. The more recent translation and publication of Gramsci's writings on culture and politics seems likely to strengthen the Gramscian influence on contemporary cultural theory; see A. Gramsci, *Selections from Cultural Writings*, Lawrence and Wishart, London, 1985.
7. For the most influential readings of Gramsci of this type, see E. Laclau, *Politics and Ideology in Marxist Theory*, New Left Books, London, 1977, and C. Mouffe, 'Hegemony and ideology in Gramsci' in C. Mouffe (ed.), *Gramsci and Marxist Theory*, Routledge and Kegan Paul, London, 1979.
8. There have, however, been a number of attempts recently to go beyond these 'outer limits', although whether the resulting formulations are meaningfully described as Marxist is debatable. See, for example, E. Laclau, 'Transformations of advanced industrial societies and the theory of the subject' in S. Hänninen and L. Paldán (eds), *Rethinking Ideology: A Marxist Debate*, International General/IMMAC, New York, 1983.
9. The failure to appreciate this is one of the most conspicuous shortcomings of N. Abercrombie, S. Hill and B.S. Turner, *The Dominant Ideology Thesis*, George Allen and Unwin, London, 1980.
10. R. Gray, *The Labour Aristocracy in Victorian Edinburgh*, Clarendon Press, Oxford, 1976, p. 6.
11. See, for example, R. Gray, 'Left holding the flag', *Marxism Today*, vol. 25, No. 11, 1982.
12. B. Brecht, *Collected Short Stories*, Methuen, London, 1983, p. 185.

Section one

Themes and Issues

Introduction

The people (oh!), the public (oh!). The political adventurists ask with the scowl of those who know what's what, 'The people! But what is this people? Who knows them? Who has ever defined them?'

Antonio Gramsci[1]

The three contributions in this first section attempt, with distinctive emphases and, we hope, without undue political adventurism, to pose and also to reformulate some of these questions on the ground of popular culture. The adventurists cited above by Gramsci were led by their scepticism to reject *any* presence of 'the people' in political and cultural processes and policy formation. The contributors here, whilst retaining a necessary scepticism with regard to a universal and essential definition of the people, the public and the popular, insist none the less that, strategically and theoretically, these are key terrains and components in both the analysis and the transformation of that field of practices, forms and structures now grouped roughly under the heading of popular culture.

The key questions, as they are reformulated here, might be framed as follows. Firstly, what, in the matrix of popular culture, might be the conditions for a politically effective and democratic articulation of 'the people' and the 'popular' within current cultural theory and practice? Secondly, what, both historically and contemporaneously, is the nature of the relationship between people, culture and the state? And finally, what are the forms and mechanisms of our 'popular' complicity with cultural forms?

Taken together these questions both condense current forms of investigation into popular culture and argue for a significant recasting of the grids of analysis and interpretation to which such forms have been submitted. In the first contribution, for example, Tony Bennett argues that within the general conspectus of left cultural theory and practice, there has been a fundamental and disabling misrecognition of the nature of the 'popular'. In a wide survey of Marxist cultural theory encompassing the work of Lukács, the Frankfurt School and contemporary cultural theory, Bennett notes that even — or perhaps especially — when there are strategic and theoretical appeals to 'the people' and the 'popular', these have tended to be marked by an essentialism which, as he demonstrates, is not sufficiently sceptical as to who or what the people, the public and the popular are. Within Marxism especially, this essentialism has tended to take the form either of a nostalgic recourse to past popular and radical traditions or of a stern and minatory condemnation of the contemporary complicities of the masses with a debased and manipulative popular or mass culture. Either way, these approaches ascribe a general form of unity either to the people themselves or to the forms of popular culture in which they are immersed. The political correlates of these theoretical positions are that either one demonstrates a general disdain for the products of contemporary popular culture or that one believes that there is, somewhere in the past, a monumental great culture to which, through enlightened leadership and political struggle, the people may eventually be led back. The fatal flaw within these conceptual frameworks, according to Bennett, lies in their inability, in Brecht's words, to theorise the 'bad new times' as opposed to the 'good old' ones.

In order to approach these 'bad new times', Bennett suggests that it is more productive to keep the key terms embodied in the notion of popular culture conceptually open and devoid of any fixed and trans-historical content and to seek instead a historically and politically variable cartography of the relationships between the terms at a given moment. This approach, he suggests, would belie the assumption, dear to many forms of contemporary cultural politics, that there exists a ready-formed oppositional culture of 'the people', a culture ready to burst out, a culture which would allow 'the people' to assume, at last, their historically repressed identity.

With different emphases, these arguments are supported by Stuart Hall's historical and theoretical overview of relations between popular culture and the state in the three key areas of the law, the nineteenth-century press and the BBC. Hall demonstrates, in his three case studies and in his exposition of the necessary theoretical coordinates for their analysis, that there is no stable, permanent and continuous relationship between people — or the 'public' — culture and the state. These relationships, he argues, are themselves the site of continuous political intervention and reformulation. Developing some of Gramsci's formulations on the relations between state and civil society, Hall convincingly elaborates the ways in which, through a series of *qualitative* transactions and negotiations and struggles, the British state has demarcated for itself a legitimated field of action in which such key components as 'the people' and 'the public' have played a fundamental and strategic role. Hall also notes that as well as being strategic in its nominal form, the adjectival form of 'the public' as counterposed to 'the private' has had decisive effects, politically and ideologically, in the formation of 'appropriate' locations for men and women within the spheres of culture and politics. Central to Hall's

3

argument here is the conception of *civil society* as sketched out by Gramsci and which he refers to, in the *Prison Notebooks*, as the site of the 'trenches and fortifications' in the 'war of position' which is constantly maintained by bourgeois democratic states.[2] This, according to Gramsci, and given substance here in Hall's case studies, is the primary site on which *hegemony* is constantly secured and maintained. Within this perspective it becomes possible to understand and analyse the strategic position which the terrain of popular culture occupies in the fields of action of modern states and societies. This field of action, as Hall demonstrates, should not be analalysed purely in terms of its repressive aspects, but also in terms of its 'positive, educative function'.

Colin Mercer's contribution takes up this theme of the 'productive' aspects of the dominant culture and attempts to weave a path through the issues of dominance and the popular by focusing on the theme of *pleasure* and the ways in which this category has, since the beginning of the nineteenth century, played an increasingly important role in the assessment and calculation of relations between people, the popular and cultural processes. Again, drawing centrally on Gramsci's work around the importance of *consent* in bourgeois democratic societies, but also combining some of Michel Foucault's insights into the nature of the 'social body', Mercer argues that within the general framework of the popular and its relationship to ideology, the issue of pleasure is a central one. But it is also a central point of resistance to certain forms of analysis. Reviewing some of the theories of pleasure in cultural forms in the work of writers such as Laura Mulvey, Mikhail Bakhtin, Roland Barthes and Pierre Bourdieu, Mercer argues that a primary site within the modern field of cultural pleasures is that of the body. He argues, for example, that an important component of consent is the process of *consensualisation* of the individual and collective body in a range of cultural forms from the daily popular newspaper through popular fiction and film to the limit case of the 'body politics' of Fascism and Nazism. Within this range of forms, however, Mercer argues that there is no basis for theoretical conceptions of pleasure which construe it as being either uniformly ideological or, as in the Marcusean conception, uniformly liberatory in its potential and effects. The author suggests, finally, that in this area, long overdue for attention from critical cultural theory, there is a need to focus on a 'plurality of special cases' concerned, in a broadly Gramscian framework, not only with the effects of construed 'dominance' but also with the points of fragility, weakness and potential resistance in the social fabric of contemporary pleasures.

Notes

1. Antonio Gramsci, *Selections from Cultural Writings*, (ed. and trans. Forgacs and Nowell-Smith), Lawrence and Wishart, London, 1985, p. 273.
2   Antonio Gramsci, Selections from the Prison Notebooks, (ed. and trans. Hoare and Nowell-Smith), Lawrence and Wishart, London, 1971 *passim*.

1

Tony Bennett

The politics of 'the popular' and popular culture

The art that the Left produces is shit. It's self-reverential garbage. The fact that Tony Banks at the GLC can give money to the Riverside Studios, an elitist outfit producing Polish mime troupers for the working class of Fulham, is ludicrous. It's awful and stupid . . . That game of constantly performing the plays about the strikes within the precincts still goes on doesn't it? It still only attracts that floating group of people who will join left-wing organizations anyway. It doesn't get further than the pre-selected audience.

Alexei Sayle[1]

The judgement is, no doubt, too sweeping and the language too harsh and dismissive. But the problem is real. The left has lost more than a political battle in recent years; it has also lost a cultural battle, the battle for the 'hearts and minds' of 'the people'. Socialist cultural initiatives — often straddled awkwardly between a modish avant-gardism and a 'workerism' of yesteryear — have remained largely peripheral to the lives of 'the people', in any majoritarian sense of that term, throughout the the greater part of the post-war period and certainly since the 1960s.

Even more depressing, many sections of the left have been simply unaware that there is a cultural battle to be fought, let alone won, so deep is the residual economism of the British labour movement. The prospect that a coherent and comprehensive cultural strategy might be developed by the Labour party, and be placed high on its list of priorities, remains unlikely. What currently passes for such a strategy is largely limited to the call for the democratisation of the media. This is obviously important, an indispensable component of any socialist cultural strategy. The massive inequalities in cultural power which result from the currently prevailing forms of media ownership and control have clearly played a major role in marginalising socialist culture and values, 'ghettoising' socialist ideas simply by systematically excluding them from the agenda for debate.[2] None the less, the call for the democratisation of the media — if posed merely as an abstracted demand, as something to be implemented by an incoming Labour government — is, by itself, radically insufficient. It is, moreover, unlikely to recruit wide support if, as is arguably the case at the moment, when the only argument advanced in its support is that of correcting the anti-Labour bias of the media, it can be represented as too closely associated with narrowly conceived sectional interests.

Nor are the suspicions to which such associations are likely to give rise entirely unfounded. There is more than a little danger, given the past record of the Labour Party in office, that such demands may be translated into statist forms of control over cultural production which will prove to be no more involving for either producers or consumers than the present arrangements. More immediately, there is also the risk that such demands may amount to little more than a recipe for doing nothing in the present. The perception that the media may need to be reformed root and branch has often been accompanied, as Brecht shrewdly noted, by a fatalistic acceptance of what they currently produce pending the day of their transformation.

The experience derived from other cultural struggles, however, has shown that it *is* possible to develop strategies which are able to exploit the manifold contradictions which undoubtedly exist within and between the various media as well as opening up new spaces for cultural activity outside them. Significantly, the most successful radical cultural initiatives of recent years — successful in terms of their ability to make any appreciable popular impact — have been developed in the context of single-issue politics (the Rock against Racism concerts of the late 1970s, for example) or by groups engaged in struggles which have been constructed to one side of and, at times, in opposition to the traditional focal points of labour and socialist politics. Feminism has been the outstanding example in this respect. In recognising the importance of cultural struggle, feminists have launched an array of initiatives across a range of cultural practices — the development of a women's press, women's theatre groups, women in rock — which have undoubtedly connected with the concerns of ordinary women and men. As a consequence, although initially the odds had seemed to be stacked overwhelmingly against it, feminism is now a major popular cultural force whose vitality seems unstoppable — even in face of the assault which Thatcherism represents.

Apart from itself being marginalised, socialist culture has also conspicuously failed to coordinate effectively — to bring together and connect — the new foci of cultural struggle which have been developed in these contexts. In thus failing to keep in step with and to take account of the new constituencies created in these struggles, socialist culture has cut itself off from some of the newer, more buoyant cultural currents and tendencies of our times. The reasons for this are no doubt complex. My concern here is with the part that ways of thinking about 'the popular' and popular culture prevalent in socialist theory have played in inhibiting the development of cultural strategies capable of coordinating a broad range of popular concerns, and thereby stitching them into an expanding socialist culture, and to suggest ways in which rethinking these concepts may contribute to the development of more adequate forms of socialist cultural intervention.

7

Rethinking popular culture

To do this, I shall be less concerned to define popular culture and the related concepts of 'the popular' and 'the people' than to explore some of the political issues which hinge on their definition. Indeed, I shall argue that the meaning of these terms and our understanding of the relations between them are not matters that can be resolved by definitional fiat. The most that one can do is to point to a range of meanings, a range of different constructions of the relations between popular culture, 'the popular' and 'the people', which have different consequences for the way in which popular culture is conceived and constituted as a site for cultural intervention.

However, whilst stopping short of advancing particular definitions for these related concepts, I shall argue in favour of a particular way of approaching these problems. Most available approaches tend to define these terms by filling them with a particular content in speaking of popular culture as being comprised of particular types of cultural activity which are held to be popular in the sense of exhibiting a particular relationship to 'the people' — where 'the people' is defined as a particular social group (usually the working class) — whether these cultural activities are directly engaged in and produced by 'the people', as so defined, or made for them without their direct or active participation. By contrast, I shall argue in favour of an approach which keeps these terms *definitionally* empty — or, at least, relatively so — in the interest of filling them *politically* in varying ways as changing circumstances may require. According to such a view, popular culture can be defined only abstractly as a site — always changing and variable in its constitution and organisation — which, since it provides one of the key terrains for the struggle over the political production of 'the people' and 'the popular', cannot be more precisely specified in terms of these concepts. The meaning of these terms, that is to say, can never be singly or definitionally fixed inasmuch as their use is always caught up in a struggle to determine precisely which senses of 'the people' and 'the popular' will carry weight politically in terms of their ability to organise different social forces into an active political alliance. As Stuart Hall has argued:

> But the term 'popular', and even more, the collective subject to which it must refer — 'the people' — is highly problematic. It is made problematic by, say, the ability of Mrs Thatcher to pronounce a sentence like, 'We have to limit the power of the trade unions because that is what the people want'. That suggests to me that, just as there is no fixed content to the category of 'popular culture', so there is no fixed subject to attach to it — 'the people'.[3]

Before further elaborating this view, however, I want to examine a number of the versions of 'the people' and 'the popular' that have proved influential in Marxist writings on the subject with a view to critically interrogating the forms of cultural politics they have formed a part of and, to some degree, helped to produce.

'What was popular yesterday is not today,' Brecht argued, 'for the people today are not what they were yesterday.'[4] Moreover, Brecht warned, it is because socialists 'so emphatically need the concept *popular*' that they must be careful how they use it for 'the history of the many deceptions which have been practised with this concept of the people is a long and complicated one — a history of class struggles'.[5] In order to use the concept productively, Brecht continues, it is necessary to oppose the 'ahistorical, static, undevelopmental stamp' it has sometimes assumed, particularly in those 'so-called poetical forms' which 'endow the people with unchanging characteristics, hallowed traditions, art forms, habits and customs, religiosity, hereditary enemies, invincible power and so on'.[6] It is worth stressing that these remarks were directed as much against left-wing as against right-wing romanticised versions of 'the people'; indeed — given that Brecht's polemic was directed primarily against the work of Georg Lukács — more so. And with good reason for — although not exclusively, but to a degree that is sufficient cause for concern — Marxist constructions of 'the people' and 'the popular' have displayed two opposing yet complementary tendencies which have militated against the adoption of that lively, adaptable, practical orientation toward the 'popular' which Brecht called for.

On the one hand, to borrow (cautiously) from McLuhan, Marxist constructions of 'the popular' have exhibited an alarming degree of 'rear-view-mirrorism', walking backwards into the future by rediscovering 'the people' in their historically superseded forms and offering these as a guide for action in the present. These have been counterbalanced by a tendency toward an 'ideal futurism' in which the only version of 'the people' that matters is one that has yet to be constructed: the ideally unified people of a projected socialist future. Sometimes, in historicist conceptions of cultural development, these two tendencies are combined in the sense that an idealised people of the future is regarded as standing in a relationship of *Aufhebung* (negation and transcendance) to an idealised people of the past, cancelling out the limitations of earlier forms of 'the people' whilst simultaneously preserving their positive qualities, but at a higher level of historical development. Whichever tendency predominates and whatever the precise pattern of their combination, however, the effect is broadly similar: 'the people', in any recognisably actual and current form, have been found wanting, viewed as a fall from what they once were and might yet be. Unsurprisingly, the cultural strategies produced by such theoretical conceptions have often proved incapable of either reflecting or contributing to the changing formation of 'the people' since they have lacked any means of connecting with them other than via the rose-tinted versions of their ideal past or future selves.

9

Tony Bennett

Walking backwards into the future and forwards into the past[7]

The editorial to the first issue of *New Left Review* in 1960 declared:

> The purpose of discussing cinema or teen-age culture in NLR is not to show, in some modish way, that we are keeping up with the times. These are directly relevant to the imaginative resistances of the people who have to live within capitalism — the growing points of social discontent, the projection of deeply-felt needs . . . The task of socialism today is to meet people where they *are*, where they are touched, bitten, moved, frustrated, nauseated — to develop discontent and, at the same time, to give the socialist movement some *direct* sense of the times and ways in which we live.[8]

That strikes me as exactly right. The first fruit of this concern with popular culture, however, was an article by B. Groombridge and P. Whannel who were particularly alarmed at the increasing popularity of rock 'n' roll. Adopting a left-inflected version of Leavis's cultural criticism, they objected to the fact that rock 'n' roll seemed to be aspiring above its station: 'There is nothing wrong with this kind of entertainment so long as it is not our sole diet. Provided also that we do not make large claims for it. Rock 'n' roll is a splendid *outlet*; it should not be something to "believe in".'[9] Moreover, they were disappointed that the BBC had abandoned the role of enlightened cultural leadership which Reith had claimed for it. Writing of the tendency of disc jockeys to use the Top Twenty charts in constructing their play-lists, they reproved: 'it can only be timidity which makes the BBC abandon its traditional function in the very sphere in which it would be most useful to encourage discrimination'.[10] This contradiction between editorial and article was symptomatic of the period. The editorial signalled a clear awareness that socialism could not afford *not* to address or take account of the significantly changing popular tastes of the times, especially those of young people. Yet the article suggested that the only terms available for doing so were those supplied by a discourse which, organised around a contrast between the 'good old days' and the 'bad new ones', hopelessly wrong-footed itself from the start.

In this respect, the terms in which contemporary popular culture was discussed and the forms in which its historical analysis was being developed were curiously complicit with one another. In a commanding essay on the subject, Bill Schwarz has usefully identified both the strengths and weaknesses of the theorisations of 'the popular' and 'the people' which informed the writings of British communist historians in the 1950s. Whilst applauding their attempts to repossess the past so as to discover within it an authentic radical popular tradition — the tradition of the free-born Englishman — which might provide an historical support for the construction of a specifically national popular politics in the present, Schwarz also notes the limitations of this approach:

it tended to turn attention severely away from contemporary cultures precisely because the reorganized structures of popular culture in the twentieth century — condensed around suspicions of Americanization (Hollywood and pulp fiction) — appeared as a barrier and impediment to this retrieval. The heroic culture of the past was seen as struggling against the contemporary cultural forms of the working class, the past against the present.[11]

'The people of the past versus the people of the present': to the degree that the noble and heroic tradition of the free-born Englishman found a distinct lack of confirmation in the grubbily material struggles of the working classes in the 1950s, what was intended as an historical aid to contemporary politics and analysis became a blockage to it. In effect, the radical popular tradition 'rediscovered' by Thompson and Hill, for example, rather than being one which could be convincingly represented as leading to and connecting with the present, came to function as a standard with which to berate it. As a consequence, 'the people' — the real active living people the historians made so much of in their excavations of the past — were nothing so much as a disappointment in their failure to live up to the standards which had been constructed for them. But, as Schwarz notes: 'The past is not a yardstick by which to *measure* the present.'[12] Nor is it a stick with which to beat it. If it is allowed to become so, there is no means by which either the successes or failures of past struggles can be made to connect productively with those of the present. The discovery of *continuities* between past and present is not worth a candle if it results in *discontinuities* being conceived moralistically or represented in the form of a fall, a failure or a lack on the part of 'the people' today.

This neglect of their contemporary popular culture by communist historians entailed the virtual surrender of the terms of debate in this area to the mass culture critique, in its peculiarly English variants, routed from Arnold via Leavis and to achieve its most influential 'leftish' condensation in Richard Hoggart's *The Uses of Literacy*. Within this tradition, popular culture and, with it, 'the people' in any recognisably contemporary form, existed only in order to be condemned, to be found wanting on moral, aesthetic and — although this more *sotto voce* — political grounds also. (Hoggart feared, following a long line of conservative critics, that the people's culture ill equipped them for their responsible role as citizens within a democracy.) Americanisation — which subsequent critics have learned to value more positively as embodying a productive irritant exerting a certain power of attrition in relation to the forms of ruling class hegemony which have traditionally prevailed in Britain[13] — was particularly likely to be singled out as the villain of the piece, cast in the role of an external agent implanted within and corroding the earlier, sturdier — if also, in Hoggart's account — slightly flatulent forms of the people's culture. Reproved by conservative critics for having sacrificed the

11

standards of 'true culture' for grossly inferior, substandard products, 'the people' found that they were cast in the terms of an equally disapproving discourse on the left, taken to task for having sold their birthright for a mess of pottage.

It is small wonder that socialist cultural discourse became progressively marginalised during this period. It marginalised itself. True, 'the people' were not held to be responsible for their own deterioration: the media, capitalist ideology and the like were clearly identified as the main culprits. However, such diagnostic subtleties failed to disguise the anti-popular sting in the tail of a discourse which could only envisage 'the people' as the innocent but also, by implication, ignorant dupes of a capitalist conspiracy. It is not surprising that, subjected to such a hectoring discourse, people stopped listening. It's not possible to win the hearts and minds of 'the people' if they are conceived as so hopelessly corrupted from the outset that no discursive space is created in which — not as some ideal construct, but in their available forms, necessarily as constituted in the midst of a capitalist culture — they can be spoken both of and to as other than simply objects to be reformed or corrected in the image of their earlier, 'truer' selves. If this does not happen, it will not be too surprising if popular impulses express themselves to one side of the terrain constituted by socialist discourse. This was precisely what happened in the 1960s when young people, especially women — hopelessly absent from socialist constructions of 'the people' at the time — moved into a variety of newly constructed cultural and discursive spaces (sub-cultural movements, the women's liberation movement, even the media construction of 'swinging Britain') in which positive forms of self-recognition and estimation could be produced.

The immediate post-war writings of the Communist Party Historians' Group exhibited another familiar tendency: that of representing the 'monumental' cultural and literary achievements of the past — the works of Shakespeare and the like — as embodying the true voice of 'the people' in their period: as, in effect, 'the people's' true cultural heritage, plundered from them by the bourgeoisie, and which it is therefore important to restore to them. In fact, this view was widespread not merely among historians but also among British Marxist critics from the 1930s through to the 1950s. In the writings of Ralph Fox, Alick West, Christopher Caudwell and the classicist George Thomson, as well as, more recently, those of Arnold Kettle, the view predominated that works now revered as classics were the genuinely popular works of their age and the product of an intimate and creative union between artist and people.

Nor has this particular construction of 'the people' and their creative cultural role been limited to Britain. Indeed, it found perhaps its most consummate expression in the writings of Lukács, whose entire theory of cultural development rests on a quite particular conception of 'the people'. For Lukács, the 'undisputed masterpieces of world literature' (Shakespeare, Goethe, Cervantes, etc.) are such because of their close association with and dependency on the culture of 'the people' of their respective periods. In the more compromised reality of developed capitalism, where the more organic ties supposedly connecting 'the people' and literature in earlier periods have been severed, it is none the less via identification — conscious or unconscious — with progressive popular forces that the writer is able to achieve the heights of realism appropriate to his age. (I say 'his age' advisedly: women writers have no place in Lukács's pantheon of world literature.) Cut that connection, and literature withers into formlessness, subjectivism and so on.

Yet, in spite of the weight it thus carries in his account of cultural development, the culture of 'the people' never figures in its own right in Lukács's works. Nor is it ever assessed in terms of its consequences for 'the people' themselves. Creative only by proxy, 'the people', in Lukács's writings, are valued only to the degree to which they furnish the necessary supports on which 'great art' can thrive. Their creativity is thus siphoned off from their own sphere of cultural activity into that of high culture. Furthermore, once 'the people' becomes a proletariat, its creativity disappears entirely. According to Lukács, it's only those cultural forms produced in pre-capitalist periods, or during the transition to capitalism, which reflect a close creative union with 'the people'. In later epochs, popular culture is too compromised by capitalist ideology to fulfil this function. All that is available to writers in such periods is the abstraction of a proletarian world-view, not a living culture. In capitalism, for Lukács, 'the people' have no culture, only a philosophy and — in the light of the distinction he proposed in *History and Class Consciousness* between the empirically given class consciousness of the proletariat and its imputed class consciousness, the consciousness it would have if it understood its situation correctly — not one they're necessarily aware of.

Equally important, Lukács's proletariat is additionally saddled with the burden of philosophical universality. The 'universal class', it neither represents nor is able to lead anything so limited as a 'national-popular'. Operating not at a national level but at the world-historical level, it stands in for 'the people as a whole' — that is, for everyone, for humanity, for the internally unified, all-embracing, post-historical subject of Man.[14] The 'imagined community', to borrow Benedict Anderson's happy phrase, of Lukács's socialism is, ultimately, world-wide and trans-historical, encompassing all subjects — past, present and future — and subordinating them to the universal sway of a yet-to-be-achieved human subject produced in a relationship of direct and unmediated unity with itself.[15]

The people's culture in capitalism is thus, for Lukács, conceived as a triple fall — a fall from the healthy (but limited) popular culture of the past, a fall from the superior standards of bourgeois art (itself viewed as a fall from the healthier art, nourished from a direct contact with the people, of the past) and a fall from the future culture of socialism when popular and great art will once again fuse and when 'the people', in becoming universal, will recognise the art of the past as their creation. This historicist consummation is vital to Lukács's theory: it is the only means by which he is able to give his account of cultural development a popular edge. 'The people' who, in between time, create nothing — or at least nothing to speak of — turn out, at the end of history, to have created everything. The trick is, of course, that 'the people' of whom Lukács speaks in earlier periods are never the 'real people', warts and all, but always and entirely the anticipations, the understudies, of this post-historical ideal people. As a consequence, the need to develop cultural strategies which can relate to and connect with 'the people' in their current and actually prevailing forms is simply overlooked. In a philosophy of history in which 'becomingness' rules the day and carries all before it, the real essence of 'the people' of today is given only in the form of the ideal people they will eventually become. Cultural strategy can only relate to this underdeveloped ideal and nourish its growth.

The negative consequences of this particular construction of 'the people' come home to roost most clearly in the gloomy prognostications of the Frankfurt School, to some degree obliged to adopt the perspective of negativity because the proletariat, in its empirical forms, had proved unworthy of the immense philosophical and cultural burden Lukács had placed on its shoulders. Marcuse, for example, in one of his later works, emphatically rejects the view that the proletariat can be deemed to represent the interests of 'the people' as a whole, let alone carry the burden of the philosophical demand for universality. Further, he argues, given that 'the proletariat is not the negation of the existing society, but to a large extent integrated into it,' there is 'no "place among the people" which the writer can simply take up and which awaits him' — a correct view which, however, inclines him to the opposite extreme in entertaining the possibility that revolutionary art may well have to become 'the enemy of the people', constructed against them, in their given form, in order to be for them, but, again, in a purely ideal sense.[16]

However, I shall not dwell on these considerations. Nor do I want to paint too one-sided a picture. There are other tendencies than those I have outlined. Apart from Gramsci, there is Brecht who sought not merely to produce a new sense of 'the popular' as the site of a critical and speculative intelligence but to create a space for it within the very structure of his epic theatre. More recently, the work of Mikhail Bakhtin has proved influential, too, enabling a reconstruction of the popular tradition of carnival and of the potentially subversive effects of its echoes in later cultural forms, popular and 'high'. However, Terry Eagleton has rightly stressed the limitations of the carnival tradition — a licensed blow-out which may facilitate accommodation to the prevailing social order no matter how much it might rupture that order symbolically.[17] In any case, the limitations of rummaging through the past for aspects of carnival whose mutated echoes can be made to be heard in the present are surely obvious.[18]

14

Although these exceptions are important, their overriding limitation — apart from the influence of Gramsci's work on the Italian Communist Party — is that they have scarcely ever impinged on the cultural policy formulations of major socialist parties, be they of the communist or labourist varieties, and least of all in Britain. Here, the two tendencies I sketched in earlier have predominated. Attention has concentrated either on constructing a radical and progressive past popular tradition in order that 'the people' might learn from and take heart from the struggles of their forebears, or on constructing 'the people' as the supports of 'great culture' so that they might eventually be led to appropriate that culture as their own. Either way, a similar orientation is produced. The struggle for 'the popular' is conceived as one of seeking to displace the current and actual forms of 'the people's' culture so as to replace it with another. It is a struggle to fill 'the people's' culture with a different content. In the case of the first tendency, this is to be done by reviving the power of those values which contributed to the formation of 'the people' in the past so that these might be set against and override those forces making for their deformation in the present. In the case of the second tendency, it's a matter of progressively leading 'the people' to replace their given culture with the 'real culture' of the bourgeois tradition, to be further developed at a higher level of historical self-consciousness in socialist society.

Whilst it is true, of course, that any socialist strategy must be centrally concerned to effect the cultural re-formation of 'the people', it is singularly inappropriate to seek to do so by taking issue with its given culture as a whole: such a strategy lacks any means of productively interacting with that which it seeks to change. Revolutionary art as 'an enemy of the people' is all very well but hopelessly inconsequential since it is, by definition, unable to connect with any social force capable of translating its truths into practice. It preserves the abstract possibility of being able to change everything only at the price of being practically unable to change anything. As Brecht once remarked, it's no use just writing 'the truth'; one has 'to write it *for* and *to* somebody, somebody who can do something with it'.[19]

But who? A further feature shared by the two tendencies I have discussed is their implicit equation of 'the people' with the working class — and usually the male working class, at that. This, in turn, has often rested on the further assumption that the tensions and conflicts which are worked out and expressed in the sphere of popular culture are reducible to a single contradiction: that between working class culture and bourgeois ideology. This fails to take account of the other, multiple contradictions and struggles which traverse the class-related aspects of cultural struggle and deeply mark the face of popular culture — the struggles of women against male domination, struggles against racism, the cultural components of Welsh, Irish and Scottish nationalisms, for example. The root weakness of the definitions of popular culture proposed by these two tendencies consists in their inability to theorise the complex, multi-dimensionality of the interacting struggles which are implicated in its constitution.

The struggle for 'the popular'

I said earlier that I would argue in favour of an approach to the study of popular culture which would keep its key terms — 'the popular', 'the people', and 'popular culture' itself — open, devoid of any particular content, rather than trying to fill them by viewing popular culture as consisting of a fixed inventory of cultural forms and practices which relate, in unchanging ways, to 'the people' conceived as a fixed subject (the working class, say). This is because the attempt to fill these terms in this way leads, ultimately, to a political closure — or, more accurately, to a range of political closures varying in their effects in accordance with the means by which their content is thus definitionally fixed. For, contrary to what appears to be its givenness and concreteness as a determinate range of cultural forms and practices, it is not possible to specify what popular culture is, or to determine what should be included within it, without first or simultaneously specifying what is *not* popular culture. As Stuart Hall has put it:

> Anybody who says 'popular culture' doesn't need to say: 'as opposed to unpopular culture, elite culture, or folk culture, traditional culture, or aristocratic culture, or whatever.' They leave that other bit absent so that it looks fuller as a term than it actually is. But unless we know what it is that it's being contrasted with, we do not get a picture of the whole field of which popular culture is, by definition, only a part . . . So you have to know what it's working along with before you know what it's doing.[20]

It is, moreover, usually 'that other bit', the absent term with which popular culture is implicitly contrasted, which determines how popular culture is defined and what it is filled with, and which, in doing so, brings a whole baggage of political presuppositions with it. This can be clearly seen in the two contrasting definitions of popular culture — related to the two tendencies discussed above — which, until recently, have held centre stage in different regions of Marxist theory. According to the first, particularly prominent in the writings of Marxist literary and cultural critics, popular culture is viewed as an imposed mass culture produced and distributed by commercial apparatuses over which 'the people', conceived as a mass of atomised yet undifferentiated consumers, have no control and which offer them no creative, productive involvement. Implicitly — indeed, sometimes explicitly — such approaches define and fix popular culture by means of a twofold contrast which is, at the same time, a double lack, a double fall. Conceived as a fall from an earlier phase of cultural production in which 'the people' took part more directly in producing the forms through which they culturally re-created themselves, the allegedly standardised, pre-packaged uniformity of such a popular culture is also represented as a lack in relation to the more critical and individuated nature of traditional bourgeois high culture.

The paradigm case here is the Frankfurt School.[21] For Adorno and Horkheimer, the role of the 'culture industry' is that of 'mass deception' under the guise of 'enlightenment'.[22] The organisation of cultural production in advanced capitalism has resulted in a total uniformity — 'culture now imposes the same stamp on everything. Films, radio and magazines make up a system which is uniform as a whole and in every part'[23] — which exerts its sway over everything: 'The whole world is made to pass through the filter of the culture industry'.[24] Such a culture produces 'the people' in its own image — a totally homogeneous mass of individuals, alike even in their pseudo-individuality, and lacking any roots in any otherness, in any socially located vision of the world, which has not been tailored to suit the requirements of the culture industry. 'The people', according to such a view, are merely, as Stuart Hall has put it, ' "cultural dopes" who can't tell that what they are being offered is an up-dated form of the opium of the people.'[25] Radically immunised against the possibility that they might be culturally re-formed, such a people forces art — idealised as the last refuge of the 'critical perspective' — into a position of transcendence, obliged to adopt a stance opposed to 'the people' and to assume a form which, in enabling it to resist the solicitations of the culture industry, also renders it inappropriable by 'the people'.

The second view, however, is scarcely preferable. According to this, most clearly developed in the work of historians and sociologists concerned with the study of the ways of life or sub-cultural practices of the working class or other subordinate social groups, 'the people' constitute the site of a culture that is spontaneously oppositional, if only in limited, relatively undeveloped ways which have therefore to be more fully elaborated so that their radical content can be more clearly heard. Here, 'genuine popular culture' is defined in being differentiated from the contrived, artifically popular culture produced by the film, television and record industries. Whereas, in the preceding definition, popular culture is equated with mass culture, here it is distinguished from it and, in the process, aligned with traditional folk culture as its contemporary variant; it is the place in which 'the people' directly speak and express themselves, in which their thoughts and feelings return to themselves without being passed through the distorting filter of the culture industry.

That is a caricature, of course: left-wing cultural populism, in its unqualified forms, is, fortunately, no longer a flourishing species. Yet, albeit hedged about with qualifications, the tendency is still a powerful one. It survives in those accounts — too numerous to detail — which construe the history of popular culture as a succession of robberies in which 'the people' were once in possession of a culture that was directly and immediately theirs — made by them, for themselves, and which was of them in the sense that it expressed their values — which has since been taken away from them, subjected to interference 'from above', and turned back to them in modified and palliated forms. Critcher's account of the development of soccer is a case in point: once 'the people's game', it has since, through a succession of stages, been taken away from them until it is, today, no more than packaged entertainment offered, via the media, to a socially undifferentiated audience.[26]

There are two main problems with such accounts. The first is that it proves impossible to locate an originating moment in which 'the people's' culture was ever directly and spontaneously theirs. It is no more possible in the past than in the present to locate a source of popular cultural activity or expression which is not, at the same time, profoundly shot through with elements of the dominant culture and, in some sense, located within it as well as against it. That is what a dominant culture does: it dominates, it constitutes the magnetic pole of the cultural field which other cultures may oppose or seek to disentangle themselves from, but which they cannot evade entirely. There is no point, as Tim Mason has shown, in the pre-history of today's soccer at which it is possible to locate a game that was ever directly and immediately 'the people's', that was not in some way caught in a nexus of social and cultural relationships — the patronage of employers' or religious organizations or, in pre-industrial society, the patronage of local notables — which made it always more than just 'the people's game'.[27] But nor, equally, is it possible to locate a moment in that history when such forms of patronage and control were not resisted, evaded, turned against themselves or used in ways contrary to those intended. More of this shortly. Meanwhile, the second limitation of such approaches consists in what they deliver politically at the level of the cultural strategies they suggest: usually, that 'the people' should struggle to reappropriate what they have lost, to take control of the terraces again. Such projects tend to overlook the fact that, in the process of the transformation of 'their culture' (if such it ever was) 'the people' have been transformed, too, and are unlikely to move back to those cultural places they once occupied, whether originally theirs or not. What was popular yesterday *cannot* be popular today for the people today do not *want* to be what they were yesterday.

In short, each of these attempts to define popular culture by filling it with a particular content, whether positively or negatively evaluated, closes in on a particular construction of 'the people' which, whether as its creative subject or its passive recipient, stands in a pre-given relationship to that culture. A different approach is suggested by those who, following Gramsci, argue that popular culture cannot be defined in terms of either the one or the other of the undoubtedly real but misleadingly one-sided emphases suggested by these two tendencies. According to such approaches, popular culture is definable neither as the culture 'of the people', produced by and for themselves, nor as an administered culture produced for them. Rather, it consists of those cultural forms and practices — varying in content from one historical period to another — which constitute the terrain on which dominant, subordinate and oppositional cultural values and ideologies meet and intermingle, in different mixes and permutations, vying with one another in their attempts to secure the spaces within which they can become influential in framing and organising popular experience and consciousness. It consists not of two separated compartments — a pure and spontaneously oppositional culture 'of the people' and a totally administered culture 'for the people' — but is located in the points of confluence between these opposing tendencies whose contradictory orientations shape the very organisation of the cultural forms in which they meet and interpenetrate one another.

Dominant culture gains a purchase in this sphere not in being imposed, as an alien and external force, on to the cultures of subordinate groups, but by reaching into those cultures, reshaping them, hooking them and, with them, the people whose consciousness and experience is defined in their terms, into an association with the values and ideologies of the ruling groups in society. Such processes neither erase the cultures of subordinate groups, nor do they rob 'the people' of their 'true culture': what they do do is shuffle those cultures on to an ideological and cultural terrain in which they can be disconnected from whatever radical impulses which may (but need not) have fuelled them and be connected to more conservative or, often, downright reactionary cultural and ideological tendencies. Similarly, resistance to the dominant culture does not take the form of launching against it a ready-formed, constantly simmering oppositional culture — always there, but in need of being turned up from time to time. Oppositional cultural values are formed and take shape only in the context of their struggle with the dominant culture, a struggle which may borrow some of its resources from that culture and which must concede some ground to it if it is to be able to connect with it — and thereby with those whose consciousness and experience is partly shaped by it — in order, by turning it back upon itself, to peel it away, to create a space within and against it in which contradictory values can echo, reverberate and be heard.

One of the decisive issues at stake in these struggles is precisely the question of 'the people' and 'the popular'. It is, ultimately, for this reason that popular culture cannot be defined in terms of some pre-given sense of 'the people' or 'the popular', for the meaning of these terms is caught up with and depends on the outcome of the struggles which comprise the sphere of popular culture. According to a familiar usage, popular culture is simply that which is 'well-liked by many people'. Clearly, this is not very illuminating unless it is further specified who 'the people' are whose liking is to be counted as pertinent. In one sense, 'the people' consists of everyone. After all, we're all people, aren't we? In another sense, as we have seen, 'the people' may be equated with the working class. In yet another sense, derived from French, Italian and Spanish usage and routed into Marxist theory via Gramsci, 'the people' refers neither to everyone nor to a single group within society but to a variety of social groups which, although differing from one another in other respects (their class position or the particular struggles in which they are most immediately engaged), are distinguished from the economically, politically and culturally powerful groups within society and are hence *potentially* capable of being united — of being organised into 'the people versus the power bloc' — if their separate struggles are connected.

These different versions of 'the people' exist not merely as abstract definitions; they are in play, in more concrete and sensuous forms, in the various struggles through and within which popular culture is itself constituted. 'The people' as everyone, as 'one nation', united in spite of our differences: many popular cultural forms do address and constitute us in this way — the World Cup, in its televised forms, for example,[28] or such public celebrations of the past as Remembrance Day.[29] Others constitute us differently — the Notting Hill carnival, for example (although now increasingly represented by the media as a pageant displaying the essential unity of police and people), or reggae. Or industrial folk-song, whose romantic 'workerism' inscribes us in the place of 'the people' of yesteryear. The question as to who 'the people' are, where they/we will be made to stand, line up and be counted, the political direction in which they/we will be made to point: these are questions which cannot be resolved abstractly; they can only be answered politically. The point is not to define 'the people' but to *make* them, to make that construction of 'the people' which unites a broad alliance of social forces in opposition to the power bloc count politically by winning for it a cultural weight and influence which prevails above others.

Notes

1. Interview with Alexei Sayle, *Marxism Today*, vol. 27, no. 6, June 1983, p. 35.

2. For a useful survey of the structure of media ownership and control in contemporary Britain, see G. Murdoch and P. Golding, 'Capitalism, Communication and Class Relations' in J. Curran, M. Gurevitch and J. Woollacott (eds), *Mass Communication and Society*, Edward Arnold, London, 1977.

3. S. Hall, 'Notes on deconstructing "the popular" ' in R. Samuel (ed), *People's History and Socialist Theory*, Routledge and Kegan Paul, London, 1981, pp. 238–9.

4. B. Brecht, 'Against George Lukács', *New Left Review*, no. 84, March/April, 1974, p. 51.

5. Ibid., p. 49.

6. Ibid., pp. 49–50.

7. Some of the points in this section have been argued at greater length in T. Bennett, 'Marxist cultural theory: in search of "the popular" ', *Australian Journal of Cultural Studies*, vol. 1, no. 2, 1983.

8. *New Left Review*, no. 1, 1960, p. 1.
9. B. Groombridge and P. Whannel, 'Something Rotten in Denmark St', *New Left Review*, no. 1, 1960, pp. 53–4.
10. Ibid., p. 53.
11. B. Schwarz, 'The Communist Party Historians' Group, 1945–56' in Centre for Contemporary Cultural Studies, *Making Histories: Studies in history-writing and politics* Hutchinson, London, 1982, p. 74.
12. Ibid., p. 81. See also, on this point, B. Schwarz and C. Mercer, 'The History Men: Popular Politics and Marxist Theory' in George Bridges and Rosalind Brunt (eds), *Silver Linings*, Lawrence and Wishart, London 1981.
13. See D. Hebdige, 'Towards a Cartography of Taste, 1935–62' in B. Waites, T. Bennett, G. Martin (eds), *Popular Culture: Past and Present*, Croom Helm, London, 1982.
14. These necessary consequences of Lukács's construction of the proletariat as the identical subject-object of history are most revealingly discussed in J. Révai, 'A Review of "History and Class Consciousness" ', *Theoretical Practice*, vol. 1, January 1971.
15. See B. Anderson, *Imagined Communities: Reflections on the Origin and Spread of Nationalism*, Verso Editions and New Left Books, London, 1983.
16. H. Marcuse, *The Aesthetic Dimension: Toward a Critique of Marxist Aesthetics*, Macmillan, London, 1979, pp. 30, 34 and 35.
17. See T. Eagleton, *Walter Benjamin, or Towards a Revolutionary Criticism*, Verso Editions and New Left Books, London, 1981, pp. 148–9.
18. The weaknesses of this approach are discussed in T. Bennett, 'Hegemony, Ideology, Pleasure: Blackpool', included later in this collection.
19. Cited in P. Slater, *Origin and Significance of the Frankfurt School*, Routledge and Kegan Paul, London, 1971, p. 141.
20. S. Hall, 'Popular Culture, Politics and History' in *Popular Culture Bulletin*, no. 3, p. 2 (mimeograph of a seminar held at the Open University).
21. For a fuller discussion of some of the themes elaborated here, see T. Bennett, 'Theories of the media, theories of society' in M. Gurevitch, T. Bennett, J. Curran and J. Woollacott (eds), *Culture, Society and the Media*, Methuen, London, 1982.
22. See T.W. Adorno and M. Horkheimer, 'The Culture Industry: Enlightenment as mass deception' in Curran *et al, Mass Communication and Society*.
23. Ibid., p. 349.
24. Ibid., p. 353.
25. S. Hall, 'Notes on deconstructing "the popular" ', p. 232.
26. See C. Critcher, 'Football since the War' in J. Clarke, C. Critcher and R. Johnson (eds), *Working Class Culture: Studies in History and Theory*, Hutchinson, London, 1979.
27. See T. Mason, *Association Football and English Society, 1863–1915*, Harvester Press, Brighton, 1981.
28. See G. Nowell-Smith, 'Television — Football — The World' in T. Bennett, S. Boyd-Bowman, C. Mercer and J. Woollacott (eds), *Popular Television and Film*, British Film Institute, London, 1981.
29. For a discussion of the role of such celebrations, see P. Wright, 'A Blue Plaque for the Labour Movement? Some Political Meanings of the "National Past" ' in *Formations of Nation and People*, Routledge and Kegan Paul, London, 1984.

2

Stuart Hall

Popular culture and the state

. . . every state is ethical in as much as one of its most important functions is to raise the great mass of the population to a particular cultural and moral level; a level (or type) which corresponds to the needs of the productive forces for development, and hence to the interests of the ruling classes. The school as a positive educative function, and the courts as a repressive and negative educative function, are the most important state activities in this sense; but, in reality, a multitude of other so-called private initiatives and activities tend to the same end — initiatives and activities which form the apparatuses of the political and cultural hegemony of the ruling classes.

Antonio Gramsci[1]

The difficulties associated with the theory of the state Gramsci develops in *The Prison Notebooks* are well known. The sphere of the state is so expanded, reaching so deeply into the recesses of civil society, that, in some of his formulations, the distinction between the two spheres evaporates entirely. The most notorious instance is an earlier passage in *The Prison Notebooks* where Gramsci defines the state as 'the entire complex of practical and theoretical activities with which the ruling class not only justifies its dominance but manages to win the active consent of those over whom it rules'.[2] For all that, the decisive significance of Gramsci's work, the respects in which it constitutes a veritable Copernican revolution in Marxist approaches to the state, consists in the stress it places on the positive, productive aspects of the state rather than seeing its functions as merely negative and repressive. Additionally, and for the first time, Gramsci placed questions of culture, and especially popular culture, at the very centre of the state's sphere of activity. The modern democratic state, Gramsci argued, forms and organises society not only in economic life but on a broad front. 'Its aim is always that of . . . adapting the ''civilization'' and morality of the broadest popular masses to the necessities of the continuous development of the economic apparatus of production.'[3] The state, according to this view, is the site of a permanent struggle to conform — that is, to bring into line or harness — the whole complex of social relations, including those of civil society, to the imperatives of development in a social formation. It constitutes one of the principal forces which mediates between cultural formations and class relations, drawing these into particular configurations and harnessing them to particular hegemonic strategies.

In this essay, I want to use this Gramscian perspective on the state to illuminate the respects in which, in different moments, the British state has always played a crucial role in conforming popular culture to the dominant culture. A detailed analysis of the history of state interventions in the sphere of popular culture cannot be attempted here. The most that can be offered is a series of 'shapshots' of different moments in the history of relations between the state and popular culture in Britain — the role of the law in mediating class cultural relations in the eighteenth century, the relations between the state and the 'free press' in the nineteenth century and the more recent development of broadcasting institutions in a relationship of 'relative autonomy' to the state. In adopting such a long historical conspectus on the relations between the state and popular culture, it is necessary to be clear that neither the state nor popular culture exhibits a continuous, uninterrupted identity throughout this long period of capitalist development. The constitution of both the state and popular culture themselves changes just as do the relations between them; indeed, their shifting constitution is, in part, an effect of the changing relations between them and of the ways in which such transformations have contributed to and been informed by more epochal shifts in the organisation of class-cultural relationships and the associated forms and mechanisms of ruling class hegemony.

I want, therefore, to argue very strongly that there is no simple historical evolution of popular culture from one period to another. The study of popular culture has been somewhat bedevilled by this descriptive approach, tracing the internal evolution of popular pastimes, from hunting wild boar to collecting garden gnomes, strung together by an evolutionary chain of 'things' slowly 'becoming' other things. Against this approach, I want to insist that, historically, we must attend to breaks and discontinuities: the points where a whole set of patterns and relations is drastically reshaped or transformed. We must try to identify the periods of relative 'settlement' — when not only the inventories of popular culture, but the relations between popular and dominant cultures, remain relatively settled. Then, we need to identify the turning points, when relations are qualitatively restructured and transformed — the moments of transition.

This will produce a historical periodisation which goes beyond the merely descriptive to apprehend the shifts in cultural relations which punctuate the development of popular culture. These turning points occur, not when the internal inventory (contents) of popular culture changes, but when cultural relations between the popular and the dominant cultures shift. This point can be made more concrete by contrasting its implications with those of two conventional 'historical' accounts of changes in popular culture. The first — stressing evolution and continuity — compares traditional village football with the modern 'association rules' version of the game. The second acknowledges change, but sees this in terms of a change of content only: here cock-fighting, bull-baiting and other rural blood sports are substituted for by modern football — all considered 'the same' in their function, because they were all popular with the popular classes of their time. Now, of course, traditional village football bears some resemblance to twentieth-century cup and league soccer. But historically the similarities tell us very little: it is the distinctions that are telling. Pre-industrial football was highly irregular, unformalised, without standard rules (the ball could be carried, thrown, snatched as well as kicked, the only prohibition being that it could not be given — i.e. in a polite manner — to a 'less beleaguered friend'!). It sometimes involved hundreds of participants, on unmarked fields or through the town streets, each game being governed by local traditions, and not infrequently, as Malcolmson notes, ending in the reading of the Riot Act.[4] By contrast, the modern game is highly regulated and systematised, administered centrally and organised according to universally observed and refereed rules. Its high points are national and international rather than parochial — though ties of locality remain strong. It has been redesigned for spectatorship rather than participation, the 'tumult' occuring on the terraces rather than on the field of play.

These contrasts bring out qualitative differences: between a rural society, regulated by custom, local tradition and the particularism of small, face-to-face communities, and an urban-centralised society governed by universally applied rules and a legal and rational mode of regulation. Nor was there any smooth evolution from one to the other. The traditional game became the object of a massive assault by the governing classes and authorities — part of a general attack on popular recreations in order to moralise the poorer classes and make them more regular and industrious in their habits. The separation of the game from local community life and space flowed from this destruction of older patterns of life and their thorough reorganization under new moral and social auspices in the second half of the nineteenth century: 'let them assemble in the Siddals or some such place, so as not to interfere with the avocation of the industrious part of the community', one Derby critic wrote in 1832.[5]

As to the second example: this traces an evolution from, say, cock-fighting (popular in eighteenth century) to football (popular in twentieth century). But this only makes sense if the activity is isolated from the cultural meanings and social relations in which it is embedded. The example changes at once if we look, instead, at shifts between the whole complex of social relations, not just the activity itself:

cock-fighting   football
gentry   bourgeoisie

rural labourers	industrial workers
village	city
parish	suburb
custom	law
common rights	property rights
local sanctions	public order

Here, we are looking at the 'evolution' of popular culture across a set of major historical transformations: a shift, not just from one pastime to another, but between historical epochs. Cock-fighting was made illegal, not only because it was frowned on by the 'polite' (it always was), but because some of the 'polite' acquired the means to impose habits and standards of a more urban character on rustic life (implying changes in law and state); and because politeness had assumed a new, sober and evangelical connotation (implying changes in religious and moral attitude).

These shifts in cultural practice and ideology reflected deep changes in class relations. Blood sports, for all their sanguinary nature, were indulged in by some sections of both the major agrarian classes of society (labouring poor and the bucolic country-gentry: no 'gentle' gentry *women* cock-fighters are recorded), within the complex tissue of customary understandings — the paternalist/plebeian relations — which framed so many of the relations between the rural classes. Let us not romanticise this 'organic' relationship. Because customary standards were set and power over their practice dispensed locally, a landlord and his tenant could meet individually at a 'cocking' without either presuming for a moment that he could really bridge the immense vertical distances separating the landed and the labouring classes. A very different web of relations and understandings mediates the classes involved in modern football. Modern soccer is no longer local in this sense — even where a strong sense of local loyalty persists. It is 'realised' as much through the mass spectatorship of the modern media as it is in direct participation. In its immediate culture of support, the defining presence is that of the urban-industrial classes (and their professional fellow-travellers). The dominant classes appear to be largely absent — though they are often present in the financing, administration and chairmanship of the game.

These two activities are only 'the same' in some obvious, meaningless and general way. Both were embedded in and helped to sustain a set of class-cultural relations; but each mediated and sustained a different set. Each was 'popular'; but 'popularity' was differently articulated in each case. The paternalism-deference of the first was part of a culture which *bound* and *separated* the fundamental classes of eighteenth-century agrarian capitalist society. The second is constructed through the *separation out* of the fundamental classes of advanced industrial capitalism and their *recombination* as a 'mass'. In this example, then, what matter, for the history of popular culture, in its full sense, are breaks, discontinuities, transformations, asymmetry: the sharply differing articulations of cultural space, in the two periods.

Like 'popular culture', there is no entity called 'the state' which unfolds across the ages while remaining the same. The field of action of the state has altered almost beyond recognition over the last three centuries. The eighteenth-century state had no regular police, no standing army, and was based on a highly restrictive male franchise. The nineteenth-century state owned no industries, supervised no universal system of education, was not responsible for national economic policy or a network of welfare provisions. There is no steady, unbroken line of development from 'small beginnings' to interventionist monolith. Under the mercantilist system, which flourished from the mid-sixteenth to the mid-eighteenth century, during which the early commercial expansion of Britain occurred, the state played a direct role in the economy, regulating commerce, establishing monopolies under charter and securing favourable terms of trade. *Laissez-faire* political economy, which displaced mercantilism as economic doctrine, and achieved its zenith in the nineteenth century, when Britain became 'the workshop of the world', was founded on diametrically opposite principles: the market flourished best when left to its own devices, without the intereference of the state.

Changes in the political composition of the state are almost as dramatic. In the eighteenth century, the great mass of the popular classes had no vote of any kind. The nineteenth century was dominated by the struggles of the popular classes to extend the franchise — a process long delayed by a series of 'last-ditch' resistances by the powerful. Full adult suffrage was not completed until the twentieth century (1928) — the resistance against female suffrage being one of the last (and most squalid) episodes of the whole struggle.

The twentieth century, it is often argued, has seen the growth of the all-encompassing state, from the cradle to the grave. Yet its role cannot be understood unless it is separated out from what it is not. The state is both *of* and *over* society. It arises from society; but it also reflects, in its operations, the society over which it exercises authority and rule. It is both part of society, and yet separate from it. Hence, there is always a line between 'public' matters (which the state claims a legitimate right to interfere in) and 'private' spheres (which belong to the voluntary arrangements between individuals, separate from state regulation). Exactly where this boundary line falls is sometimes difficult to establish. It certainly changes from one period to another, or one society to another. In the nineteenth century, the domestic privacy of the 'home' was an Englishman's (private) castle; *his* wife was so deeply ensnared in the 'private' that she could not own property, vote or stand for public political office. In the twentieth century, the family has progressively become the site of extended state intervention, and has thus been drawn increasingly into the 'public' sphere. Under *laissez-faire* capitalism, the economy, education and the press were privately owned, organised and managed: they belonged to 'civil society'. Today, under advanced capitalism, the economy is largely private, though there is a significant 'public' or state sector; education is substantially 'public' — though the 'public schools' are still private! And the press is privately owned (could it be 'free' otherwise?).

We can see here how the *theoretical* problem which Gramsci's work raises regarding the relations between the state and civil society is, at the same time, a historical problem. The shifting boundary line between state and civil society is one whose very shifts tell us a great deal about the changing character of the state. It is a significant moment, for example, when culture ceases to be the privilege and prerogative of the cultivation of *private* individuals and begins to be a matter for which the state takes public responsibility. In this light, it is worth recalling that Gramsci's expanded definition of the state was intended to apply specifically to the modern democratic state and the expanded range of functions it abrogated for itself, reaching so deeply into civil society as to unsettle the confident nineteenth-century distinction between state and civil society, rather than as a theory of state forms in general. This is not to suggest that the development of state forms can be viewed as one of the incessant, step-by-step encroachment on the terrain of civil society. The development of the state's role in relation to popular culture from the eighteenth to the twentieth century bears witness not merely to a quantitative increase in the state's role in cultural regulation but also to a series of qualitative transformations in state—culture relations.

Law, class and culture: an eighteenth-century example

The class which primarily benefited from the Hanoverian settlement of 1688 was the 'landed interest'. This was composed of men of substantial landed property, whether aristocrat or gentry, who gradually established themselves as a 'superbly successful and self-confident capitalist class'.[6] They secured their annual incomes by rents and agricultural improvements, expanded their estates by judicious marriage settlements and enclosures; ventured into trade and commerce for the growing markets at home and abroad; and began to develop domestic and small-scale manufacturing. Land, trade, commerce and the market created an immense belt of agrarian capitalist wealth, property and power: the material basis of a class 'profoundly capitalist in style of thought . . . zestfully acquisitive and meticulous in their attention to accountancy'[7] — i.e. the first 'bourgeois culture' the world had ever seen.

The eighteenth-century state was, in the view of many historians, a parasitic formation: small, compact, reflecting the cohesion of and vertical ties between the small élite who constituted the 'political nation'. As Namier has shown, it was divided by factional rivalry, but solidified

27

through nepotism, patronage, favour, advancement, the purchase of office, and the free play of bribery and corruption.[8] The independent country-genry kept themselves at home. The grandees and their networks of clients and hangers-on more strenuously involved themselves in manipulating the state to their advantage, exploiting the narrow factionalism of eighteenth-century party politics. The state was therefore homogeneous, but weak. Large tracts of social life remained largely outside its effective control. State power had devolved to the local bastions of the gentry who ruled, regulated and judged in their country seats and parishes. Central state control over a tumultuous and riotous labouring population was fitful and uncertain. Sometimes power was maintained through a complicated balancing act of negotiation between the different factions; sometimes by draconian measures, excursions into the ungovernable areas and bouts of judicial terror, supplemented by the Riot Act, the threat of militia and the gallows. Yet this unique and parasitic formation — what Cobbett called 'Old Corruption' — presided over an astonishing growth in trade, the amassing of great estates and fortunes; it successfully pursued an expansionist policy abroad and, as Anderson notes, secured for the propertied at home an astonishing social stability, without the aid of either a standing army or a regular police.[9] How was this achieved? Partly through the law — 'the strongest link of the body politic' in the eighteenth century.

Was the law, then, simply a branch of the eighteenth-century state? Yes and no. Yes, because the 'rule of law' was already established. Courts and judges derived authority from state and crown. The state enforced the 'due legal process'. No, because the law was so much at the disposal of private individuals, and so thoroughly imprinted with the class relations of eighteenth-century civil society.

Seen from above, the law was a mighty, terrible engine. It was also haphazard, irregular and uncodified: a jumble of ancient common law and hastily enacted statute. It was arbitrary, with no relation between offence and sentence, and severe. The principal punishment for serious offences was death by public hanging. Judges often exercised their wide powers of discretion — but, according to Hay, in an unpredictable manner.[10] The exercise of legal power was under the practical monopoly of the leading social classes. They used it to defend and advance their rights and properties and to enhance their authority. During and after the English Revolution, the independent gentry had used the principles of the rights of free-born Englishmen, guaranteed under law, to advance their cause against crown and court. By the 'free-born' they meant themselves — since the term did not include women, domestics or the mass of the labouring poor. To them, the 'rule of law' meant the maintenance of public order, the protection of property and the preservation of liberty — their order, property, liberties. These had to be secured through the procedure and constraints of the law, and this had contradictory consequences. On the one hand, rule 'by law' further enhanced their authority. They identified themselves with it, thereby appropriating its majesty. The awe aroused in the populace by the pomp and ceremony of the law became vested in them. They used the courts to preach secular sermons on the virtues of established authority, the need for respect and the necessity for obedience. Public trials and strict procedure, at least in the higher courts, were offered as formal proof that all men were equal before the law, despite its lack of observance in practice. On the other hand, having affirmed the rule of law as the free-born Englishmen's rightful inheritance, it became increasingly difficult to refuse to extend it to poor and powerless Englishmen. And though in practice the law rarely worked in the latter's favour, they were free to put themselves 'at law', to claim justice and seek redress of grievance. And they sometimes were rewarded — not often enough ever to lose sight of the class nature of the justice they received, but often enough not to regard the 'rule of law' as an empty sham. So, as Thompson has shown in convincing detail, the law came to provide a framework in which the liberties of the landed classes and the injustices against the poor were negotiated, struggled over and fought through.[11]

The exercise of justice thus presents us with a picture of the massive social power of the dominant classes — but legalised power: power that had acquired a measure of legitimacy and consent because it was articulated through the law — but also for that very reason, subject to its constraints. The law was therefore never simply and exclusively an instrument of ruling-class oppression. A plebeian version of the 'rule of law' gradually took root in popular attitudes and culture, contesting more patrician interpretations. Not only were social struggles framed by overlapping conceptions of law and justice. Legal language and precedent could be expropriated into and reworked as part of popular conceptions of 'grievance and justice'. If the popular classes were bound to power and property, through law, they could also use it to bring pressure to bear against property and power. Paradoxically, though, the very fact that conflicts were played out within the framework of law helped to hold an unequal and tumultuous society together:

> Those in authority knew that protests about specific grievances were intended to provoke a remedial response, and not to challenge authority *per se*. Such an assumption was only possible as long as the aggrieved had some faith in authority's willingness to be bound by the law and the ideals it was supposed to embody. Negotiation, of course, was not carried on between equals.[12]

The delicate balances on which this negotiation depended may be observed in the judicious mixture of legal and illegal means which the popular classes used to bend the rule of law in their favour. When the price of bread rose or the supply dropped away, the labouring poor would often seek redress from a magistrate, requiring him to 'fix a fair price'. If he did not, riot and tumult frequently followed. The century was constantly interrupted by these bread riots by the hard-pressed poor who, when 'negotiation with the law' failed, took to 'bargaining by riot'.[13] Yet these riotous occasions were subject to a high degree of popular discipline. Corn sacks were ripped open, the grain scattered, butter, cheese and bacon sold at a 'fair price' — the crowd returning the money to the miller. Bread riots were highly ceremonial and disciplined occasions. Processions were decorated with flags, emblems, ribbons and favours; the crowd, led by a woman ringing a bell, or by horns and drums; the loaves draped in black crepe or smeared with blood. This was the 'theatre' of popular justice.

These cultural practices secreted alternative moral ideas and social conceptions. Rural society was still in considerable part regulated by custom, tradition and unwritten precedent. But as property, trade and the free market in goods and labour began to impress their patterns on social life, transforming rural England into a fully-fledged agrarian capitalism, the society was gradually tutored, bludgeoned, driven and enticed along a road away from 'custom' and towards the 'law' of property and the market forces. The law became one of the principal instruments of this transformation — entailing a shift from economic self-sufficiency to marketing for profit, from custom to law, from the 'organic compulsions of the manor and guild to the atomized compulsions of the free labour market . . . a comprehensive conflict and redefinition at every level, as organic and magical views of society gave way before natural law, and as the acquisitive ethic encroached upon an authoritarian moral economy'.[14] One of the principal things at stake in this historic transformation was precisely the customs, practices and ideas — the culture — of the 'common people'.

Custom informed real economic practice: for example, the decision as to what was a 'fair price'. But it was also inscribed in ideology and belief: the notion that there could be something like a fair price; that, in times of scarcity, there was a *moral limit* to the miller's or the merchant's right to profit at the expense of the poor; the belief that there was, as Thompson calls it, a 'moral economy', larger and more compulsive than the pure laws of the market.[15] That whole customary culture had to be actively dismantled, and refashioned into one based on the 'morality' of the free market. The law was one means by which a culture of custom and paternalism was reshaped into a culture of law, property and the free market. This transformation required that the older plebeian culture be broken up and set aside, so that new patterns, attitudes and habits could be formed in its place. It involved the destruction of one culture, and the 're-formation' of society, the re-education of the people, into 'a new type of civilization': the civilization of a fully-developed agrarian capitalism. The fracturing of this older culture and the construction of the habits of regular 'free labour', of private property and the laws of political economy among the popular classes was conducted, in part, through the mediation of the law and the state.

This is, of course, no more than a 'snapshot' of the relations between the law and popular culture in the eighteenth century. None the less, we can see how the state, through the law, intervened in the relations between the classes and the cultures. It helped to define and fix relations of power, authority and consent between the dominant (i.e. landed) and the dominated (i.e. labouring) classes. It also mediated the cultures (paternalist/deferential; plebeian and patrician; the authoritative-legal conceptions of 'rights' and 'justice' versus popular conceptions). It played an educative/ideological as well as a repressive/coercive role. It transformed practices — legal (from customary regulation to the formal law) and moral ones (setting a 'fair' price; 'bargaining' by riot), as well as economic. It was part of a major historic transformation. It was also an instrument through which society was 'conformed' to certain historical imperatives — the formation of a fully-formed bourgeois society; the shift from a 'natural' to a 'market' economy; the transition into agrarian capitalism. It transformed cultural habits, ideas and practices — breaking and reorganizing popular customs. It nevertheless sustained a particular type of authority (the 'rule of law'), which mediated and contained social struggles and secured a particular type of legitimacy and consent to the authority of a particular social bloc. The 'cultures' of the dominant and the popular classes were a critical site in this whole process.

The liberties of the press and the voice of the people

In this second case study, we shift our attention from the law to a cultural apparatus in the more direct sense: the press. We consider the role of the state in the formation of a national popular press. Through the organs of the press, the different classes of society are given a voice. Through these organs, the people and 'popular opinion' are represented to the state. The organs of public opinion therefore institutionalise a particular set of social and cultural relations. This configuration is underpinned by an ideological model — the model of the 'free press'. It is crucial for this model that, unlike the law (which derives from the state), the press belongs to the terrain, not of the state, but of civil society. In democratic class societies, the whole *raison d'être* of the 'free press' is that it is *not* directed by, owned by, or bound to the state. It operates freely and voluntarily. Its only limits are the laws of libel and commercial viability. Indeed, it is *because* the press is 'free' in the market sense that it is said to be the bulwark of 'the people' against the power of the state, the defender of English liberties and the independent voice of the nation. In the nineteenth century this was a *new* cultural model, a new configuration of cultural power. It organised the elements in the state—culture—class equation into a new 'equilibrium of

31

authority and consent' on the basis of a new articulation of the relations between state and civil society.

The reading public, the market and the Fourth Estate
The rise of an independent 'public opinion', literary production for the market and a free press were all associated with the growth of the urban bourgeoisie. The expansion of reading in the second half of the eighteenth century was very rapid. The new reading public included self-taught and pious working people, small shopkeepers, skilled journeymen, independent tradesmen, the artisan classes and clerical workers. Women of all classes constituted a significant element in this new reading public. 'General literature now pervades the nation through all its ranks', Dr. Johnson observed in 1779.[16] But it was the expansion of those ranks associated with commerce and manufacture and their domestic counterpart in the home — now, increasingly for this class, separated from the masculine world of work — that 'altered the centre of gravity of the reading public sufficiently to place the middle class as a whole in a dominating position for the first time'.[17]

Not yet a politically cohesive force, the middle classes nevertheless discovered, through this expanded 'public sphere' in civil society, a significant 'voice', a source of cultural power and a means of self-definition as a class. New forms and practices — the novel, the great literary periodicals, the newspapers, writing and publishing for profit, reviewing — were created *for* this new public, *about* this new public: forming their experience, giving expression to their cultural ideas and aspirations. The famous periodicals of the time — the *Tatler*, the *Spectator*, the *Gentleman's Magazine* — helped to mould the social taste and manners of men in the image of the bourgeois 'gentleman'.

Conduct books, pamphlets of religious guidance, the polite journals and the novel served, in the same way, to help create a 'private' culture and to define a domestic ideal for the bourgeoisie as a whole, and especially for women — guardians of the hearth and homes of 'fit and proper' (male) persons. The world of the new middle ranks acquired a very particular cultural definition through the newly created institutions of voluntary association (civil society). It was divided and punctuated into the great 'separate spheres' of public and private, around which urban bourgeois culture cohered. The organs of the press were paradigm instances of these new social institutions: developed outside the state, in the voluntary world of civil society, helping to constitute the classes whom they addressed, as a public cultural force. The fortunes of this rising class depended on the application of keen *laissez-faire* principles and they extended this new political economy to the world of publishing — writing for profit rather than patronage; printing and selling books like other commodities in the market-place; catering for the private tastes of an expanded buying and reading public; and providing a channel for the classified commercial advertiser to address his clientele.

One great, new commercial publishing form was the newspaper. The state licensing system for newspapers was abolished in 1695. Thereafter, newspapers of all types, kinds and sizes expanded phenomenally. By the 1770s, there were nine London daily papers. In 1746, 2,500 copies of each issue of the *London Daily Post* were printed. The market was also flooded by an army of unstamped dailies and thrice-weeklies, often circulating at half price. Distribution within the city was supported by a 'floating and semi-destitute population of hawkers'.[18] By 1790, 4,650 copies of London papers were passing by way of the Post Office into the country. A similar distribution system developed for the provincial papers.

This rapidly expanding cultural industry constituted the 'reading public' as a *cultural market* for the first time. It introduced the standards of sales and popularity, piracy and 'scribbling', alongside the high standards of literary canon and judgement, into culture. And it helped to fashion the independent middle classes as a political, social and cultural force.

By modern standards, this was a highly regulated 'independence', for in the early stages the state was still heavily involved. For many years, the Secretaries of State acted as the principal retailers of London newspapers. In the 1760s, the extention of MPs' privilege to send franked post through the mail was used to distribute newspapers. In one week in June 1789, 63,177 copies were distributed in this way. In 1712, the first of a series of stamp duties was introduced, designed as a means of policing the press, forcing up the price of newspapers. Newspaper proprietors undertook extraordinary dodges to circumvent stamp duties — registering as pamphlets, or switching to thrice-weekly publication. Alongside the 'stamped' press arose a mass of smaller illegal papers. But in the 1740s this 'unstamped press' was undermined by a legal assault on the hawkers, their only means of distribution, and later on the publishers themselves.

At the same time, the political establishment, curbing the press with one hand, through the state, were active, as private individuals, buying themselves into positions of influence with the other. In the earlier period, the Prime Minister, Walpole, bought up the anti-government *London Journal*, turning it into a vehicle of government propaganda, set up the *Free Briton* and the *Daily Courant*, largely written by government employees, and later, the *Daily Gazeteer*. He spent over £50,000 of Treasury funds on propaganda — largely in the London newspapers. Yet, as the whole economy was gradually transformed by the universal application of the law of free-market profit-maximizing political economy, the independence of the press came to be even more highly prized than its dependability as a kept instrument. This independence was identified with a system whereby opinions circulated, like other commodities, in the market place outside the direct control and supervision of the state.

Indeed, in the heroic version of 'Progress', which dominates popular historical writing to this day, the formation of the *middle classes* as the leading social element in society, the creation of the *free market* as the leading principle of commercial organisation, and the growth of an *independent press* as a 'Fourth Estate' separate from the state, are the essential ingredients of a heroic narrative. This story explains how state restrictions were set aside and the middle classes, basing themselves on the free market, founded a national press; and how only in this way were the liberties of the English people maintained. In fact, between the 1790s and 1830s, and again during Chartism, the ascendancy of this cultural model was powerfully challenged by *another* kind of press, articulating a *different* culture, the voice of a *different* class. This was the press that flourished as part of the radical artisan culture of the 1790s and emerged alongside the institutions of the first industrial working class in the years up to the mid-nineteenth century: the radical press, the 'unstamped', the 'poor men's guardians'. Like the plebeian culture of the eighteenth century, this alternative set of popular institutions had to be actively dismantled before 'freedom' of a quite different kind could be left to organise the opinions of 'the people'.

The challenge: the radical press and popular culture
The existence of a wide and highly 'literate' culture among the popular classes in this period has been greatly underestimated. The radicalising of political class-consciousness in the period of industrial unrest, political agitation and revolutionary wars helped actively to expand and develop that culture. Paine's *Rights of Man* sold 50,000 copies within a few weeks in 1791. Cobbett's *Address to Journeymen and Labourers* sold 200,000 in 1826, his *Political Register* sold up to 44,000 copies at twopence weekly. Wooler's *Black Dwarf* sold 12,000 in 1820 when the circulation of *The Times* was no more than 7,000.

This radical working-class press was labelled by the authorities and established classes as a subversive force. Edmund Burke called it 'the grand instrument of the subversion of morals, religion and human society itself'.[19] Lord Ellenborough, justifying the new Stamp Act of 1819, stated quite clearly that 'it was not against the respectable press that this Bill was directed, but against the pauper press'.[20] In the turbulent period between the 1790s and the Reform Act of 1832, this 'pauper press' was subject to extensive harassment and intimidation. In 1799, all printing presses were required to be registered. The press was severely curtailed in the period of the Six Acts, and again by the 'Gagging Bills' of 1819—20, which extended the scope of the stamp duty and strengthened the seditious libel law. Despite this attack, Doherty's *Voice of the People* and *The Pioneer*, Carlile's *Gauntlet* and Hetherington's *Poor Man's Guardian* all ran to several thousand readers, the first two to above 10,000.[21] The leaders of London radicalism in the 1790s were constantly before the courts on charges of seditious libel in this period. In fact, as Thompson has remarked (and quite contrary to the myth):

There is perhaps no country in the world in which the contest for the rights of the free press was so sharp, so emphatically victorious, and so peculiarly identified with the cause of the artisans and labourers. If Peterloo established (by a paradox of feeling) the right of public demonstration, the rights of a 'free press' were won in a campaign extending over fifteen or more years, which has no comparison for its pig-headedness, bloody-minded and indomitable audacity.[22]

This popular agitation resulted in the repeal of the 'taxes on knowledge' — without which no free press could exist. The duty on pamphlets was abolished in 1833, on advertising in 1853. The stamp duty was reduced from 4*d*. to 1*d*. in 1836, and abolished in 1855. This victory for 'freedom of opinion' was one in which the radical popular press had been greatly instrumental. Yet it was not this, but the commercial bourgeois press that inherited its fruits. How did this occur?

Synthesis, transformation, incorporation
In fact, a new cultural model, and a new set of class-cultural relationships prevailed. In this formation, 'freedom' was redefined. It no longer meant 'free from the tyranny of established authority'. Instead, it came to mean that opinion was regulated *exclusively* by the laws of the market, free competition, private ownership and profitability. Such a market is *formally* 'free', in the sense that the state or the law prohibits no one from owning or publishing a newspaper and expressing views and opinions — provided they have the capital. The state 'interferes' with this freedom only externally and negatively — by insisting that the laws of libel, obscenity competition and fair trading, and so on, are not infringed. Of course, this type of formal 'freedom' also has its own very real positive limits. Gigantic accumulations of capital are required to own, publish, distribute, capitalise and maintain a modern newspaper. The vast majority of people are, basically, free only *to consume* the opinions which others provide.

In fact, the new commercial press which expanded in the wake of the abolition of the 'taxes on knowledge' *did* increasingly depend on the popular classes: but as a reading and buying public, not as a popular cause which it championed. So the 'free market' did build the popular classes into the newspaper business, but only as a necessary economic support. At the same time and by the same process, it *incorporated* them in a *subordinate* position, politically, culturally and socially within a set of relationships institutionalised by the principles of capital investment and free-market competition. Within this class-cultural relationship, 'freedom' acquired a special but restricted meaning: it meant freedom from state intervention, freedom to compete and survive: freedom for the laws of capital accumulation, private appropriation and market competition to operate unhindered. It established no positive *collective* right to express opinions and had little radical-popular content. This definition of freedom is not democratic but *commercial*.

This type of relationship gradually came to dominate the press from the mid-nineteeth century onwards. It contained the seeds of a cultural pattern which became dominant in the modern relations between the state, the classes and public opinion. It hastened the separation of the society into two, distinct and simplified 'publics': the small, 'élite' public, important not because of numbers but because of the strategic nature of its power and influence (attractive, for this reason to advertisers), and the 'mass public' who compensate for their lack of influence by their sheer numerical strength.

This pattern was then reproduced as a cultural distinction — between the 'quality' and the 'popular' press. The latter first began to discover its characteristic cultural form — or formula — in this period. This formula was, in essence, a cultural solution to the problem of the power, rights and opinions of the popular classes — that is, the problem of *democracy*. The problem was essentially this: how to contain the popular classes within the orbit and authority of the dominant culture, while allowing them the formal right to express opinions. To do this, a press was created that *reflected* popular interests, tastes, preoccupations, concerns, levels of education (sufficient, that is, to win popular identification and consent); but which *did not become* an authentic 'voice' of the popular interest, which might then be tempted to voice its opinions independently, and thus forge a unity as a social and political force (as the Chartist press had attempted to do). The new 'popular' press was a press *about* and *bought by* but not *produced by*, or *committed to the cause of*, the popular classes. The formula for this type of cultural incorporation was generated out of a synthesis between two earlier models: the Sunday press and the popular miscellanies.

The 'Sundays' had often had larger circulations than the daily press, with a wider social readership. They were fully commercial enterprises, reflecting the largely non-political concerns of urban popular culture, giving prominence to crime and violence, sex and scandal, sensation and titbits. As the century advanced, this formula provided the model for the new commercial 'popular press'. For the Sunday formula represented a synthesis between the old, non-political tradition of popular chap-book, criminal confession, life-of-the-highwayman or 'dying speech', and the more recent political radicalism of the Unstamped and Chartist press: 'It was an important half-way stage in the development of the modern popular press; but the commercial pressures inherent in its appeal to a mass audience resulted, too, in a significant dilution and manipulation of the many traditions of the earlier radical press.'[23]

This formula *synthesised* traditional and radical elements: the 'plain-spoken bluntness' of the radical tradition was diluted into a style ('The Daily . . . is not afraid to call a spade a bloody shovel . . .') and the 'vigour' of traditional popular culture appeared as a dispersed sensationalism

('Read all about it'!). These elements were, however, synthesised on the ground of capitalist commercial principle and organization. John Cleave's highly successful *Weekly Police Gazette*, for example, combined popular radicalism and police court cases. *Lloyds,* with a very similar mix, was the first to sell a million copies.

In summary, then, we can see how, in the transition of the press from state to market regulation, a new (and highly contradictory) configuration of class and cultural elements emerged. This formation was very different from that which prevailed a century before. It was achieved through a new cultural institution — the 'free' commercial press (i.e. the *withdrawal* of the state from the sphere of competition). This, in turn, institutionalised a new set of class-cultural relationships (that is, gave them a 'permanent' form, regularised, stabilised, and fixed them in a certain pattern). The heart of this relationship was the constitution of the popular classes as an economically essential but culturally and ideologically dependent and subordinate element. They were bound to, or incorporated into, the ascendancy of the dominant classes, through a *new form*: the so-called 'popular press' formula. This formula transformed and reworked old elements (radical and traditional) into a new synthesis. This is the origin and basis of the modern discourses of the popular press and popular commercial journalism. Through the operation of these discourses, the press was subdivided into two unequal parts: the 'quality' and the 'popular', each carrying a different cultural value or index. 'Quality' is serious; 'popular' is entertaining but trivial. The whole terrain of cultural practices and relationships in contemporary British society is *mapped into* these mutually exclusive, polarized binary opposites. What is 'popular' cannot be 'serious'. What is 'quality' must be powerful. What is entertaining cannot be 'quality', and so on. The readers are also constructed as two distinct kinds of public: highbrow and lowbrow. Through these processes, a new 'equilibrium of power' was established. The popular classes entered the free market in opinions under the leadership and authority (hegemony) of bourgeois opinions: the latter were secured in their place of dominance (ideologically) by the 'logic' of commercial capital (economic).

State, culture and public authority: the case of broadcasting

The class-cultural relations institutionalised through the free press/free market principle have survived into the twentieth century. The principle that culture should be largely organised on the private choice/market competition/private profitability system, outside the state, remains a powerful one. Thus, even today, the British state plays a far less extensive role in cultural matters than in other European societies. Eastern European — and some Western — countries have their Ministries of Culture; Britain has only the Department of Education and Science. France's 'academies' define national standards in scholarship in ways to which the British Royal Society does not aspire. Britain keeps no regular cultural statistics, as other UNESCO member-states do, as indicators of the direction of 'cultural development' or 'life-long education'. We do now have an Arts Council financed through state subsidy, and other bodies to protect the national heritage. But attitudes to the Arts Council are notoriously ambiguous. Though financed by the state, its detailed policies are defined by 'independent committees' — the famous British 'mixed' system.

Of course, the British state has assumed wide responsibilities for the *conditions for culture* in a broader sense. Especially through its education systems, it assumes responsibility for the definition and transmission of cultural traditions and values, for the organization of knowledge, for the distribution of what Pierre Bourdieu calls 'cultural capital' throughout the different classes; and for the formation and qualification of intellectual strata — the guardians of cultural tradition. The state has become an active force in *cultural reproduction*.

What is more, in critical areas, the voluntary private market-dominated system of organization ceased for much of the twentieth century to be the dominant one through which class-cultural relations are arranged (though in the 1980s its dominance in culture is being vigorously restored). New sources of cultural authority and new models of cultural hegemony were developed, constituting new class-cultural relations and cementing a new 'equilibrium of authority'. And all of these were in the early and middle decades of the twentieth century, much more directly mediated by and through the state. In our third case, we look at one such development, focusing on another period of historical transition — that which occurred at the end of the nineteenth and beginning of the twentieth-centuries.

The containment of democracy

This is a period of profound historical transformation. It precipitated a social crisis, the main elements of which were as follows. Firstly, Britain's industrial and commercial dominance ended with the industrialisation of the other major powers, and the intensification of economic competition and imperialist rivalry. Secondly, this was reflected in a loss of leadership in the field of economic production, as UK productivity levels were surpassed by Germany, Japan and the US. Thirdly, this break-up of past economic supremacy triggered off a fragmentation and reconstruction of political parties, formations, and philosophies. *Laissez-faire* political economy and political individualism, which had been pivotal to the parties and ideas of liberal reform (the dominant political philosophy of the middle of the century), lost their hegemony and new political formations emerged, totally transforming the political scene. The modern forms of mass-industrial labour first appeared in this period, giving rise to new types of labour organisation (the *general* trade unions for semi-skilled and unskilled labour, replacing the craft unions and skilled 'aristocracies of labour' which had dominated trade union and radical-liberal politics in the earlier period). Eventually, this social force broke its alliance with the radical tail of the Liberal party and emerged on the political stage as an independent 'party of labour' — the Labour Party. Women entered the struggle for mass political enfranchisement.

What condensed these different levels of social and economic crisis into a problem of *class authority* was the shift in the balance of social forces which came to be defined as 'the problem of democracy'. The struggle to widen the political franchise to all adult males was at last near its end. And, as the great majority of the men in the popular classes entered the 'political nation' fully enfranchised as citizens, the challenge of democracy to the old class alliances and political leaderships assumed a new thrust. This was compounded by the emergence of a vigorous and determined feminism, struggling to win the same rights of representation for adult women.

The 'rise of democracy' shook earlier models of class and cultural authority to their foundations. The state could no longer be the arena in which the established classes simply 'took note of' and accommodated the views and interests of the unrepresented parts of the nation. It had become, formally at least, fully representative (one man, and shortly thereafter, one person, one vote) and its rule had, therefore, to assume the appearance of universality — treating all its citizens, equally. This posed quite new problems of political, social and cultural management. The leading social classes and their interests had to sustain their position of dominance — yet, somehow, within a state which claimed that political power had been equalised and 'democratised'. The question, then, was how to *contain* democracy while, at the same time, maintaining popular consent, in the circumstances of economic upheaval and intensified international rivalry. This required a programme of social reconstruction — to modernise, renovate and restructure society and the state, while retaining the existing hierarchy of power and authority, and securing to this national programme the cohesion of popular consent: a problem, in short, not of 'democracy' but of hegemony! The only force capable of imposing authority and leadership in these circumstances was a new type of state: the universal neutral state, representative of all the classes; the 'representative state', the state of 'the people', the common good, the 'general interest'; the state that could steer, incite and educate society along certain definite pathways, while retaining its appearance of universality and class independence — 'above the struggle', party to none.

Such a profound reconstruction of the British state did, indeed, occur: in true pragmatic British fashion, not all at one stroke; not all in the same period; with backwards and forwards movements, accreting itself, as Middlemas has put it, through the slow growth of a 'collectivist bias' rather than by the brutal imposition of a Prussian-type state solution.[24] The question of how democracy could be contained was also a cultural one: how to create, above the contending class-cultures and interests, a source of national cultural authority which could defend the leadership of the dominant class-cultural formations, but so stamp it with the 'seal of general social recognition' as to incorporate into it the respect and consent of other classes.

This period is, consequently, massively cross-cut by varieties of new doctrines about society and the state: encroaching into, borrowing from, distinguishing themselves in strident debate against one another. These proliferating discourses and ideas were united, *negatively*, by their desertion of the old ground of liberal-individualism and *laissez-faire; positively*, by their subscription to new models of social collectivism, at the centre of which stood a new conception of the 'ethical' role of the state. This new conception of the state was articulated through a range of doctrines: Social Imperialism, 'national efficiency', tarrif reform, 'new' liberalism, Fabian socialism, Lloyd George coalitionism, Social Darwinism, ethical Christianity, and other philosophical schools and political tendencies which contributed to the formation of a new collectivism, based on the ideal of a universal, interventionist state.

In the cultural sphere, this had been germinating for some time. As early as 1867, in the sound of the Hyde Park railings being rattled during the reform agitations, Matthew Arnold thought he heard the approach of democracy. But, like so many of his cultivated contemporaries and successors, he interpreted it as the harbinger of 'anarchy'. In *Culture and Anarchy*, Arnold's principal theme was how to create an alternative centre of authority to democracy and the costs which the nation would have to pay for leaving the resolution of the problem to a straight struggle between the aristocratic, middle and working classes. These needed, in troubled times, he argued, something that could transcend the ding-dong, establish criteria of excellence and intelligence — a realm of the ideal, of 'sweetness and light', beyond, above and against immediate cultural-class interests. This ideal — which he called 'Culture' — could not, in his view, be constructed unless it were founded squarely on an authority which could abstract itself from each class and stand for or represent only society's 'best self'. The source of this authority must be the state.[25]

The brute force of monopoly

This ideal was set in place in the management of opinion and consent via the assertion of state regulation of the new and developing means of communication. The period from the later years of the nineteenth century to the 1920s saw the birth, in rapid succession, of the still photograph, moving photography and the cinema, cable telegraphy, wireless telegraphy, the phonograph, the telephone, radio and finally television. The technical and commercial pioneer of wireless and radio was the great international Marconi Company, founded in 1897. But 'broadcasting of speech and music', first made in 1906, seemed trivial, at first, in comparison with the commercial potential of 'telegraphy without connecting wires', quickly dominated by Marconi — an oligopoly of a quite new type. The strategic role of wireless only became obvious during the First World War. But this introduced a new factor: the question of control. Its strategic importance made wireless a subject of great interest to the military and defence establishment. By the Wireless Telegraphy Act in 1904, 'all transmitters or receivers of wireless signals had to have a licence, the terms and conditions of which were laid down by the Post Office'. Amateur radio broadcasts were banned between 1914 and 1919. The Imperial Communications Committee complained in 1920 that the Marconi broadcasts were 'interfering with important communications'.[26] The state had already established 'an interest', even though the general shape of broadcasting remained chaotic, its full potential unperceived.

Then several factors converged to reshape this chaos into a very definite and novel formation. First, the producers wished to consolidate their commercial dominance against the competition from amateurs and smaller rivals: but to do so they first had to subordinate competition between themselves to the consolidation of their monopoly. This was done by an amalgamation of the 'big six' (Marconi, Metropolitan Vickers, General Electric, Radio Communications, Hotpoint and Western Electric), with the 'small two' companies (Burndept and Siemens), a development that the government actively encouraged. This formed the commercial-industrial base of the British Broadcasting Company. This was a powerful and restrictive amalgamation; a less polite name for it was a cartel.

To this was added a second element. The 'boom' conditions in which radio expanded in the United States in the early period (1914–20) came to serve as an awful warning. American radio was a riotous and unregulated competition, leading to problems of airwave congestion and 'jamming'. Broadcasting became an open race for the 'radio business', a field for lucrative investment and a channel for competitive advertising. On the one hand, this commercial competition precipitated 'interference and overlapping, a jumble of signals and a blasting and blanketing of rival programmes'.[27] On the other, the unregulated quality of broadcast material precipitated a 'frivolous' use of the medium — a 'toy to amuse children rather than the servant of mankind'.[28]

The Post Office and the government in Britain set their face against this 'chaos of the ether', which they attributed to the unlicensed and unregulated nature of commercial competition (indeed, the very same market that was claimed to have served the freedom of the press so well), on which no public interest or serious social purpose could be stamped. Accordingly, once the commercial interests had sorted themselves out into an amalgamation — a monopoly with which the state could deal — the state itself entered into a sort of cultural partnership with it. It was, therefore, to the amalgamated British Broadcasting Company that the Post

Office granted, in January 1923, an exclusive licence to broadcast 'news, information, concerts, lectures, educational matter, speeches, weather reports, theatrical entertainment and any other matter . . . within the scope or orbit of the said Licence . . .'.[29] This extraordinary hybrid beast became the basis of public broadcasting in Britain: a 'broadcasting authority thinly disguised as an arm of private enterprise yet bearing a curious resemblance to an officially blessed monopoly.'[30] J.W.C. Reith was appointed as the first General Manager of the Company to guide its cultural fortunes.

The BBC was a cultural institution of a quite new type. Regulation by 'pure market forces', by open and unhindered competition — which had served to 'free' the press — was no longer adequate to substain a new locus of cultural authority in a mass democracy based on a technical medium of such immense social and political power. What was required was a new kind of partnership between monopoly capital, the people, and the state. Such an institution also required a new 'philosophy'. And it was Reith, above all, who provided it. High-minded and public-spirited, in the Arnoldian way, though morally narrower and more self-righteous, Reith was convinced that, in the face of the 'chaos' of rival parties, forces and doctrines in a democracy, society needed firm moral guidance, respect for the traditional values and a 'best self'. The consent and confidence of the people must be won for an authority which would not merely *reflect* public tastes and values through the medium of the free market, but educate, steer, guide and *shape* public taste and values towards 'higher things'. Reith thus imposed on broadcasting a high, austere, idealist and traditionalist ethical regime. But such a task, a vocation, could not, in his view, be achieved without the full authority of the state. Only the state could stamp broadcasting with the legitimacy of cultural leadership. Reith, in this sense, though in no way a 'collectivist', was nevertheless a new kind of intellectual guardian — an organic state intellectual. This new instrument of cultural education required, in his view, an ideal of public service, a sense of moral obligation and assured finance. None of this was possible without what he called 'the brute force of monopoly'.[31] And so the man appointed as General Manager of a licensed monopoly gave the Crawford Committee the critical evidence which convinced them to convert the 'Company' into a 'Corporation': a public authority — with Reith himself as its first Director-General! The formula for this new kind of cultural institution was, as usual, delicately but precisely formulated by Reith: 'a public service, not only in performance but in constitution — but certainly not as a department of state'.[32] This delicate positioning — *in*, drawing authority *from*, but not *of* the state — has been the basis of the BBC's cultural operations, the foundations of both its 'dependence' and its 'independence', ever since.

Like the state, whose development in a sense it has mirrored, the BBC's whole thrust has been 'centralising'. The range and variety, achieved in the press through free and unregulated competition, had to be somehow *designed* as a matter of *strategy* within the mixed programming *policies* of a corporate institution. The variety of 'publics' and interests and tastes and differences of opinion had to be orchestrated into a corporate unity. Broadcasters — its cultural guardians — had to discharge the public responsibility of reflecting the culture of the whole people as an organic *national* culture while, at the same time, defending traditional values and standards and educating popular taste towards its 'better self'. This was a conception of national cultural policy modelled on the state itself (which is supposed to balance all interests within itself, and act disinterestedly) rather than on the market.

An instrument of the national culture
Between its re-construction as a 'public service' channel and the Second World War, the BBC became a national cultural institution. Two words which became associated with the BBC in this period provide a shorthand clue as to how this cultural ascendancy was accomplished. The BBC was regarded as an 'authority'. And it was a 'corporation'. Both words have to be understood in their literal as well as their metaphorical sense.

Literally, the BBC had been authorised — i.e. licensed — to broadcast to the nation. But figuratively it established an ascendancy (that is, an authority) over its publics. Its standards, its particular combinations of programmes, its received pronunciations, its musical tastes, literacy and entertainment judgements, its 'broadcasting manners' (for a time, all of Reith's newcasters wore evening dress and black ties, though they could not be seen!) set the authoritative criteria by which public service broadcasting itself was judged.

Again, literally, it was a 'corporation': it incorporated into one body or institution all the elements deemed necessary to provide a national broadcasting medium. But, figuratively, it incorporated — drew together into an organic, though diverse, unity — all the publics in the nation: regional, local, metropolitan; and all the tastes and interests in the nation: Home, Light, Third and World. It was also integrative in the sense that it found a place for all these classes and publics — but it arranged and organised them within a particular hierarchy. Its centre of gravity was the educated, broad-minded, serious, cultivated, public-spirited, disinterested middle classes. Arnold's guardians. But it designed an acceptable, though subordinate, place for — and thereby incorporated into the national audience — the many regional and working-class audiences.[33] In these ways the BBC identified itself with a certain representation of the nation — a national (that is, not a sectional) medium for a national audience. Then, in its programmes and policies, it set out to address the nation it had so constructed, reconciling the many English voices into its 'Voice'. The whole gamut of 'national voices' was reflected back to the nation through the medium of the sound waves. Yet the Standard Voice — the 'received' accent, pronunciation and tonal pitch of the 'BBC voice' — circumscribed and *placed* them all. This was not, of course, 'Cockney' or 'Scouse' or even, quite, 'Oxbridge'. It was a variant synthesis of the educated, middle-class speech of the Home Counties. It was this Voice that read the news, introduced the programmes, described the symphonies, interviewed spokespersons, made the announcements, filled the gaps between programmes and provided broadcasting with its vocal cement.

In its other area of programming — its political, rather than its cultural role — much the same process unfolded. Here, too, the BBC represented itself as the Voice, not of the state, the government, or even 'the people', so much as of the nation. One key episode in this transformation into a national institution was the General Strike. During the General Strike, in 1926, the country was deeply divided along class and political lines. Baldwin's Cabinet, egged on by Churchill, seriously considered commandeering the BBC, as it had done the press. Reith, though sympathetic to the government side, fought hard to maintain the BBC's 'independence'. The BBC's relative autonomy from the state, secured through the principles and practices of 'impartiality and balance', were first powerfully enunciated and defended in this moment. Reith, in a confidential letter to senior staff once the Strike had ended, expressed the delicate balances on which this autonomy rests in memorable words. By remaining independent, Reith argued, 'we had secured and held the goodwill and even the affection of the people; . . . been trusted to do the right thing at all times; . . . were a national institution and even a national asset . . .'. 'On the other hand', Reith continued, 'since the BBC was a national institution and since the Government in this crisis were acting for the people . . . the BBC was for the government in the crisis too . . .'. Briggs comments that this intricate statement of principle clarifies the desire of the BBC to convey 'authentic, impartial news', while at the same time remaining in every sense of the word 'an organization within the constitution'.[34] The complicated balancing act through which the BBC remains both inside, and yet independent of, the state — both for the government and of the nation — are writ large in these richly ambiguous formulations.

In very brief outline, this is the story of how BBC radio forged for itself an identity as a national cultural institution: how it served, at one and the same time, to maintain the cultural standards and values of the dominant class-cultures by organizing them into a single 'voice', while incorporating the other class and regional 'voices' within its organic and corporate framework. The story of how the BBC then became not simply a 'national' but a popular institution, temporarily identified with the fate and fortunes of the whole British people, is really a story of the great ascendancy it established during the years of the Second World War, when it came positively to symbolise many of the things for which the British people believed they were fighting.

Broadcasting — the 'shadow state'

However, as soon as the spirit of 'national unity' in the face of the enemy ebbed, the model on which the BBC had been founded, and which it had matured over three decades, began itself to be challenged. The lure of a new, and highly lucrative, alternative medium to radio first emerged in the early 1950s with the new experiments in television; and the questions about the most appropriate models of cultural leadership once more surfaced. The fact that an ITV (commercial), rather than a second BBC (public authority), television channel was chosen in 1954 suggests that the regulation and ordering of culture through the free market remains as an active alternative to state 'incorporation' for societies like Britain, even in the latter half of the twentieth century. Indeed, the preference for market rather than state regulation has become more, not less, popular since the 1950s. This, in turn, suggests that the leading social classes remain divided between at least two different and competing cultural and economic 'models': free-market and state-sponsored. It also reminds us that, though the state is the necessary point through which the many conflicting lines of policy are drawn together and shaped into a more coherent thrust of government, its 'unity' is never complete. The state remains contradictory, riven by conflicting perspectives and policy interests; and these often reflect the real divergencies among and within the different sections of the dominant class.

The Conservative Party, for example, was deeply split on the question of whether the second channel should be structured in a 'public service' or a 'market-commercial' way. Selwyn Lloyd, in opposition to the more 'paternalist' members of his own party (such as Lord Hailsham), signed a minority report to the Beveridge Committee, favouring the market principle. A Conservative backbenchers' pressure group in alliance with the same sort of commercial interests that had struggled to colonise the BBC in the early days (equipment manufacturers, advertising agencies, large investors, and so on) eventually carried the day when the Television Act 1953, which established the ITV network, was finally drafted. The second channel was financed through the sale of advertising time, not through a public licence. It had therefore to submit to the logic of the market. This meant catering more explicitly to the mass-popular audience in its consumer form, with programmes which might make an immediate appeal to existing audience tastes. Thus, for the first time in Britain since the birth of the radio and television era, two kinds of cultural institution, founded on two competing cultural models, orchestrating the relations between the classes and the cultures in two, contrasting ways — the 'paternalist' BBC, the 'populist' ITV — vied with each other for cultural leadership in a period of intense competition.

The effects of competition were, however, complex. The BBC was obliged to become more populist, more demotic, more calculatingly competitive in its struggle to secure a majority of the audience. But ITV

45

also broadened and varied its ouput over time, producing a higher proportion of 'quality' material, in the face of public criticism. In the event, the two channels have come to resemble one another more than they differ.

On the other hand, this 'peaceful coexistence' (i.e. fierce competition) between the two elements of the duopoly which has dominated national television since can be easily misread, so far as the state's involvement in culture is concerned. For the ITV (like the new fourth channel) is not and never has been a pure instance of the commercial free-market model, as the nineteenth-century press was. Though independently organised and financed, it had imposed on it, by the terms of the Act (in principle) and by the regulation 'authority' of the Independent Broadcasting Authority (IBA) set over it, many public service standards, criteria and requirements. In its own ways, ITV is also required to 'serve the nation', to meet a public service ideal. It, too, must meet certain required programme standards; must offer to serve a broad range of public interests and tastes; that is, address itself to the nation. Its practices are monitored through the IBA. Its applications for franchise have to meet certain requirements (though the details remain private) and, in the area of news and current affairs, the requirements of 'balance, neutrality, impartiality' — the terms on which broadcasting is allowed to be both 'independent' and yet 'within the constitution' — are broadly the same as those governing BBC practice. Actually, they are more clearly and formally stated in the ITV's Act than they are in the BBC's Charter.[35]

In these different ways, then, television is linked, in a multitude of visible and invisible, direct and indirect, ways, to the state. While retaining a great deal of day-to-day independence, broadcasters and the general strategies of broadcasting are organised within the state's field of force. The definitions of political reality which are assumed as 'legitimate' within the state provide the limits within which broadcasting's versions of reality move. The broadcasters will not immediately reproduce a government's views; they are not, in that sense, the mere mouthpieces of the political party in power. But, just as the state does not favour one manufacturer against another, but does maintain the system of private enterprise *as a whole*, so broadcasting does not illegally swing its weight behind one political party or another, but it does respect and cherish the whole ideological framework, the basic structure of social relations, the existing dispositions of wealth, power, influence, prestige, on whose foundations it ultimately rests. In debating any of these questions, broadcasting's starting point, parameters and frames of references will be the same as those established for society through the state. Sensitive points for the state (Northern Ireland, picketing, trade union power, nuclear strategy, inflation, left advances in the political parties) are also, sooner or later, broadcasting's sensitive points. The broadcasting institutions constantly orientate and acclimatise themselves to the shifts and trends in the established political culture. When controversial issues have to be debated, what the established definition of a problem is, within the state, is what any broadcaster with an instinct for survival will take as the starting point. And when the nation divides, or problems drive the parties and the classes apart, the only point of rest or ultimate authority, which secures for broadcasting some element of legitimacy, and licenses it to continue to broadcast, is whatever is left of the consensus as represented through the state.

In general, it seems that in this new broadcasting model both BBC and ITV behave like, or model themselves on, and tend to reproduce the practices of, the state, though to different degrees. In periods of relative calm or national unity, it is the general consensus (which, in liberal-democratic theory, is supposed to be represented by the state) which provides broadcasting with its authority, legitimacy and practical guiding light. In periods of controversy and social or political division, the broadcasters ride out the rifts in the consensus by adopting — as state civil servants do — a position of impartiality and neutrality, 'above the struggle'.

This set of underlying parallels between broadcasting and the state (especially strong in the areas of news, current affairs and political coverage) can be traced through to the actual practices of particular programmes. Current affairs television programmes, as a form, thus signify nothing so much as the source of their coherence: the state. They are organised as if the BBC really were a sort of 'shadow state': the studio, a microcosm of Parliament; the TV compère, none other than the 'Speaker of the House' himself; and its 'expert' commentators, the equals of senior civil servants and departmental permanent secretaries with their neutral briefs — disinterested guardians of the 'public interest'.[36]

Conclusion

I have tried, in this essay, to show how cultural institutions and practices institutionalise (settle, fix, secure, stabilise) a particular pattern of relations between the cultures and the classes in society. These configurations shift in line with much broader and more far-reaching 'epochal' shifts and historical transitions. They are not, however, simply rearrangements of an existing pattern. They establish new 'relations of force' between the classes and the cultures. They remodel and refashion the nature of cultural leadership in society. They mobilise consent and help to win popular support for, and thus secure, different types of class-cultural authority. The restructuring of these relations is central to the processes by which hegemony — a condition of social ascendancy, of cultural, moral and political leadership by a particular social bloc — is, or is not achieved, in particular historical periods. I have thus shown how, in each of the three

47

cases considered, a different model of cultural authority was in the course of formation, how that model achieved a sort of dominance, for a time, and thus secured (again, for a time) the cultural leadership of a particular social force or alliance of social forces, positioning and fixing the dominated classes in the place of subordination. I have also outlined the pressures that led to the eventual disintegration of each of these models and its supersession by an alternative model.

Clearly, there is no simple, linear progression in the transitions between these models, in the cultural role of the state. Even in the twentieth-century model of broadcasting, the state-culture relations have been differently organised, within even clearer evidence — accumulating rapidly under Thatcherism — of acute ruling class dissension as to how they *should* be organised. None the less, the general tendency — the main point in Gramsci's expanded view of the state — for hegemony to become increasingly reliant, in mass democracies, on the enlarged cultural role of the state is undeniable.

Notes

1. A. Gramsci, *Selections from The Prison Notebooks*, Lawrence and Wishart, 1971, p. 258.
2. Ibid., p. 244.
3. Ibid., p. 242.
4. See R. Malcolmson, *Popular Recreations in English Society, 1700–1850*, Cambridge University Press, 1973, p. 40.
5. Ibid., p. 143.
6. E.P. Thompson, 'Peculiarities of the English', in *The Poverty of Theory and Other Essays*, London, Merlin Press, 1978, p. 43.
7. Ibid., p. 43.
8. See L. Namier, *The Structure of Politics*, Macmillan, 1929.
9. See P. Anderson, *Arguments within English Marxism*, Verso/New Left Books, 1980, p. 92.
10. See J. Hay, 'Property, authority and the criminal law' In Hay, Linebaugh and Thompson (eds), *Albion's Fatal Tree*, Allen Lane/The Penguin Press, 1975.
11. See E.P. Thompson, *Whigs and Hunters*, Allen Lane, 1975.
12. J. Brewer and J. Styles (eds), *An Ungovernable People*, Hutchinson, 1980, pp. 18–19.
13. See G. Rudé, *The Crowd in History*, Wiley, 1964; and E. Hobsbawm and G. Rudé, *Captain Swing*, Allen Lane/The Penguin Press, 1975.
14. E.P. Thompson, 'Peculiarities of the English', *loc. cit.*,
15. See E.P. Thompson, 'The moral economy of the English crowd', *Past and Present*, no. 50, February 1971.
16. Cited in R. Altick, *The English Common Reader*, University of Chicago Press, 1957, p. 41.
17. I. Watt, *The Rise of the Novel*, Peregrine, 1963, p. 49.
18. M. Harris, 'Structure, ownership and control of the press, 1620–1780', in J. Curran (ed), *Newspaper History: From the Seventeenth Century to the Present Day*, Constable, 1978, p. 9.

19. Cited in A. Aspinall, *Politics of the Press, 1780–1859*, Harvester, 1973, p. 1.
20. J. Curran (ed) *Newspaper History*, p. 46.
21. See E.P. Thompson, *The Making of the English Working Class*, Penguin, p. 789.
22. Ibid., p. 791.
23. V. Berridge, 'Popular Sunday papers and mid-Victorian society' in J. Curran, *Newspaper History*, p. 247.
24. See K. Middlemass, *The Politics of Industrial Society*, André Deutsch, 1980.
25. See M. Arnold, *Culture and Anarchy*, Cambridge University Press, 1963, p. 204.
26. A. Briggs, *The Golden Age of Wireless*, Oxford University Press, 1961, pp. 48–9.
27. Ibid., p. 64.
28. Ibid., p. 48.
29. Ibid., p. 127.
30. A. Boyle, *Only the Wind will Listen*, Hutchinson, 1972, p. 128.
31. A. Briggs, *Wireless*, p. 238.
32. J. Reith, *Into the Wind*, Hodder, 1949, p. 102.
33. For further details of this moment in the BBC's history see the essay by David Cardiff and Paddy Scannell in this collection and their 'Serving the Nation: Public Service Broadcasting before the War' in B. Waites, T. Bennett and G. Martin (eds), *Popular Culture: Past and Present*, Croom Helm, 1982.
34. A. Briggs, *Wireless*, pp. 365–6.
35. See K. Kumar, 'Holding the middle ground' in J. Curran, M. Gurevitch and J. Woollacott (eds), *Mass Communications and Society*, Edward Arnold, 1977.
36. See, for a fuller discussion of these aspects of current affairs television, S. Hall, I. Connell and L. Curti, 'The "Unity" of Current Affairs Television' in T. Bennett, S. Boyd-Bowman, C. Mercer and J. Woollacott, *Popular Television and Film*, British Film Institute, 1981.

3

Colin Mercer

Complicit pleasures

In a brief and tantalising commentary on the movie *Jaws*, Stephen Heath, in characteristic understatement, insists that 'analysis must grasp this pleasure-meaning-commodity complex'.[1] The film as entertainment, the film as a system of meanings and the film as box-office hit. Nicely and roundly put; but there is, at present, a large gap between the last two terms of the triad — commodity and meaning — and the first — pleasure. The question — the problem — of pleasure has emerged or erupted recently precisely because of a perceived insufficiency within cultural analysis. Pleasure as an *area* rather than as a concept has signalled, at least within the repertoires of Marxism and critical theory, a failure not only to answer questions but even to *pose* them. This is in part a historical problem and in part an analytical one. It is historical insofar as pleasure and its accomplices — entertainment, the comic, laughter, enjoyment — have been relegated by a hard-nosed and minatory Marxism to the realms of surplus or excess. For good historical reasons no doubt. But, and this is where the analytical is necessarily imbricated with the historical, it is precisely because of the success and persuasiveness of the analysis of the last two terms of the triad that the theoretical horizon of the first term now needs to be established and developed. If we now accept that the field of popular culture is important, that, at the base line, its existence has certain determinate political, ideological and economic effects then it is absolutely crucial that we engage with its currency, with the terms of its persistence, its acceptability and its popularity: crucial, in other words, to engage with the specific ways in which we *consent* to the forms of popular culture.

This question of consent, of a complex and negotiated position in relation to the forms of a culture, has not been very high on the agenda of cultural analysis. If a consenting relationship is acknowledged then it tends to fall into one of two possible alternatives. Either this consent is — paradoxically — *forced* by means of a legitimising 'dominant culture' or the force is *consented to* via a liberal conception which holds that the mainspring of consent resides in the sovereign and legal category of the individual. Either way the site of consent is reduced to a vacuous timidity and its cousins 'pleasure' and the 'popular' are similarly assimilated to either ideological effects or personal preferences. Any form of cultural analysis with critical and transformative ambitions must take these issues seriously. It must recognise, for example that the powerful, though uneven, political reality of consent is strongly shaped by a highly *elaborated* culture: a culture which is simultaneously coercive and productive. Commenting on this notion of elaboration in a passage from Gramsci, Edward Said notes that this has two 'apparently contradictory but actually complementary dimensions'. The first of these is that a culture works towards a dominant conception of what a society should be like and secondly that culture has a highly complex (elaborate) mode of existence with a 'density, complexity, and historical-semantic value that is so strong as to make politics possible'. Said concludes that 'Gramsci's insight is to have recognised that subordination, fracturing, diffusion, reproducing, as much as producing, creating, forcing, guiding, are all necessary aspects of elaboration'.[2]

It is important to hang on to this 'productive' and 'persuasive' dimension of culture. Since the notions of 'culture', 'pleasure' and 'the people' (the substantive of 'popular' should we forget it) converged in the nineteenth century from key sectors of ascendant intellectual strata, the agenda for consent has been organised quite distinctively around ways of *including* (rather than repressing or excluding) people and their pleasures in a common national culture. From Bentham's elaborate calculus for the social measurement of 'pleasure and pains' to Matthew Arnold's stern indictments of 'doing as one likes' the issues of pleasure and consent have been inextricably linked in a combative reformulation of a culture's 'historical-semantic' complexity.

To approach this complexity I now need to modify the rather caricatural image of Marxism which I provided at the beginning. There have been exceptions within this tradition of analysis which have transgressed and taken, respectively, consent, pleasure and the popular seriously. The names of Brecht, Bakhtin and Barthes figure largely in relation to the latter two categories and have provided us with some partial, some more systematic insights into the nature of our *contract* — the complex nature of our complicity — with cultural forms. Some of this work will seep into the present analysis. The fundamental theoretical and political emphasis however, derives, as partially signalled above, from the work of Gramsci insofar as this provides a basis for connecting regional analyses of pleasure to the more general but no less pressing and resilient problem of consent, not, as Gramsci says 'generic and vague' as in elections but organised or, if you like, *elaborated*. The fundamental insistence of the concept of hegemony in Gramsci's work, the scandalous emphasis on 'active consent' and the scrutiny of the uneven but negotiated contours of a 'common culture' are primary points of departure for any form of cultural analysis which 'takes pleasure seriously'.

Play-time

Gramsci recognised the fundamental importance of taking on the dominant ideology at its strongest, rather than at its weakest points: 'the defeat of the auxiliaries and the minor hangers-on is of all but negligible importance. Here it is necessary to engage battle with the most eminent of one's adversaries'.[3] But simultaneously the whole direction of the concept of hegemony and Gramsci's deployment of it is not only to attack head on the field of forces as they are perceived to exist on the 'ideological front' but also actually to rethink the composition of that field, to realise that such forces might not be laid out as clearly as we imagine. That the 'obvious targets' might not be the ones where ideological strength is operated. When Gramsci writes of the 'ethical dimension' of the state and the importance of civil society he is not just reprising an old debate but insisting on the importance of those processes, functions, forms traditionally located at the periphery of, or in the interstices of the perceived 'hard centres' of political and economic power: common sense, folklore, popular culture. But, as Gramsci was to learn to his cost, it was precisely on these edges, in these interstices, that, for example, Fascism was able to articulate a persuasive and consensual version of the 'new man'. It was right in the heart of popular cultural forms, in the *Dopolavoro* (afterwork) organisations, that Fascism achieved one of its most significant and far-reaching victories. By establishing and maintaining a concerted 'war of position' on the terrain of popular culture and leisure time, Mussolinian Fascism could represent itself as the harmoniser — at last — of the work and leisure activities in the mass, and indeed popular, *Dopolavoro* organisations organising popular theatre, opera, bowling, excursions. In coordination with the mass women's and youth organisations and the Ministry of Popular Culture, Fascism effectively colonised — for a time at least, and not without engendering mass contradictions — the strategic zone of civil society. And part of the reason it was able to do this was precisely that in the theoretical horizon of the Italian labour movement this area was effectively and tragically perceived as marginal.[4] By harnessing together the key concepts of production and leisure and thereby displacing the previously foregrounded contradictions of class and ownership, Fascism condensed, temporarily (but 20 years is long enough!), a whole network of interstitial ideologies and forms of common sense around a state-controlled 'pleasure dome'.

It is perhaps as well to remind ourselves of the strategic importance of the terrain of pleasure as the inner cities and suburban towns witness the arrival and growth of 'pleasuramas' populated mostly by the unemployed. And, funnily enough, these sites of pleasure are now only rivalled in high streets across the country by building societies and video shops! The privatisation of pleasure and the privatisation of ownership mark out some of the distinctive contours of the Thatcherist vision of Britain in the future.

This is a *strategic* terrain and not necessarily an immutable sign of things to come. If it is strategic, then it should be possible to recognise and analyse the elements and mechanisms of pleasure-production and to intervene there. But this is probably easier said than done.

Recent approaches to the question of pleasure have indeed recognised its strategic ideological importance and, drawing on traditions of analysis from semiotics and psychoanalysis, have begun to work, with delicate tools, at the apparently unassailable because 'spontaneous', 'natural', 'personal' edifice of pleasure. Laura Mulvey, for one, has had a go at the profound ideological imbrication of pleasure and sexuality (or a particular version of it) in traditional narrative cinema. But her argument stops precisely at that point where pleasure is at its most resilient, at the point of what she calls the 'sentimental regret' with which women will view the decline of the traditional film form.[5] Quite apart from the problem that the traditional film form is not declining *in general* — for every innovative and aware production for the cinema there are a thousand traditional TV movies — it is precisely in these interstices of regret, desire, ambition, identification, nostalgia that pleasure does its *work*. This is the matrix of the 'popular' resilience of received pleasures, this is its *economy* and as such it demands a patient and resourceful work of disarticulation rather than a search and destroy mission.

As a starting point in this we might question the inevitable coupling, within Marxist and other critical discourses, of pleasure and ideology in the analysis of cultural forms. We would have to reject, I think, the argument that a cultural form is ideological (product or expression) *per se*. Ideology certainly cannot be reduced in, say, film to the intentions of the director, the producer, the production company, the screenplay writer or, indeed, to an amorphous Hollywood or British cinema. Nor can it be reduced to the reception by critics and audiences of the film, nor to the contexts in which it is shown. Take all these together and you have something like a map of the ideological field in which it operates but this is only a snapshot of a historically movable field of force relations. As a limit case, if you showed *Birth of a Nation* to an audience in Alabama and then to an audience in New Jersey, you would have quite different inflections within that field. This is not just saying that 'one man's meat is another man's poison', it is also saying that ideologies of pleasure and, indeed, the pleasures of ideology, do not necessarily fit and correspond to each other in a pre-given relationship of mutual support. They constitute precisely a field of forces in the case of the cinema, a whole 'pleasure machine'. It is not that a different interpretation of a given film or book changes the whole of this field — the historical, institutional and subjective constraints of its genesis remain — but that it alters it significantly enough for us to be wary of the assignation of the term 'ideological' to it. Is it the 'form' of the film which is ideological, for example? Or is it the 'message'? Or is it the nature of its reception by a given audience? These questions pose a larger problem: that the general notion of 'the ideological' cannot answer specific questions like these without assuming a generalised response across different locations. The general category needs to be broken down into more manageable segments. We might begin this by following, for example, a procedure which would interrogate the specifics of the *site* of a given form (the various positions from which its 'transmission' is possible and legitimate); its *status* (how and by whom it is seen, heard, read and its cultural 'authority' to be thus received;) and the *subjectivities* which its addresses and assumes (this may address questions of male or female desire, utopian ambitions, individual and collective identification and so on).[6] Clearly these need to be analysed simultaneously and in relation to each other: there is no generalised status or site of, say, a film. A local film club, for example, works on a quite different cultural economy to that of the ABC in the High Street and significantly different coordinates come into play with the different weightings of site, status and subjectivity. I stress different *weightings* there rather than an infinitely variable set of differences because, by the very act of selection of these three coordinates I am accepting that, in general, these are 'hard-core' coordinates which function according to certain principles of *dominance*: there are dominant sites, statuses and subjectivities. The forces of industry, production, personnel and the pressure of 'giving the people what they want' have a head start here but they do not necessarily converge into a vortex of ideological persuasion. The point about questioning the unity of what is assumed to be 'the ideological' here has as its analytical and political basis firstly a recognition of the complexity of our relationship to cultural forms and secondly the recognition of fissures, points of 'non-communication' and of resistance in what is sometimes called the area of 'mass communications'. Contemporary concerns with pleasure have, albeit in a vague and sometimes too cryptic way, signalled a beginning of this interrogation of 'the ideological':

The concern with pleasure, then, is a corresponding interrogation of the 'fact' of ideology. It suggests a rejection of the ascribed unity and omniscience, of its depth and homogeneity, of its stasis within a given cultural form. Barthes has it that 'ideology passes over the text and its reading like the blush over a face (in love, some take erotic pleasure in this colouring)'[7] and this signals something of the contemporary concern for the contradiction *play* of ideology. There is a general unease that, within the plethora of ideology analysis which has emerged in recent years, something has quite crucially been missed out: that it may now be important to look over our shoulders and try to explain a certain 'guilt' of enjoyment of such and such *in spite of* its known ideological and political provenance. Again, it is Barthes who has captured this mood well when he states that

> All socio-ideological analyses agree on the *deceptive* nature . . . of literature
> . . . These analyses forget (which is only normal since they are hermeneutics
> based on the exclusive search for the signified) the formidable underside of

writing: *jouissance: jouissance* which can erupt, across the centuries, out of
certain texts that were nonetheless written to the glory of the dreariest, the
most sinister philosophies.[8]

Any analysis of the pleasure, the modes of persuasion, the consent
operative within a given cultural form would have to displace the search for
an ideological, political, economic or, indeed, subjective, *meaning* and
establish the coordinates of that 'formidable underside'. And I think that
we have to take the concept of *jouissance* (orgasm, enjoyment, loss of stasis)
with a pinch of salt as a sort of 'nudge' in a certain direction because what
we are really concerned with here is a restructuring of the theoretical
horizon within which a cultural form is perceived. The new terms of
enquiry, if they are to engage with pleasure must, as Franco Moretti has
recently put it, 'approach the text not as if it were a vector pointing neatly in
one direction, but as if it were a light source radiating in several directions
or a field of forces in a relatively stable equilibrium.[9]

Spirals of pleasure and power

Every relation of force, Foucault argues, 'implies at each moment a
relation of power (which is in a sense its momentary expression) and every
power relation makes a reference, as its effect but also as its condition of
possibility, to a political field of which it forms a part'.[10] We could envisage
a metaphor for the relationship between pleasure and power in a given
cultural form as a double helix with points of immediate contact, points of
wide separation and points of varying proximity. Or, to put it another way,
points of persuasion, points of resistance and points of negotiation. But, the
spatial metaphor will not hold: it is also a question of active processes of the
generation and holding into consent, into acceptability, of that strong
relationship between pleasure and power which is, we remember, only a
'momentary expression'. And it is momentary not because the relationship
is annulled or is only coincidental, as liberal thought would have it, but
because the 'strength' can draw its resources form elsewhere in the field
without losing the opportunity of returning to its strongest expression and
point of persuasion. We have only to look at the most frequent resources
and strategies of a popular newspaper to see how this works.

Popular newspapers are a disposable commodity *par excellence*. They are
read over breakfast, on the train or bus or at a coffee break and then end up
discarded in the bin or on the seat. There is a ritualised dimension to the
reading of them, as Hegel observed when he compared them to morning
prayers for which, in his own time, they became a substitute. They do
indeed constitute either a preamble or a break in the routine of the day but
not in the sense of an escape, more in the direction of setting a frame, a
tissue of confirmations, beliefs and expectations. And they are, indeed,
constructed in a ritualised way which is fully aware of this power. It is a

power constructed not through the persuasion of a leader comment, nor through traditions of serious reportage (there is nothing to hold on to in a tabloid, no articles to cut out and save, no pursual of the main lines of political and historical movement) but through the *montage* of elements. It is only in relation to the lead story of adultery in showbiz, promiscuity in the office, road accidents and developments in the world of crime and so on *held together* that the identifiable political line of a tabloid works. It operates within the tissue of *doxa*, of common sense: the language, the interleaving discourses — abbreviated 'titbits', 'spots' of local and eccentric news textually coordinated with exclusives on 'sad mums', and a bestiary of human 'monsters' and 'beasts' and 'animals' — provide all the strongest coordinates of this tissue of pleasure and persuasion. The *sexualisation* of social life is a dominant discourse operative within popular British newspapers. The *Sun* is, of course, emblematic here and the 'page-three girl', now institutionalised, is central to this. But this is not, or not only, an example of sexist voyeurism. The image of the woman here functions as a lead metaphor in a field of rhetoric which disperses, encircles and returns to the point of sexuality and which holds, as its self-confirming image, the reader (and not just the male reader) in its elaborated grid of events and happenings and comments. The traditional masculine pleasure of the look at the body of the woman, spectacularised, is only part of the economy of the 'personal' and the 'private', which is itself only a part of a more generalised voyeurism of the social and political scene which is the aim of these papers. Thus, metonymically as it were, the 'page-three girl' is encircled on the same page by various 'sexy' stories (wayward vicars, Joan Collins, houses which are too small to make love in) but metaphorically the connotative chain is prepared for, for example, 'The Real Paul McCartney' or for the 'Reagan You Never Hear About', the 'family-man noted for being generous, easy-going, thoughtful, with a marvellous line in stories and a cool line in humour'. The sexualisation of the social is thus far from being purely glib or sensational, or even 'sexy' as the *Sun* calls itself: it is a primary and constitutive form of the persuasive rhetoric which returns all events ultimately to the level of the personal, or rather which posits the personal as the ground for all presuppositions, as its primary pole of interpretation. Thus, the complex space between 'the people' and 'politicians' is sutured by a *vow*: "I Won't Free Moors Monsters"; "Brittan vow to sad mum". Person to person, body to body, the pleasures of this contract are resilient: the complexities of the social and political spheres are occulted (literally) through a structure of discourses analogous to the eagerly sought and read mechanisms of the horoscope which are persuasive not because of any link they may have with astrology but because they are appropriate and homologous 'psycho-histories' for the assumed (and real) reader. They are an ideal and fitting part of the syntax and semantics of pleasure in a tabloid newspaper: usually towards the end of the paper they are, as it were, its ideological full stop, reconstituting and reinforcing the pleasures of identification and 'capture' ('my horoscope today was really accurate') as you leave it on the seat of the train or bus.

The 'information' such papers carry is minimal: it can be reduced literally to what is on TV in the evening and who is running at Plumpton in the 2.45. It is in the *play* of their language that the pleasure is constituted: 'Independently of all information, the simple play of language establishes between individuals certain relations of collaboration, struggle, domination and dependence.'[11] Out of this set of relations, or rather because of their interdiscursive play, there emerges a dual and complementary process common to all forms of language *as discourse*: the combination, in linguistic terms, of a *preconstruction* and a 'support effect'. The preconstructed is the discursive form of the taken for granted, the natural, the spontaneous and the obvious. The support effect is the action, the process of 'doubling-back, as the construction of the effects of sense and certainty; construction along and across the possible paraphrases that constitute a discourse'.[12] Thus, for the headline announcing the sinking of the General Belgrano and the loss of 300 Argentinian lives in the Falklands War, the *Sun* uses the single word 'Gotcha' rather than, say, 'Belgrano Sunk' precisely because it works, even as a single word, discursively by combining the 'information', the preconstruction (this is a war, lives will be lost, ships will be sunk, etc.) and the 'support effect' (a condensation of half-humorous colloquialism, onomatopaeia, the language of a one-to-one confrontation) in a pernicious but also, given the context, 'persuasive' capture of a preferred subjectivity of 'mind and body'. 'Gotcha' is, in this sense, well chosen: a word always on the border between enunciation and physical action as if you were catching a child hiding behind the door.

The politics of the 'leader comment' or the headline does not depend on its own resources but on strengths drawn silently from elsewhere in the field of meaning of a popular newspaper: from the grammar of sexuality, entertainment, action, intrigue, horror and revelation which provide its points of 'capture', the terms of its contract — points of condensation of meaning, points of multi-layered and sedimented resilience and pleasure. Nowhere more evidently than in the popular newspaper is it true that 'discourse produces within one domain of thought another domain of thought *as if* this other domain had already been introduced'.[13] The subject is held vicariously within this field of meaning.

For the analysis of pleasure, though, we would then have to ask what are the terms of this capture, how complete is the circle of subjection and 'imaginary unity'? How far do unconscious operations of the sort implied here simply coincide with the intentions of a dominant ideology or discursive formation, how far does 'ego' correspond to 'super-ego' and 'subject' (individual) with 'Subject' (the Other, Order, the Symbolic, Culture)? If we are concerned with 'spirals' of pleasure and power rather than direct ideological capture, these questions — of the instability of preferred forms of identification, of points of resistance and negotiation —

must be returned to the terrain of consent or, perhaps more appropriately, to the processes of *consensualisation*.

The body in question

Commenting on some of these problems in the work of the discourse analyst Michel Pêcheux, Colin MacCabe argues that '[a] first step in the rectification of Pêcheux's position would necessitate a greater emphasis on the other practices imbricated with the interdiscourse and, in particular, the positioning and representation of the body'.[14] This sort of emphasis, MacCabe argues, would, because the body cannot be exhausted in its representations, provide a material basis from which 'the unconscious of a discursive formation disrupts the smooth functioning of the dominant ideologies'. This is positive in its stress on the importance of the body as a strategic site but also too general in its enthusiasm for the 'radical heterogeneity of the Lacanian Other' to which it, and a host of theories like it, ultimately resort. It is both too optimistic about the body and too general about its forms of positioning and potential for disruption.

The positioning of the body is indeed at the centre of questions of pleasure and is, in the sense that the body does not coincide quite so neatly with the 'subject', a possible point of dislocation and resistance. But before abandoning ourselves to the libidinal economy of desire and to the evacuation of history we have to pay quite close attention to the formation of particular conceptions of the body, to the specific forms of power and pleasure in which that body has been involved and assess more precisely the nature of the force relations operative there. We need also to ask questions about the nature of this 'hold' on the body, about the nature of the power involved: whether it is just a question of capture, submission and subjection or whether it is something rather more complex than that.

These are the sorts of question posed, for example, by Foucault when he argues that the emphasis on the body specific to the modern period

> should undoubtedly be linked to the growth and establishment of bourgeois hegemony: not, however, because of the market value assumed by labour capacity, but because of what the 'cultivation' of its own body could represent politically, economically and historically for the present and future of the bourgeoisie.[15]

In various works, Foucault has demonstrated how, through various 'disciplines' — penology, clinical medicine, psychiatry — the body has become a strategic site of 'power relations'. He is not so much concerned with a pre-given body which then becomes the site of competing definitions and repressions, as with the ways in which the conceptions of the body itself, of its possibilities, its limits, its areas of control and observation and disorder, were 'spoken' into existence by the various discourses which encircled and defined it. This was broadly congruent also with emergent conceptions of 'man' or the 'human' as in 'the human sciences' (or, more appropriately in French, *'les sciences de l'homme'*). And the key word for Foucault here is not the negative one of prohibition but rather of *production*: the nineteenth century did not prohibit sexuality, it virtually *invented* it by producing a whole series of discourses about it (pornography, titillation, social fears about masturbation and, symptomatically, the concept of hysteria are all nineteenth-century discursive innovations). Thus, Foucault's terms to define this are all nouns of *process*: psychiatrisation, hysterisation, etc. In order to be able to pose the sort of future question of 'new pleasures' it is crucial to understand the past complexities of the specification of pleasure around the body. This holds for the whole corpus of culture and is, in effect, one of the determining matrices for the division of culture into its sedimented categories of high and low, popular and serious, and so on. From the moment of its genesis in Kantian aesthetics the body has been a key and strategic discriminator in the reception of a hegemonic culture.

'Nothing' argues Pierre Bourdieu, 'more radically distinguishes popular spectacles — the football match, Punch and Judy, the circus, wrestling or even in some cases the cinema — from bourgeois specta-cles, than the form of the participation of the public.'[16] For the former, whistles, shouts, pitch invasions are characteristic, for the latter the gestures are distant, heavily ritualised — applause, obligatory but discontinuous and punctual cries of enthusiasm — 'author, author' or 'encore'. Even the clicking of fingers and tapping of feet in a jazz audience are only a 'bourgeois spectacle which mimes a popular one' since the participation is reduced to 'the silent allure of the gesture'. A certain *distance*, Bourdieu argues, has been central in the bourgeois economy of the body: a distance between 'reflexion' and corporeal participation.

The agenda for this was set by Kant and it was he, not Barthes, who first attached a politico-philosophical importance to the terms of *plaisir* and *jouissance* in *The Critique of Judgement*. For Kant, though, it is *jouissance* — enjoyment-pleasure — with all its sexual and oral connotations which is the negative and repressive term and *plaisir* — pure contemplative pleasure — which is the positive and liberatory term. If *plaisir* is derived from 'pure intuition', then *jouissance* is lined up with the vulgar, the distracting, the 'agreeable' and the corporeal. Symptomatically, *jouissance*, 'flatters' and 'seduces'; it reduces the subject to the realm of involuntary needs and desires and, we should add, to the realm of recognition of a field of forces, tastes, influences — in brief, to *history*. Commenting on this aesthetic, Bourdieu suggests that it instils and threatens a violence on the subject: that the submission to *jouissance* held the body in its rhythm and captured the mind in its intrigues, suspenses and surprises. It is the basis of a certain *horror*:

> This horror, unknown to those who abandon themselves to sensation, results
> fundamentally from the abolition of a distance where liberty can be affirmed
> between the representation and the thing represented. It results . . . from the
> loss of the subject in the object, from the actual submission to the immediate
> present which is determined by the enslaving violence of the 'agreeable'.[17]

This distance or space between the representation and the referent is, of
course, the space of the subject: the nascent bourgeois subject. Elsewhere
Bourdieu acidly comments that this 'bourgeois' space and its occupant are
still with us even in contemporary intellectuals' dispositions for 'Brechtian
distanciation' and in the fact that, whereas the intellectual sees a 'new
movie by Raoul Walsh', the popular audience faced with the same product
sees 'a Victor Mature' movie: intellectual product of an *auteur* on the one
hand, bodily display of an *acteur* on the other.

The 'enslaving violence of the agreeable' is, in one very immediate
sense, what the study of popular culture is all about, and though we might
want to put it in different terms it is generally true that in the body politic
popular culture and its modes of reception have been located somewhere
below the belt. One response to this, and a mistaken one, is to 'go for the
vulgar', to sing the glories of an *essential* and corporeal popular art over the
'bourgeois' religions of quiet appreciation and distance or, in some cases,
to sing the glories of *carnival*, citing Bakhtin as they go. This is inimical to
the analysis of both popular culture *and* pleasure and is wrong on two
counts. First of all it is *essentialist* in its ascription of the predicates
'bourgeois' and 'popular' to particular *forms* of culture and secondly, as
Tony Bennett argues elsewhere in this collection, it is a misunderstanding
of Bakhtin's notion of carnival. Like mooning down the street at midnight
it might be a laugh but not much else.

Under another name, Bakhtin writes: 'The organism and the outside
world meet here in the sign',[18] and the dialogic theory of the utterance
insists on this variable complicity. There is no sense in which the
'carnivalesque', anymore than its privatised associate *jouissance*, can be
allocated an essentially radical status. Indeed — and to return for a
moment to my original example — there is no clearer case of the negative
possibilities of the carnivalisation of the social sphere than in popular
newspapers. These particular cultural forms eminently recognise the
potential of the sign as a meeting point for the 'organism' and the 'outside
world' as they daily transfigure the dimensions of historical and ideological
processes around a licensed carnival of the woman's body (page three or
five or wherever), physical confrontation (an arrest, a fight, a war),
interpersonal commitments (a threat, a vow, a pledge), the languages of
spectacle (showbiz and sport), a voyeurism of the famous (Ronald Reagan,
Princess Diana, Randy Andy), and the figuration of excess (cartoons,
comic strips, caricatures). The whole ensemble is marked or framed in a
grammar of visceral hyperbole: 'Frustrated', 'Delighted', 'Randy',

'Insatiable', 'Fiery', 'Sizzling', 'Sexy', 'Flirty', and a series of sub-semiotic phatics : 'Cor', 'Ooh', 'Oomph', 'Wow', 'Crash' and so on (all of this a selection from just one paper on one day). Binding mind and body, 'gut' and 'head' it is nowhere more accurate to say that '[t]he discourse of carnival knows no neutral terms; caught up in ambivalent evaluations of praise and abuse, marked by shifting dualities of tone, it is always speech received back from the other to whom it was addressed in the first place'.[19] Needless to say, the ideologically committed popular newspaper will attempt to marginalise those ambivalences and those dualities of tone or, as Voloshinov puts it, 'to impose a supraclass eternal character on the ideological sign' in order to extinguish the 'multiaccentual' contact between the organism and the outside world. But this is a process which is never quite completed, always in some sense unstable.

The analysis of pleasure in the forms of popular culture necessitates the recognition of the instability of this spiral : it involves a complicity — of beliefs, 'gut feelings', common sense — but also the shadowy recognition that this complicity is transacted in an unstable medium of dialogue in which the response might not fit with the original mode of address. The metaphor of the carnival is, in its most important sense, precisely a way of figuring this double bind of complicity and dialogue and, in some interpretations might be seen, as Terry Eagleton puts it, 'as a prime example of that mutual complicity of law and liberation, power and desire, that has become a dominant theme of contemporary post-Marxist pessimism'.[20] But it is also possible to be neither post-Marxist nor a pessimist and insist that this recognition is, none the less, a fundamental starting point for the analysis of popular culture and pleasure and the forms of their possible transformation into other relationships. It is a necessary recognition of where we are, as Gramsci never ceased to argue, 'in the subsoil of popular culture as it is, with its tastes, its tendencies, etc., with its moral and intellectual world'.[21]

Modern times, modern pleasures

In his autobiography, Roland Barthes remembers the films of Chaplin where, he confesses

> he found a kind of delight in this art at once so popular (in both senses) and so intricate; it was a *composite* art, looping together several tastes, several languages. Such artists provoke a complete kind of joy, for they afford the image of a culture that is at once differential and collective: plural. This image then functions as the third term, the subversive term of the opposition in which we are imprisoned: mass culture *or* high culture.[22]

First, Chaplin's films deploy, perhaps more than any other, the resources of the *gestus*: they are, in one sense, precisely about the 'imbrication of the body and the social'. They are about intricate, frustrated and excessive movements : the funny walk, the unanswered gaze at the loved woman, the impossibility of coordination with the machine (*Modern Times*), the staccato strutting of the dictator (*The Great Dictator*), the punch which misses and the custard pie which connects. Chaplin's body, and those of Harold Lloyd and Buster Keaton who took the forms, respectively, to corporeal excess and zero degree, are *economies* of frustrated and excessive expenditure, therefore funny/pleasurable because we conserve our own physical expenditure in the face of it. But then, in order to avoid an ahistorical Freudianism, we have to pose questions as to the *currency* of *this* economy. Such questions would need to consider, for example, the implications of this new filmic capture of the body made possible by the 1895 invention of the cinematograph and before that of devices such as the zoopraxiscope which made possible the detailed, moment by moment photography of human actions and movements. Such 'machines of the visible', as Stephen Heath has called them, clearly represented a distinctively new economy of representation and constituted, simultaneously, both the possibilities of surveillance and of pleasure: a new spiral of pleasure and power. The possibility of filming a Chaplin in his detailed movements is also the possibility of filming a suspect, a populace, a demonstration in their detailed and equally significant movements. The problem is that, with few exceptions, critical cultural theory and practice has only responded to and engaged with the coercive movement of this spiral. It produces a 'counter-surveillance' in the deployment of film as an oppositional political weapon. But it has not engaged adequately with the consensual movement, with the ways in which it might be possible also to produce 'counter-pleasures'.

Secondly — and this is intricately connected to our first point — the nature of Chaplin's films as 'looping together several tastes, several languages' as the source of their 'complete kind of joy'. A critical cultural theory and practice needs more insistently to recognise this complexity and pluralism, the multivocality of contemporary cultural forms. There is a tendency to work within a frame set by an assumption of unified voices: of oppression, domination, resistance. These are blunt and ineffective weapons against what must be counted, as I noted above, as a formidably *elaborated* culture. We would need then not only to recognise the simultaneously coercive and productive nature of cultural forms but also, and within that complexity, to register the existence and effect of differential codes, of differently inflected voices which cannot be assumed to have unified meanings. Part of the pleasure which Barthes is hinting at here consists in the fact that these 'different languages' do, indeed, hang together persuasively. But not just randomly. This is not an argument for recognising a limitless pluralism or heterogeneity. We would still have to pose questions of the mechanisms by which these 'voices' hang together in *this* way and not that. In recognising, both theoretically and in cultural practice, the elaborated nature of culture as it exists and the corresponding need for an equally elaborative intervention, we are also acknowledging that there is a *hierarchy* and a reproducible *structure* which persists in defining how things hang — or loop — together. It would then be possible to 'unloop', to disarticulate, some of those languages in defining new forms of pleasure and developing new cultural capacities.

Third, what Barthes calls, both crudely and hopefully, the 'subversive term of the opposition in which we are imprisoned' between mass culture *or* high culture. Given some of the cautions announced in the first two points we need to be careful about this. There can be no automatic and guaranteed 'subversion' within these terms anymore than there can be an effective 'destruction of pleasure as a radical weapon' or, indeed, *pace* many, a 'cultural revolution'. The insistence upon recognising 'spirals of pleasure and power' in cultural forms also entails an acknowledgement of constantly shifting and restructured boundaries between 'mass' and 'high'. Not only that, it entails the recognition of other oppositions and boundaries which cut across that between mass and high culture such as the entrenched but moveable distinction between 'public' and 'private'. To be sure, women's writing is more immediately concerned with the investments of pleasure in the latter distinction than it is in the former. The point I am making here is that in the elaboration of appropriate theoretical coordinates for the analysis of pleasure and in the development of other forms it is important to resist the tendency to identify and locate given points of subversion and assume automatic cultural or political effects. That point of subversion, in the absence of a more general theory and strategy, may turn out, as with Marinetti and the Italian futurists, to be much more supportive of a regressive politics than we had imagined. Who, after all, could be more 'subversive' in his gestures, actions, jokes than Kenny Everett? And how better could this 'subversion' be used than to appear at a Young Conservative rally with enormous ears and hands and to open with the line 'Bomb Russia'?

Taken together, these analytical cautions and formulations may provide us with ways of approaching both the specificity of pleasure in contemporary cultural forms and its elaborative complexity. Such a form of analysis would, at the point where body, pleasure, culture and power are most complicit, allow us to confront, for example, a historically — and hegemonically — formed configuration of sexuality which is central to many of the more modern forms of popular culture. Here, clearly and insistently, the body is in question:

> held, worked through and resolved on a general terrain of medical-sexological-psychological-novelistic representation, worrying over the phallus and its order of men and women, responding to challenges to its identities of men and women, fixing things up.[23]

This is how Stephen Heath puts it, insisting on the relationships of power and complicity — as well as pleasure — which persist across a range of forms from the medical (including medical and hospital romances in which the persona of the doctor and his/her assumed capacities assume key narrative functions) to the 'psychological novel', through film, television, popular music, 'agony aunts' and forms of pseudo-theorising about sexuality, men and women, children and so on. The elaborative and persuasive power of these 'discourses' of pleasure, the complexity and force of the interrelationships between the different forms is resilient and persistent. Perhaps one of the most difficult but politically resonant questions to be posed to it is that formulated by the French feminist, Helene Cixous: 'How do I have pleasure? What is female *pleasure*, where does it happen, how is it inscribed on her body, in her unconscious? And then how do we write it?'[24] But then, though immediate and persistent, these questions, considerable in their implications, also need to be located in the context of others concerning modern forms of pleasure. As feminism has shown, questions of female pleasure can only be posed in relation to questions of male pleasure. And, in turn, these questions must be formulated in relation to the whole ensemble of cultural mechanisms by which contemporary pleasures are produced.

This returns us to the general question of the specification of the body in contemporary forms and to that matrix of disciplines which Stephen Heath outlines above. For it is not only true that a distinctive feature of contemporary cultural forms is an obsession with 'fixing things up' for the sexual body, but also, literally, with *fixing* that body, ascribing it certain capacities, and establishing it in a new relationship to its ideological environment. This is true, with varying degrees of intensity, of the new moral technologies of writing and representation which emerge in the nineteenth century — photography, cinema, detective and police novels, pornography and, of course, the 'popular' newspaper initiated by Lord Northcliffe's *Daily Mail* in 1896. This last form would draw upon and condense many of the other genres and provide the most compact and powerful of daily pleasures.

Redefining and investing the body with new pleasures is, in a very strong sense, what detective fiction is about. This new focus is represented, for example, in Poe's work, as a constitutive ambivalence between, on the one hand a specification of the body and its capacities and, on the other hand, a need to prevent it from being dissipated in the traces of a new social complexity. His 'The Man of the Crowd' is probably the most acute moment of genesis of this ambivalence. The concern with fragmentation of the body is persistent in his work: disembodied hearts and hands, the teeth of a loved woman, the story of the man who was nothing but a composite of artificial limbs, eyes, hair, etc. The concern with control of the body is insistently there in the obsession with the catatonic trance which leads to premature burial in *The Fall of the House of Usher*. Frequent references to the 'loss of self' in Poe's work (and even more frequent ones to fear of the vagina dentata) are perhaps more fruitfully related not to an existential crisis but to a struggle for a new form of writing the relationship between the individual and the social.

This is clear from 'The Man of the Crowd' where the man in question is followed by the narrator through the streets of London, the pursuit spurred on by the glimpse of a diamond and a dagger; the subject, who 'looked at all objects with a wild and vacant stare' follows a meaningless path, retracing his steps, going into shops with no apparent object. Finally the narrator breaks off from his pursuit with the words

> This old man, I said at length, is the type and genius of deep crime. He refuses to be alone. *He is the man of the crowd*. It will be in vain to follow; for I shall learn no more of him, nor his deeds.

In the final sentence, the narrator compares this 'worst heart in the world' with a German book of which it is said that *'es lässt sich nicht lesen'* — it does not allow itself to be read. It cannot be read, we might add, because there are not the forms in which this 'mystery' can yet be represented. But this is not a point of resignation for Poe but a starting point for the emergence of a new technology of writing and of constituting, reordering and momentarily capturing the subject in the new social topography of the metropolis. This is not just a 'literary history': it is a question also of a whole series of responses to the 'progressive societalisation of human relations' and to the contradictions which emerged from that large-scale elaborative work which shaped industrial societies into modern democracies. On the one hand the problem of *specification* of the individual and on the other the problem of *collectivisation* within a preferred hierarchy of social relations. This ambivalence transposes and figures in fictive terms the boundaries of a perceived social duality of, on the one hand, a 'totalitarian' desire to make everything visible (as in Bentham's *Panopticon*) and in the other the sense that in this social complexity, to paraphrase Marx, the 'content goes beyond the gaze'. This is especially appropriate in *The Purloined Letter* where it is precisely the multiplicity of 'points of view' which makes the all-important clue invisible to the investigator even though it is situated in an obvious place. By the time of *Sherlock Holmes*, this oscillation had been firmly, if temporarily, fixed to the point of total ultimate visibility. *Every* clue is now open to Holmes's deductive reasoning, the secret of disruption in the work of the guilty party is available to the investigator and the defeat of the criminal is 'the victory and the purge of a society no longer conceived as a "contract" between *independent entities*, but rather as an organism or social *body*'.[25] The clinical gaze transmuted to the social *corpus*. This dubious 'utopian' aim is, of course, part of the pleasure of a Sherlock Holmes: a pleasure of complicity in a generalised tissue of surveillance.

Moretti has it that '[d]etective fiction does not found mass culture: it *prepares* it, by erasing the preceding hegemonic culture'.[26] That is rather too momentous and sweeping but it does suggest some of the contours and coordinates of pleasure in contemporary culture: a complex and negotiated 'fix' on the individual within the social framework, in the urban space, in the city. The basic social and political necessity of a 'bind' between individual and social assumes new forms, new relations which suture a contract across a whole range of discursive forms. Within this new matrix '[t]he self is minimal but not isolated, it is held in a texture of relations more complex and more mobile than ever'.[27] At another point in this emergent cartography of new pleasures and new 'fixes', we might cite the example of photography which, as John Tagg has demonstrated, literally figures the bind of the body and the social in precisely a 'more mobile' texture. Starting out as parasitic upon portraiture in order to preserve the image of the bourgeois in his or her personal realm, its processes were quickly developed in relation to the new science of criminology and 'social welfare' — the two *necessary* poles of a hegemonic culture — in order to develop simultaneously a 'record' of a person and as case history which firmly locates that person as the subject of 'legal memory', inspection and surveillance. Photography not only captured the person or 'represented' the bourgeois (as coercive theories of culture have it) but also, combining pleasure and power, presented, specified, defined and produced the framework within which that individual could be thought. The snapshot and the case history thus being the *recto* and *verso* of 'the transmision of power in the synoptic space of the camera's examination'.[28] The photographic image of the individual, in a variable set of power relations, thus functions as a sort of narrative insofar as it can provide both description and detail, binding and separation, stasis and movement, the pleasure of fixity and the pleasure of process, not as 'general phenomena' of narrative *per se* but within a particular set of relations fixing a whole range of contracts across the individual and the social body.

Foucault tantalisingly sketches something of this movement when he writes of the ways in which 'different instances and stages in the transmission of power were caught up in the very pleasure of their exercise. There is something in surveillance . . . which is no stranger to the pleasure of surveillance, the pleasure of the surveillance of pleasure, and so on'.[29] For the analyst of cultural forms it is a question of specifying those 'different instances and stages' and their interrelationships at given moments of power, of negotiation, of complicity and resistance. Photography, film, detective fiction can be taken as key instances in the contemporary cartography of pleasure. They, amongst others, constitute a plurality of powers and potentials, a technology of the body and of the social which makes up — elaborates — a dense texture of complicities, of subjectivities which are formed not just 'in the head' but across the space of the body too.

But the plurality distinctive to modern cultural forms is not without limits and the body is not therefore the site, as some contemporary theorists have it, of a limitless to and fro of desire. We have to recognise a certain powerful hierarchy in the ordering of preferred images of the body. There is a range of terrains both historical and actual on which the image of the body has been fundamentally strategic. To take the most obvious examples we only have to look at the 'body politics' of Italian Fascism and German Nazism where, as Benjamin observed, the aim was to 'aestheticise politics'. Mussolini bare to the waist, the Aryan body, the identification of 'impurities' in Judaism, the blood, the race as *person*, the virile figure all loom enormously over the cultural politics of those forms of power. There are other — by no means coterminous but powerful in their own terms — representations of the 'utopian body' in contemporary advertising, soft porn, traditional Hollywood movies, Busby Berkeley spectaculars and, more recently, the image of a young woman gymnast in the foreground of a picture at the Port of Liverpool which, after years of neglect and deindustrialisation and recent riots is now 'The Slim, Trim Port' without, as Lytton Strachey once said, 'an ounce of redundant flesh'. But this is only one point on the spiral. If the emphasis on the body either in authoritarian forms of power or in the contemporary 'will-to-fitness' of aerobics, jogging, marathons, breakdancing and 'burning' might in some curious and worrying way fit here with a more generalised social image of the rejection of the days of 'welfare excess' and lazy 'state socialism', then it also inscribes the potential for another type of assertion of control over the body and control over the environment in which it operates.

This is not an appeal for a 'release' of suppressed pleasures or for the mobilisation of liberatory desires. The problem is both more modest and more 'technical' than that. It is more modest in that 'pleasure' like 'experience' is not some 'thing' which can actually be suppressed or released. Commenting, for example, on the category of experience, Wittgenstein once noted that

> Here we think we are standing on the hard bedrock, deeper than any special methods and languages games. But these extremely general terms have an extremely blurred meaning. They relate in practice to innumerable special cases, but that does not make them any *solider*; no, rather it makes them more fluid.[30]

Similar misrepresentations of pleasure either as *solidly* ideological/ repressive or *solidly* liberatory have marked contemporary critical approaches to the issue from Marcuse to (in different terms) Laura Mulvey. We have simply to state, against this, that there is no *general* form of pleasure with ascertainable political and cultural effects. The 'technical' nature of the problem relates then to the 'innumerable special cases' in which pleasures, capacities for pleasure and conceptions of pleasure are mobilised. Perhaps, though — and here we might have to part company with Wittgenstein — they are not quite *in*numerable. Part of my argument has been that although there is a plurality of special cases, there are, none

Colin Mercer

the less, ascertainable points of convergence, points of dominance and, of course, points of fragility in the elaborated culture in which we live.

Notes

1. S. Heath, '*Jaws*, Ideology and Film Theory' in T. Bennett *et al.* (eds), *Popular Television and Film*, British Film Institute, London, 1981, p. 200.
2. E. Said, *The Text, The World, The Critic*, Faber, London, 1984, p. 169.
3. A. Gramsci, *Selections from the Prison Notebooks*, ed. Hoare and Nowell-Smith, Lawrence and Wishart, London, 1971, p. 433.
4. See V. de Grazia, *The Culture of Consent: Mass Organization of Leisure in Fascist Italy*, Cambridge University Press, 1981.
5. L. Mulvey, 'Visual Pleasure and Narrative Cinema' in Bennett *et al*, *Popular Television and Film*, p. 215.
6. The procedure is adapted from M. Foucault, *The Archaeology of Knowledge*, Tavistock, London, 1972.
7. R. Barthes, *The Pleasure of the Text*, trans. R. Miller, Cape, London, 1975, p. 31.
8. Ibid., p. 39.
9. F. Moretti, *Signs Taken for Wonders*, New Left Books/Verso, London, 1983, p. 22.
10. M. Foucault, *Power/Knowledge*, ed. C. Gordon, Pantheon Books, New York, 1980, p. 189.
11. Oswald Ducrot, cited in R. Robin, *Histoire et Linguistique*, Armand Colin, Paris, 1973, p. 26
12. Colin MacCabe, 'On Discourse', *Economy and Society*, vol. 8, no. 3, 1979, p. 300.
13. Ibid.
14. Ibid., p. 303.
15. M. Foucault, *The History of Sexuality*, Pantheon Books, New York, 1978, p. 125.
16. P. Bourdieu, *La Distinction*, Editions de minuit, Paris, 1979, p. 569.
17. Ibid., p. 570.
18. V.N. Voloshinov, *Marxism and the Philosophy of Language*, Academic Press, London, 1976.
19. T. Eagleton, *Walter Benjamin or Towards a Revolutionary Criticism*, New Left Books/Verso, London, 1981, p. 149.
20. Ibid.
21. A. Gramsci, *Quaderni del carcere*, ed. V. Gerratana, Turin, Einaudi, 1975, p. 1822.
22. R. Barthes, *Roland Barthes*, trans. R. Howard, Macmillan, London, 1977, p. 54.
23. S. Heath, *The Sexual Fix*, Macmillan, London, 1982, p. 110.
24. Cited in ibid., p. 111.
25. Moretti, *Signs Taken for Wonders*, p. 135.
26. *Op. cit.* Ibid., p. 155.
27. J.F. Lyotard, *La Condition Post-Moderne*, Paris, 1979, p. 31.
28. J. Tagg, 'Power and Photography' in Bennett *et al., Culture, Ideology and Social Process*, Baksford London, 1982, p. 110.
29. M. Foucault, *Power/Knowledge*, p. 186.
30. Cited in I. Hunter, 'After Representation', *Economy and Society*, November/December, 1984, p. 420.

Section two

Popular Culture: Historical and Social Relations

Introduction

It is not enough to know the *ensemble* of relations as they exist at any given time as a given system. They must be known genetically, in the movement of their formation.

Antonio Gramsci[1]

In this, one of the most frequently cited passages from the *Prison Notebooks*, Gramsci's immediate concern is with the forces and pressures shaping the forms of the human personality. 'For each individual', he continues, 'is the synthesis not only of existing relations, but of the history of these relations. He is a précis of all the past.' Abstracted from this specific context, however, the argument has been granted a more general pertinence as a critique of structuralism *avant la lettre*. The currency of the argument, applied to the concerns of cultural studies, is roughly to the effect that neither the organisation nor the functioning of cultural practices can be understood if these are examined only from the point of view of their current forms and contemporary social articulations. They need also to be considered 'in the movement of their formation', as the product of a history which, to use another famous Gramscianism, 'has deposited . . . an infinity of traces, without leaving an inventory'.[2] By recovering this inventory, it is then argued, our understanding of both the make-up and current socio-political affiliations of cultural practices is significantly enriched.

This bias in favour of historical analysis is shared by each of the essays collected in this section of the anthology — not in the trival sense that each essay is concerned with forms of popular culture which are historical in the sense of belonging to the past; rather, in each case, the emphasis is upon 'the movement of the formation' of the practices under examination. While importantly similar in this respect, they differ quite markedly with regard to the specific fields of socio-cultural relations which constitute their respective points of focus.

In 'The Tale of Samuel and Jemima: gender and working class culture in early nineteenth-century England', Catherine Hall's concern is with the contradictory pressures bearing on the formation of the culture of radicalism, particularly as these affected the position, aspirations and self-definitions of women in that culture. However radical its protocols might have been in class terms, Hall argues, the culture of working-class radicalism was deeply tainted by middle-class assumptions concerning the relations between the public and the private sphere, the 'proper' division of labour between the sexes, and so on. The definition of the political role of women radicals resulting from these conceptions was an auxiliary one: women were to play a supporting role in relation to class struggles that were conceived as essentially masculine; women's stake in political struggle was an indirect one — they served their own interests by supporting those of their fathers, husbands and brothers. However, Hall's purpose goes beyond pointing to this contradiction. Rather, by tracing the ways in which it was registered, felt and experienced by women, and the ways in which they sought other terms of defining their own role and place in political struggle, she is concerned precisely with the part this contradiction played in the ongoing movement and formation of the culture of both working class radicalism and feminism.

David Cardiff and Paddy Scannell's interests centre on the changing styles and forms of programming developed by the BBC during the last war. Focusing particularly on developments in light entertainment broadcasting, and the use of broadcasting in relation to both morale boosting during the war and initiating debate on the future of Britain after the war, Cardiff and Scannell examine these in the light of changing organisational relations between the BBC and the government and, indeed, of organisational tensions within the BBC itself. The ultimate context for their analysis, however, is provided by a discussion of the changing relations between state and society during wartime Britain. Arguing that the need to mobilise the whole population in support of the war effort entailed 'a gradual, but significant, change in the nature of political, social and cultural relations in Britain — a movement away from the exercise of direct leadership and rule by dominant political and cultural alignments, towards negotiated agreements in which the apex of the social pyramid must win the consent and agreement of the base for its actions' (p. 116), Cardiff and Scannell outline the respects in which changes in BBC programming both contributed to and were shaped by these developments.

In the last two essays, the focus shifts to an examination of the national and regional aspects of popular culture. Colin McArthur's subject is the form of the national exhibition, particularly as exemplified by the 1937 Glasgow Empire Exhibition. What contradictions, McArthur asks, does the exhibition form pose for nations like Scotland whose dominant international imagery is as the romanticised and exoticised Other of England? In answering this question, McArthur relates his discussion to the current development, in Scotland, of forms of cultural nationalism which refuse such a subservient identity. In a similar vein, Tony Bennett's analysis of Blackpool is concerned with the relations between subordiante regional cultural identities and dominant national ones. In examining the ideological organisation of the main forms of popular pleasure and entertainment in Blackpool, and considering these in 'the movement of their formation' over the period from the mid-nineteenth century to the present, Bennett argues that they offer evidence of a distinctive 'regional-popular'.characterising the way in which, at least until recently, the local hegemony of the Lancashire bourgeoisie was secured precisely by differentiating itself from the national bourgeoisie.

Notes

1. A. Gramsci, *Selections from The Prison Notebooks*, Lawrence and Wishart, 1971, p. 353.
2. Ibid, p. 324.

4

Catherine Hall

The tale of Samuel and Jemima: Gender and working-class culture in early nineteenth-century England

Samuel Bamford, the radical weaver, described in his famous auto-biography *Passages in the Life of a Radical* his experience of the Peterloo massacre in 1819. The account has rightly become a classic. Bamford first recounted the gathering of the procession in his native town of Middleton. At the front were

> twelve of the most comely and decent-looking youths, who were placed in two rows of six each, with each a branch of laurel held presented in his hand, as a token of amity and peace, — then followed the men of several districts in fives, — then the band of music, an excellent one, — then the colours; a blue one of silk, with inscriptions in golden letters, 'UNITY AND STRENGTH', 'LIBERTY AND FRATERNITY'. A green one of silk with golden letters, 'PAR-LIAMENTS ANNUAL', 'SUFFRAGE UNIVERSAL'; and betwixt them on a staff, a handsome cap of crimson velvet, with a tuft of laurel, and the cap tastefully braided with the word LIBERTAS in front.

Next came the men of Middleton and its surroundings, every hundred with its leader who had a sprig of laurel in his hat, the three thousand men all ready to obey the commands of a 'principal conductor', 'who took his place at the head of the column with a bugleman to sound his orders'. Bamford addressed the men before they set off, reminding them that it was essential that they should behave with dignity and with discipline and so confound their enemies who represented them as a 'mob-like rabble'. Bamford recalled the procession as 'a most respectable assemblage of labouring men', all decently if humbly attired and wearing their Sunday white shirts and neck-cloths. The Middleton column soon met with the Rochdale column and between them, Bamford estimates, there were probably six thousand men. At their head were now about 200 of their most handsome young women supporters, including Bamford's wife, some of whom were singing and dancing to the music. The demonstrators had as their keywords 'cleanliness', 'sobriety', 'order' and 'peace' and the women symbolised these virtues. The reformers arrived in Manchester, having changed their route following the personal request of Orator Hunt that they lead his group in. This did not particularly please Bamford, who had elevated views of his own dignity as leader and was not overly sympathetic to Hunt, but he agreed and then while the speeches were going on, he and a friend, not expecting to hear anything new, went to look for some refreshment. It was at this point that the cavalry attacked and that the great demonstration was broken up with terrible brutality. Hundreds were wounded, 11 killed. Bamford managed to get away and after much anxiety met up with his wife, from whom he had been separated for some hours.

The human horror of Peterloo was differently experienced by Jemima Bamford, for from the moment of realising that something had gone badly wrong her anxieties and fears were focussed on her husband's safety. As a leader of the reformers he was potentially particularly subject to persecution and indeed he was arrested and charged with high treason soon afterwards. Reform demonstrations were predominantly male occasions, as we can see from the description of the Middleton procession. There was usually a good sprinkling of women present and 'a neatly dressed female, supporting a small flag' was sitting on the driving seat of Hunt's carriage. Mary Fildes, President of the Female Reform Society of Manchester, was on the platform, all dressed in white. Over a hundred women were wounded in St Peter's Fields and two were killed but nevertheless the majority of participants, speakers and recognised leaders were men.

When Bamford first began to worry as to where his wife was he blamed himself that he had allowed her to come at all. In her account she says that she was determined to go to the meeting and would have followed it even if her husband had not consented to her going with the procession. She was worried before the event that something would go wrong and preferred to be near Samuel. He finally agreed and she arranged to leave their little girl with a 'careful neighbour' and joined some other 'married females' at the head of the procession. She was dressed simply, as a countrywoman, in her 'second best attire'. Separated from her husband and the majority of the Middleton men by the crowd she was terrified when the soldiers started the attack and managed to escape into a cellar. There she hid until the carnage was over when she crept out, helped by the kindly people in the house, and went in search of Samuel, who was first reported as dead, next said to be in the infirmary, then in the prison, but with whom she eventually managed to meet up safely. At the end of the tragic day, Bamford tells us,

> Her anxiety being now removed by the assurance of my safety, she hastened forward to console our child. I rejoined my comrades, and forming about a thousand of them into file, we set off to the sound of fife and drum, with our only banner waving, and in that form we re-entered the town of Middleton.[1]

Peterloo was a formative experience in the development of popular consciousness in the early nineteenth century and Bamford's account takes us into the question of the meanings of sexual difference within working-class culture. In E.P. Thompson's classic account of the making of the

English working class, that process whereby groups of stockingers and weavers, factory workers and agricultural labourers, those in the old centres of commerce and the new industrial towns came to see themselves as having interests in common as against those of other classes, Peterloo is seen as one of the decisive moments, significantly shifting disparate individuals and groups towards a defined political consciousness. By 1832, Thompson argues, working people had built up a sense of collective identity and shared struggle, had come to see themselves as belonging to a class. Central to this process, he argues, was the development of a distinctive working-class culture, with its own beliefs, its own practices and its own institutions.[2] That was the culture to which Bamford belonged, a culture that originated with artisans but extended to factory operatives, a culture that stressed moral sobriety and the search for useful knowledge, that valued intellectual enquiry, that saw mutual study and disputation as methods of learning and self-improvement.

Such a culture placed men and women differently and the highlighting of these forms of sexual division can give us some access to the gendered nature of popular culture in the early nineteenth century. Men and women experienced that culture very differently, as we can see from Bamford's story. He had been involved with the organization of the day, with the training of the men so that they would march in disciplined procession, with the arrangements as to the route, with the ceremonial and ritual which would help to give the reformers a sense of strength and power. He belonged unambiguously to the struggle; as a leader he was concerned to articulate the demands of honest weavers, to help to develop strategies which would make possible the winning of reform. For his wife it was a very different matter. She too had a commitment to the cause but it was her husband who wrote down her tale, hoping that it would not be 'devoid of interest to the reader'. Her anxiety to go to Manchester stemmed from her fears for him. Her arrangements were to do with their child; her first concern, once she knew that her husband was safe, was to get back to the child. Like the majority of female reformers at the time she positioned herself, and was positioned by others, as a wife and mother supporting the cause of working men. The men, on the other hand, like her husband, entered the political fray as independent subjects, fighting for their own right to the vote, their own capacity to play a part in determining forms of government. It is this distinction, between men as independent political beings and women as dependents which the tale of Samuel and Jemima vividly illustrates.

The emergence of the working man as a political subject in his own right was part of the process of the development of male working-class consciousness. Eighteenth-century society had not primarily been dominated by class issues and class struggles. It was King Property who ruled eighteenth-century England and the hegemony established by the land-owning classes and the gentry rested on an acceptance of a patriarchal and hierarchical society. Consent had been won to the exercise of power by the propertied in part through the shared acceptance of a set of beliefs and customs, the 'moral economy' of the society, which unlike the new political economy of the nineteenth century, recognised communal norms and obligations and judged that the rich would respect the rights of the poor, particularly when it came to the issue of a 'just price' for bread. When that moral economy was transgressed, eighteenth-century crowds believed they had the right to defend their traditional customs. Bread riots, focused on soaring prices, malpractices amongst dealers, or just plain hunger, were one of the most popular forms of protest. Women were often the initiators of riots for they were the most involved in buying and inevitably the most sensitive to evidence of short weight or adulteration. Their concern was the subsistence of their families. Similarly, women were heavily involved in protests against enclosure, which threatened the survival of families and undermined those traditional rights associated with the moral economy.[3] Men were engaged in these protests along with women. They too were concerned to articulate and defend customary and communal practices.

It was the turbulent decade of the 1790s that was to fracture the established consensus and begin the movement towards a new sense of distinctive interests, of class interest, not only for working people but for aristocrats and entrepreneurs as well.[4] The degree of sympathy which food rioters had been able to expect from some magistrates disappeared and more punitive strategies began to be adopted by the authorities especially in the light of the revolutionary example from France and after the start of Jacobin activities in England. The repudiation of customary rights by those in power meant that such expectations had to be rethought and reinterpreted. It was the writings of Tom Paine and the revolutionary ideals of liberty, equality and fraternity which inspired the 1790s version of the 'free-born Englishman' and the creation of new traditions of radicalism and protest. In the clubs and the meeting places of the 1790s serious reformers gathered to discuss the vital subject of the day — parliamentary reform. As Thomas Hardy, the first secretary of the London Corresponding Society, wrote in his autobiography describing their first meeting:

> After having had their bread and cheese and porter for supper, as usual, and their pipes afterwards, with some conversation on the hardness of the times and the dearness of all the necessaries of life . . . the business for which they had met was brought forward — *Parliamentary Reform* — an important subject to be deliberated upon and dealt with by such a class of men.[5]

The artisans and small tradesmen of the reforming societies had come to the conclusion that their demand must be for political representation. It was Parliament which carried the key to a better future. With the moral consensus eroded and the refusal of the rich to take their responsibilities seriously, whether in the field of wages, the customary control of labour, or poverty and hunger, the only solution could be to change the government for the better. It was men who were in the forefront of formulating such demands. Drawing on and reworking the established traditions of English liberalism and dissent they defined themselves as political agents whilst their wives, mothers and daughters were defined as supporters and dependents. The shift from the communal forms of protest of the eighteenth century to the class struggles of the nineteenth century carried with it a sharper distinction between the interests and identities of men and women. As bread riots gave way to new forms, whether constitutional societies, demonstrations for reform or machine smashing, the old emphasis on the common interests of the whole community was replaced by more sectionalised and gender-specific forms of politics. In this process working men increasingly saw themselves as the main breadwinners and the representatives of their families. Radical working-class culture came to rest on a set of common-sense assumptions about the relative places of men and women which were not subjected to the same critical scrutiny as were the monarchy, the aristocracy, representative forms of government and the other institutions of old corruption.

What were the beliefs, practices and institutions of this working-class culture that emerged in the early nineteeth century and in what ways did they legitimate men and women differently? It was the reform movement that lay at the heart of that culture. This does not of course mean that there were not other extremely significant elements within popular culture. Methodism, for example, provided one such alternative discourse, intersecting at some points with the beliefs of serious and improving artisans, as in their shared concern to challenge the evils of alcohol, but at other points having sharply different concerns. Meanwhile heavy drinking and gambling remained very popular pastimes for sections of the working class, however much the sober and respectable disapproved of them. But it was the characteristic beliefs and institutions of the radicals which emerged as the leading element within working-class culture in the early nineteenth century, carrying more resonance and with a stronger institutional base, than any other. The main thrust behind the reform movement, Thompson argues, came from the 'industrious classes' — stockingers, handloom weavers, cotton-spinners, artisans, and, in association with these a widespread scattering of small masters, tradesmen, publicans, booksellers and professional men. These different groups were able to come together and on the basis of their shared political and industrial organisation, through the Hampden Clubs, the Constitutional Societies, the Trade Unions, the Friendly Societies, the educational groups and the self-improvement societies they were able to come to feel an identity of interest.[6] Such clubs and societies were, therefore, central to the task of building a common culture but such locations offered a much easier space for men to operate in than for women.

Bamford tells us of the Hampden clubs and their importance:

Instead of riots and destruction of property, Hampden clubs were now established in many of our large towns, and the villages and districts around them; Cobbett's books were printed in a cheap form; the labourers read them, and thenceforward became deliberate and systematic in their proceedings. Nor were there wanting men of their own class, to encourage and direct the new converts; the Sunday Schools of the preceding thirty years, had produced many working men of sufficient talent to become readers, writers, and speakers in the village meetings for parliamentary reform; some also were found to possess a rude poetic talent, which rendered their effusions popular, and bestowed an additional charm on their assemblages, and by such various means, anxious listeners at first, and then zealous proselytes, were drawn from the cottages of quiet nooks and dingles, to the weekly readings and discussions of the Hampden clubs.[7]

Bamford is describing male gatherings; the men who had learnt to read and write in the Sunday Schools of the late eighteenth century made use of their new talents, spoke to others, sometimes even in popular poetic form, and built up weekly reading and discussion meetings. Work on literacy rates suggests that working-class women lagged significantly behind men.[8] Teachers were less likely to give them time and energy. They were less likely to have time or space or freedom to pursue study and discussion. As David Vincent has shown, the difficulties associated with women writing are reflected in the autobiographical material which has survived. Of the 142 autobiographies which he has analysed only six were by women. He attributes this silence to the lack of self-confidence amongst women for who could possibly be interested in their lives? We remember Jemima Bamford, writing her few notes to be included in her husband's story. Vincent also points to women's subordinate position within the family. Men could demand that their wives and children recognise their need for quiet and privacy in circumstances where such conditions were almost impossible to obtain. The wife would hush the children and quell the storms whilst her husband struggled with his exercises in reading and writing. Such efforts were rarely forthcoming for women. Furthermore, self-improvement societies were normally for men only. It was hard for women in these circumstances to have the same kind of commitment to intellectual inquiry and the search for useful knowledge, values which were central to radical culture.[9]

But this subordinate position of women within the family was not given. Customary assumptions about 'a woman's place' were rethought and reworked in this period. As Dorothy Thompson has argued the replacement of the more informal and communal protests of the eighteenth century with the more organised movements of the nineteenth century resulted in the increasing marginalisation of women.[10] As formal societies with constitutions and officers replaced customary patterns of crowd mobilisation, women withdrew. Many meetings were seen as occasions for male conviviality and women were excluded informally if not formally. Meetings might be at times when they could not go, for once they were removed from the street the automatic participation of men, women and children was broken. They were often held in places to which it was difficult for them to go, for pubs were coming to be seen as unsuitable places for respectable women. If they did manage to get there they might well feel alienated by the official jargon and constitutional procedures so beloved by some radical men.[11]

Radical men were certainly sometimes happy to welcome women as supporters of their demands. In the Birmingham Political Union, for example, resuscitated in 1839 after its triumphs in the lead up to the Reform Act of 1832, a Female Political Union was established through the efforts of Titus Salt, a leading radical, who argued that the support which women could provide would be invaluable. At a giant tea-party held by the Female Political Union in the grand new town hall in the city the male leaders of the BPU demonstrated the ambiguous and contradictory nature of their feelings about women's engagement in politics. Tea and plum cake were served to the assembled thousand and then the men on the platform delivered their addresses. Thomas Attwood, the hero of 1832, spoke first. 'My kind and fair and most dear countrywomen,' he began, 'I most solemnly declare my affection for the women of England has been mainly instrumental in causing all my exertions in the public cause, not that I do not feel for the men, but I have a stronger desire to promote the comforts of the women.' The women, according to the report of the *Birmingham Journal*, the mouth piece of the radicals, were suitably grateful for his efforts on their behalf. After Attwood came Scholefield, the first MP for the city, elected after the triumph of Reform. Scholefield proceded to enunciate his contradictory impulses to his audience. 'It was gratifying to him to meet so many excellent and intelligent women', he began, 'who, by their presence showed very plainly that they took a lively interest in all that concerned the welfare of their husbands, fathers, brothers and sons, and which also', he added, 'deeply affected their own welfare.' Scholefield went on to argue for women's politics, citing the importance of the women's storming of the Bastille. He concluded, however, that 'He was far from wishing that politics should ever supersede the important duties of social and domestic life, which constituted the chief business of the female; but he also hoped the women of Birmingham would never become indifferent to politics.' Titus Salt followed Scholefield, arguing that by their good conduct the women had won over everybody to the cause of female unions and that, 'by a continuance of the same conduct, and the force of moral power, they would gain all they required'. All these radical men wanted support from women. Their capacity for fund raising was particularly welcomed. But in seeking this support they were breaking in part with the old assumptions abouts politics being a male sphere. Not surprisingly they had mixed feelings about this. So, indeed, did many women. Attwood's patronage of his female audience, Scholefield's insistence that they were involved primarily for their menfolk, Salt's emphasis on good conduct and moral force as the ways in which women could be politically effective, all point to the difficulties arising from the mobilisation of women, the tensions generated by the spectacle of a thousand women in the Birmingham Town Hall and what they might do. Would they properly recognise that Attwood had achieved reform for them, would they be content with acting for their fathers, husbands and sons, would they continue to behave well and conduct themselves according to female propriety, could the men control them? Would Mrs Bamford have gone to Manchester without her husband's permission? What was a woman's place? They were certainly not willing to be rendered silent. At a subsequent Female Political Union meeting with a Mrs Spinks in the chair, Mr Collins, a prominent BPU member, spoke. Birmingham had at last achieved incorporaton and the right to representative local government. Mr Collins said 'He could not but congratulate them on the glorious victory that had been that day achieved in the Town Hall by the men of Birmingham'. A woman in the meeting, resenting this slur on her sex, piped up: 'And by the women, Mr Collins, for we were there'. Mr Collins had to admit 'the assistance the women had rendered'.[12]

Given the institutional framework of radical working-class culture it was difficult for women to engage straightforwardly in it as political agents in their own right. Nevertheless they were there, in considerable number and with considerable strength, in Female Reform Associations, in the Owenite communities and amongst the Chartists.[13] For the most part it seems that they sought primarily to advance the cause of their menfolk, and, in the case of Chartism, to asure that the male voice could be properly represented in Parliament. But there were sounds of discord. Discussion as to the nature of womanhood was an ever present feature of both working-class and middle-class society in this period. Debates over the character of woman's moral influence, over her potential for moral inspiration, over the tension between spiritual equality and social subordination, over the proper nature of woman's work, permeated both political and literary discourses. Radical circles provided no exception to this. Attempts by feminists such as Mary Wollstonecraft to open up questions of sexual difference and sexual equality in the 1790s had met with a barrage of hostility. But those women who wanted to question the primacy of women's status as wives and mothers, who wanted to argue for women to have rights for themselves, not only the right to improve men through their spiritual inspiration, but to be independent workers in the vineyards of radical and socialist culture, were able to use and subvert the language of moral influence to make new claims for themselves as women. As Barbara Taylor has shown, the most sustained attempts to interpret political radicalism as centrally to do with not only class politics but also gender politics, came from the Owenite feminists.[14] Owenism provided less stony ground than other varieties of radicalism and socialism for the development of new forms of socialist feminism. Its commitment to love and cooperation as against competition and its critique of the relations of domination and subordination, whether between masters and men or men and women, meant that the Owenite analysis potentially focussed on all the social relations of capitalism, including the institutions of marriage and the family.

But the Owenite moment was a transitional political moment. Owenite men were not immune to the sexual antagonisms fostered by new methods of production which aimed to marginalise skilled men and make use of the cheap labour of women and children. Even within the movement Owenite feminists had to struggle to be heard and as Owenism declined in strength and Chartism increasingly occupied centre stage within radical culture, feminist voices were quietened. The institutions of radical working-class culture, as we have seen, tended to centre around men and legitimate male belonging. The self-improvement clubs, the debating societies, the Hampden clubs and the mutual education evenings were more accessible to men than to women. If the institutional framework positioned men as agents and women as supporters, what of the belief system?

Paineite radicalism was central to the political discourses of working people at this time. With its stress on radical egalitarianism, its rejection of the traditions of the past, its conviction that the future could be different, its belief in natural rights and the power of reason, its questioning of established institutions and its firm commitment to the view that government must represent the people, it gave a cutting thrust to radical demands.[15] Mary Wollstonecraft was to build on that radical egalitarianism and extend the demand for individual rights to women. In her new moral world women would be full agents, able to participate as rational beings, no longer tied into the constraining bonds of a frivolous femininity. But her cause won few adherents, the countervailing forces were too strong and her ideal of woman's citizenship, whilst it survived in feminist thinking and debate, was lost in the more public discourses of radicalism in the next 50 years.[16]

Paine's stress on individual rights and on the centrality of consent to representative forms of government drew on the classical tradition of Locke, which was itself built on the inalienable Puritan right to individual spiritual life. This tradition had attained considerable power in eighteenth-century England. But Locke's concept of the individual agent never extended beyond men. For him the origins of government lay in the consent of the propertied. The only people who were qualified to give consent were those propertied men who would take responsibility for their dependants, whether wives, children or servants. Political authority for Locke rested with men. Locke then further reinforced the differences between men and women by arguing that within the family men would inevitably carry greater authority than women. In line with the political

81

break he represented with Filmer and conservative ideas of the divine and patriarchal nature of kingly authority, he insisted that marriage was a contractual relation to which both partners had to consent. To this extent Locke was arguing *for* individual rights for women. The husband was not seen as having any absolute sovereignty within the family. But Locke saw it as only to be expected that in every household someone would take command. Both parents had obligations to their children but the superior ability of the husband would give him the right to act as head and arbiter. This was a *natural* outcome. Locke thus distinguished between the 'natural' world of the family in which men would emerge as more powerful than women, and the political world of civil society in which men consented to forms of government.[17] This distinction between the two spheres, the family and civil society, with their different forms and rules, was played upon and developed by Enlightenment thinkers in the eighteenth century. As Jane Rendall has argued, writers across England, France and Scotland elaborated theories of sexual difference which built upon this primary distinction. They stressed that woman's nature was governed more by feeling than by reason; it was imaginative rather than analytic, and that women possessed distinctive moral characteristics which, in the right setting, could be fulfilled. Thus Rousseau combined his critique of the moral and sexual weakness of women with a belief that women could act as sources of moral inspiration and guidance, if they were allowed to blossom in their domestic worlds. The domestic sphere, Enlightenment thinkers argued, could provide a positive role for women but a role which was premised on an assertion of difference from rather than similarity to men.[18]

Radical thinking was embedded in these assumptions about sexual difference. Mary Wollstonecraft herself argued for the rights of women as wives and mothers and thought that most women in the new world would put those duties first. For her such a view was balanced with her belief that women should have the right to fulfilment for themselves. For others it was only too possible to combine a clear commitment to political radicalism with a deep and entrenched social conservatism. William Cobbett, the writer and journalist who Thompson sees as the most important intellectual influence on post-war radicalism, was in the forefront of such tendencies. It was Cobbett who created the radical culture of the 1820s, Thomspon argues,

> not because he offered its most original ideas, but in the sense that he found the tone, the style, and the arguments which could bring the weaver, the schoolmaster, and the shipwright, into a common discourse. Out of the diversity of grievances and interests he brought a Radical consensus.[19]

But Cobbett's radical consensus was one which placed women firmly in the domestic sphere. He came to be categorically in favour of home life and what he saw as established and well-tried household patterns. Wives should be chaste, sober, industrious, frugal, clean, good-tempered and beautiful with a knowledge of domestic affairs and able to cook. The nation was made up of families, argued Cobbett, and it was essential that families should be happy and well managed, with enough food and decent wages. This was the proper basis of a good society. In writing *Cottage Economy* Cobbett hoped to contribute to the revival of homely and domestic skills which he saw as seriously threatened by the development of a wage economy. He offered precise instructions on the brewing of beer, not only because it could be made more cheaply at home but also because a good home brew would encourage men to spend their evenings with their families rather than at the tavern. A woman who could not bake, Cobbett thought, was 'unworthy of trust and confidence . . . a mere burthen upon the community'. He assured fathers that the way to construct a happy marriage for their daughters was to 'make them skilful, able and active in the most necessary concerns of a family'. 'Dimples and cherry cheeks' were not enough; it was knowing how to brew, to bake, to make milk and butter that made a woman into 'a person worthy of respect'. What could please God more, asked Cobbett, than the picture of 'the labourer, after his return from the toils of a cold winter day, sitting with his wife and children round a cheerful fire, while the wind whistles in the chimney and the rain pelts the roof?'[20] Given that so much depended on it, men should take care to exercise their reason as well as their passion in their choice of a wife. Wives should run the household and forget the new-fangled 'accomplishments' of femininity with which he had no patience. Men should honour and respect their wives and spend their time at home when not occupied away. Cobbett shared the commonly held view that women were more feeling than men and he saw that women had more to lose in marriage, for they gave up their property and their person to their husband. Husbands should consequently be kind to their wives but there was no question that wives were subject to the authority of their husbands, that they must obey and must not presume to make decisions. Reason and God, thundered Cobbett, both said that wives should obey their husbands; there must be a head of every house, he said, echoing Locke, and he must have undivided authority. As the heads of households men must represent their dependants and themselves enjoy the most salient right of all. There could be no rights, Cobbett belived, without that most central right 'the right of taking a part in the making of the laws by which we are governed'. Without that, the right to enjoy life and property or to exert physical or mental powers meant nothing. Following directly in the tradition of Locke, Cobbett argued that the right to take part in the making of laws was founded in the state of nature:

> It springs out of the very principle of civil society; for what compact, what agreement, what common assent, can possibly be imagined by which men would give up all the rights of nature, all the free enjoyment of their bodies and their minds, in order to subject themselves to rules and laws, in the

making of which they should have nothing to say, and which should be enforced upon them without their assent? The great right, therefore, of every man, the right of rights, is the right of having a share in the making of the laws, to which the good of the whole makes it his duty to submit.

Cobbett argued strongly, breaking entirely with Locke at this point, that *no* man should be excluded from this 'right of rights' unless he were insane or had committed an 'indelible crime'. He would have no truck with the view that it was property in the sense of landownership which conferred the right. For Cobbett it was those properties associated with 'honourable' labour and property in skill which gave men the right to vote. Minors he saw as automatically excluded from such privileges since the law classified them as infants. But the rights of women to share in the making of the laws, to give their assent to the abandonment of the rights of nature and the free enjoyment of their bodies and their minds, he disposed of in one sentence. Women are excluded, he wrote, from the right of rights because

> husbands are answerable in law for their wives, as to their civil damages, and because the very nature of their sex makes the exercise of the right incompatible with the harmony and happiness of society.

There was no escape from this. Single women who wanted to argue that they were legal individuals with civil rights were caught, when it came to political rights, by their *nature*. Women could only become persons 'worthy of respect' through their household skills. Society could only be harmonious and happy if they behaved as wives and daughters, subject to the better judgements of their fathers. By nature the female sex was unsuited to the public sphere.[21]

***

The positioning of women as wives, mothers and daughters within radical culture at the same time that men were positioned as active and independent agents was in part connected to similar processes within middle-class culture. The period from the 1790s to the 1830s also saw the emergence of the English middle class, with its own beliefs and practices, its own sense of itself as a class, with interests different from those of other classes. The middle class defined itself in part through certain critical public moments; the affair of Queen Caroline, the events of 1832 and the repeal of the Corn Laws in 1845; but it also defined itself through the establishment of new cultural patterns and new institutional forms. Central to its culture was a marked emphasis on the separation between male and female spheres. Men were to be active in the public world of business and politics. Women were to be gentle and dependent in the private world of the home and family.[22]

The two most important cultural and intellectual influences on middle-class formation were serious Christianity and political economy. Both, in their own ways, emphasised the different interests of men and women and articulated the discourses of separate spheres. For the serious Christians, led by the Evangelicals who constituted a powerful reforming group within the Anglican church, the interest in sexual difference was highly explicit. They believed that mankind was damned by the fall and that the only hope lay in conversion and salvation. Given the debased nature of manners and morals in the late eighteenth century, men and women who had been converted had the best hope of living a good Christian life within the safe sanctum of a religious family. The family became for them, as it had been for the Puritans before them, the basic social unit. Within the family the woman, untouched as she was by the immorality of the outside world, was more susceptible to spiritual inspiration than the man who had to survive in the public world. Women, therefore, had a special role as the moralisers, the teachers of their children, the consciences of their husbands and fathers. This did not mean that women were the equals of men. St Paul was explicit on this point. Wives should obey their husbands. It did mean, however, that the proper spheres of men and women were different. A man's most important task was to order and support his Christian household through being active in the world. A woman's was to maintain a benevolent moral influence within the home. Her job was to be a Christian wife, mother and mistress.[23]

Political economists and Utilitarians were not concerned in the same way with male and female spheres; indeed, most of them had very little to say on the subject (except John Stuart Mill, who challenged the orthodoxies). But they worked with assumptions about sexual difference, about the superior rationality of the man and the more emotive nature of the woman, for example, from which they concluded that a man's place was in the market and a woman's place in the home.[24]

Middle-class men from the late eighteenth century were striving to establish their power and influence in the provinces, long before they achieved full national recognition. They sought to make their voices heard in both town and countryside, to influence Parliament on matters that concerned them, to intervene in different forms of local government, to establish and maintain religious and cultural institutions, to exercise their charity and to build new mercantile, financial and commercial associations. In every field of interest they were active and energetic, fulfilling the precept that 'a man must act'. Their initiatives were multiple, their fields of enterprise boundless. Assumptions about sexual difference permeated all their schemes. Their political committees excluded women, their churches demarcated male and female spheres, their botanical gardens assumed that men would join on behalf of their families, their philanthropic societies treated men and women differently, their business associations were for men only. In defining their own cultural patterns and practices the men and women of the middle class had a significant impact on working-class culture. The middle class was fighting for political and cultural pre-eminence. In rejecting aristocratic values and the old forms of patronage and influence, they sought to define new values, to establish new modes of power. In the process they were both defining themselves as a class, and asserting dominance. In many areas, particularly new industrial towns where aristocatic interest was not well entrenched, they were able to occupy the field, to be the providers of education and philanthropy, to establish whole new ranges of institutions which bore their imprint.

In Birmingham, for example, large numbers of schools, Sunday Schools and charitable ventures were established in the late eighteenth and early nineteenth centuries, which all operated with middle-class notions of what were properly male and female. In recommending domestic values to Sunday School pupils, charity-school girls or aged and infirm women, middle-class women at one and the same time defined their own 'relative sphere' and their sense of the proper place of working-class women. That proper place was either as servants in the homes of their betters, or as respectable and modest wives and mothers in their own homes. The Birmingham Society for Aged and Infirm Women sought money on behalf 'of those who have discharged the relative duties of a wife and mother' and were left, perhaps deserted, in their old age. The organisers paid the strictest attention to establishing whether the women really deserved such assistance, whether their lives had been humble and respectable.[25] Schools taught boys and girls separately, often in different buildings and with emphasis on different achievements.[26] Self-improvement societies and debating societies, such as the Birmingham Brotherly Society, were for men only.[27] The new Mechanics Institute was exclusively male and aimed to train men to become better husbands, servants and fathers. As the first report of the Birmingham Institute stressed, a man's whole family would benefit from his involvement with such an establishment. He himself would become more 'sober, intelligent and tranquil' they claimed,

> his presence at home will diffuse pleasure and tranquillity through out his household. His own improvement will be reflected in the improved condition of his family. Perceiving the benefit of a judicious economy, he will still be able to command a larger expenditure in the education of his children, and in the accessories of rational enjoyment. Cheerfulness, cleanliness, and the smile of welcome will constantly await his approach to his domestic fireside. Beloved at home and respected abroad, it will not be too much to assert, that he will become a better servant, husband and father; a higher moral character; and consequently a happier man, from his connection with the MECHANICS INSTITUTE.[28]

These were grandiose claims indeed! Not surprisingly working-class men and women were not miraculously transformed into respectable and sober men, domestic and home-loving women, by the action of institutions inspired by the middle class. But, as many historians have demonstrated, nor did they simply refuse the values of this dominant culture. As Gray has shown in his perceptive study of the aristocracy of labour in Edinburgh, a process of negotiation took place between dominant and subordinate; negotiation which resulted in the emergence of distinctive concepts of dignity and respectability, influenced by middle-class values yet holding to a belief in Trade Union action, for example, and a strong sense of class pride.[29] Similarly Vincent, in his study of the meaning of 'useful knowledge' to working-class autobiographers, has demonstrated the independence from middle-class meanings of the term and the creation of a separate and class specific concept.[30] The same story could be told in relation to male and female spheres. Working class men and women did not adopt wholesale the middle-class view of a proper way of life. But aspects of both religious and secular discourses on masculinity, femininity and domestic life did have resonance in some sections of the working class, did make sense of some experiences and appeal to some needs.

Take the case of temperance. Temperance, it has been argued, provides a prime example of the successful assertion of middle-class hegemony. Working men became volunteers in the cause of middle-class respectability. They aimed to improve themselves, to educate themselves, to raise themselves to their betters. The initiative for the total abstinence movement had come from class-conscious working men and there were many connections between them and the Chartist movement, but the radical belief in individual improvement was extremely vulnerable to assimilation to the cultural patterns of the middle class[31]. Arguments against drink made heavy use of an appeal to home and family, for one of the major evils associated with alcohol was its propensity to ruin working-class families and reduce them to depravity. In the famous series of Cruikshank plates entitled *The Bottle*, for example, the first image was of respectable and modest working-class family enjoying a meal in their simple but clean and comfortable home. They represented the model happy family with clothes carefully mended, a family portrait, the young children playing, a fire burning cosily in the grate and a lock on the door ensuring that the home would remain a place of refuge and security. Then the man offered his wife a drink and in scene after scene Cruickshank documented the horrifying destruction of the home and family ending up with the husband insane, having murdered his wife with a bottle, the youngest child dead and the other two a pimp and a prostitute.[32] It was a cliché of temperance lecturers to rely on the comparison between the unhappy home of the drunkard and the contented domestic idyll of the temperate worker. As a reformed drinker poetically declared:

I protest that no more I'll get drunk —
For I find it the bane of my life!
Henceforth I'll be watchful that nought shall destroy
That comfort and peace that I ought to enjoy
In my children, my home and my wife.[33]

Such protestations did not simply imply the acceptance of middle-class ideals of domesticity, for working men and women developed their own notions of manliness and femininity which, whilst affected by dominant conceptions, nevertheless had inflections of their own. As John Smith, a Birmingham temperance enthusiast, argued:

> The happiness of the fireside is involved in the question of temperance, and we know that the chief ornament of that abode of happiness is woman. Most of the comforts of life depend upon our female relatives and friends, whether in infancy, in mature years, or old age.[34]

Here he touched on a vital nerve for the comforts of life for the working man did indeed depend on female relatives. But those female relatives needed different skills from their middle-class sisters. Whilst middle-class idealogues stressed that the moral and managerial aspects of womanhood for wives were to provide moral inspiration and manage the running of their households, working-class blueprints for the good wife and mother emphasised the practical skills associated with cooking, cleaning and bringing up children. Dignity and self-worth for women lay in doing those tasks well.

This elevation of woman's domestic role coincided with the emergence of working women as a publicly defined 'social problem'. As Sally Alexander has argued, the period of the 1830s and 1840s saw the confirmation of men as responsible political subjects whilst women were largely condemned to public silence.[35] An important aspect of this was the emergence of the idea of the 'family wage', a wage which a male breadwinner would earn, sufficient to support his wife and children.[36] Such an ideal of male support and female dependence was already firmly established within middle-class culture but was to become embedded in working-class practice as well through, for example, the bargaining procedures of skilled trade unions.[37] Again, this did not involve the straightforward acceptance of middle-class standards but rather 'an adaptation and reshaping of class-specific notions.

In the early 1840s, to take one case, middle-class fears and anxieties about the employment of women in unsuitable work reached a pitch over the issue of women's work in the mines. The commissioners appointed to enquire into the incidence of child labour underground were shocked and horrified at the evidence that emerged of female conditions of work. Bourgeois views of femininity were violently assaulted by the spectacle of women in various stages of undress working alongside men. The affront to public morality and the fears generated as to the imminent collapse of the working-class family and consequently working-class morality, led to the campaign, spearheaded by the Evangelicals, for the exclusion of women from underground work. Working miners supported the ban that was subsequently imposed but not for the same reasons as the middle-class campaigners. As Angela John has shown, they did not accept the judgement of commissioners such as Tremenheere that female exclusion was 'the first step towards raising the standard of domestic habits and the securing of a respectable home'.[38] They resented middle-class interlopers who told them how to live their lives and organise their families. They emphasised working-class control over their own culture. They argued for better lives for their wives and daughters and insisted that if the wives of the owners could stay at home then so should theirs. They stressed that their wives were entitled to a decent life above ground and attacked those coal-owners such as the Duke of Hamilton, who continued to employ women illegally. But the miners had another powerful motive for supporting exclusion. The Miners Association of Great Britain and Ireland was formed in 1842, three days before the date designated for the exclusion of females under 18. As clearly stated in the *Miners Advocate* the union was firmly against female employment from the start. They sought to control the hours of labour and obtain the highest possible wages. For women to work was seen as a direct threat to this enterprise for women's work kept down wages. For their own reasons men in the mines preferred, as an ideal, to be able to support their women at home. The women, unable to speak publicly for themselves, were lost. They hated the conditions of work but they needed the money. But their voices were not heard and in one of the major public issues of the 1840s, blazoned across the press, men were legitimated as workers, women as wives and mothers, by the state, by middle-class philanthropists and by working men.

Samuel and Jemima went together to Peterloo. They shared the excitement, they shared the horror and the fear. But they experienced it differently on account of their sex. Men and women did not occupy the culture of their class in the same way. Ideologically their differences were emphasised, institutionally they were often segregated. The complexities of the relations between class and culture have received much attention. It is time for gender and culture to be subjected to more critical scrutiny.

Notes

Thanks to Stuart Hall, Leonore Davidoff and David Albury for comments on an earlier version of this paper.

1. S. Bamford, *Passages in the Life of a Radical*, Oxford, Kelley 1984. The account of Peterloo is on pp. 141–56.
2. E.P. Thompson *The Making of the English Working Class*, London, 1963.
3. On the eighteenth-century crowd see E.P. Thompson, 'The moral economy of the English crowd in the eighteenth century', *Past and Present*, no. 50, 1971. See also E.P. Thompson, 'Eighteenth century English Society: class struggle without class?', *Social History*, vol. 3, no. 2, 1978, and 'Patrician Society, Plebeian Culture' *Journal of Social History*, vol. 7, no. 4, 1974.
4. The literature on class in the early nineteenth century is extensive. See H. Perkin,

The Origins of Modern English Society 1780–1880, London, 1969; R.J. Morris, *Class and Class Consciousness in the Industrial Revolution,* Humanities Press, London, 1980; A. Briggs, 'The language of "class" in early nineteenth century England' in A. Briggs and J. Saville (eds), *Essays in Labour History* London, 1960; J. Foster, *Class Struggle and the Industrial Revolution: Early Capitalism in Three English Towns,* London 1974; G. Stedman Jones, *Languages of Class. Studies in English working class history 1832–1982* Cambridge 1983.

5. T. Hardy, *Memoir of Thomas Hardy . . . Written by Himself,* London, 1832, p. 16.
6. E.P. Thompson, *The Making of the English Working Class,* particularly chapter 16 'Class Consciousness'.
7. S. Bamford, *Passages in the Life of a Radical,* p. 14.
8. T.W. Laqueur, 'Literacy and Social Mobility in the Industrial Revolution in England', *Past and Present,* no. 64, 1974.
9. D. Vincent, *Bread, Knowledge and Freedom: a Study of Nineteenth Century Working Class Autobiography,* London, 1981.
10. D. Thompson 'Women and nineteenth century radical politics: a lost dimension' in J. Mitchell and A. Oakley, *The Rights and Wrongs of Women,* Harmondsworth, 1976.
11. For a delightful example of such constitutional practice see E.P. Thompson, *The Making of the English Working Class,* pp. 738–9.
12. *Birmingham Journal,* 5 January 1839; 12 January 1839, and 2 February 1839.
13. On women's militancy and engagement with radical politics see I.B. O'Malley, *Women in Subjection: A Study of the Lives of Englishwomen before 1832,* London, 1933; B. Taylor, *Eve and the New Jerusalem. Socialism and Feminism in the Nineteeth Century,* London, 1983; M.T. Thomis and J. Grimmett, *Women in Protest, 1800–1850,* London, 1982; D. Jones, 'Women and Chartism' *History,* no. 68, February 1983. There is an excellent introduction to the literature in J. Rendall, *The Origins of Modern Feminism: Women in Britain, France and the United States 1780–1860,* London, 1985.
14. B. Taylor, *Eve and the New Jerusalem.*
15. T. Paine *The Rights of Man,* New York, 1963. The best discussion of Paine in the context of English radicalism is in E.P. Thompson, *The Making of the English Working Class.*
16. M. Wollstonecraft, *Vindication of the Rights of Woman,* Harmondsworth, 1982. There is a voluminous literature on Mary Wollstonecraft. For an excellent recent analysis, see M. Poovey, *The Proper Lady and the Woman Writer. Ideology as style in the works of Mary Wollstonecraft, Mary Shelley and Jane Austen,* Chicago, 1984.
17. J. Locke, *Two Treatises of Government,* ed. P. Laslett, Cambridge, 1965; G. Schochet *Patriarchalism in Political Thought, The Authoritarian Family and Political Speculation and Attitudes, especially in Seventeenth Century England,* Oxford, 1975; S. Moller Okin, *Women in Western Political Thought,* London, 1980; R.W. Krouse, 'Patriarchal Liberalism and beyond: from John Stuart Mill to Harriet Taylor' in J.B. Elshtain (ed) *The Family in Political Thought,* Brighton, 1984; E. Fox-Genovese 'Property and Patriarchy in Classical Bourgeois Political Theory', *Radical History Review,* vol. 4, nos. 2–3, 1977.
18. J. Rendall *The Origins of Modern Feminism,* chapter 2. For a discussion of the related problems of the distinction between public and private see J. Habermas 'The public sphere: an Encyclopedia article', *New German Critique,* vol. 1 no. 3, 1974; J.B. Elshtain *Public Man, Private Woman,* Oxford, 1982; T. Eagleton, *The Function of Criticism,* London, 1984.

19. E.P.Thompson, *The Making of the English Working Class*, p. 746.

20. W. Cobbett, *Cottage Economy*, London 1822, pp. 60, 62, 63, 199.

21. W. Cobbett, *Advice to Young Men, and Incidentally to Young Women in the Middle and Higher Ranks of Life*, Oxford, 1980, see particularly chapters 4 and 6. For a discussion of the importance of 'honourable' labour and property in skill to working men's claims for manhood, see S. Alexander 'Women, Class and Sexual differences in the 1830s and 1840s: some reflections on the writing of a Feminist History', *History Workshop Journal*, London, no. 17, 1984. On independence and self-respect see T. Tholfsen, *Working class radicalism in mid-Victorian England*, London 1976.

22. On gender and middle-class culture see L. Davidoff and C. Hall 'The Architecture of Public and Private Life: English middle class society in a provincial town 1780–1850' in D. Fraser and A. Sutcliffe (eds), *The Pursuit of Urban History*, London 1983; L. Davidoff and C. Hall, *The Firm of Wife, Children and Friends: men and women in the English provincial middle class 1780–1850*, forthcoming; C. Hall, 'Gender divisions and class formation in the Birmingham middle class, 1780–1850' in R. Samuel (ed.), *People's History and Socialist Theory*, London, 1981; C. Hall, 'Private persons versus public someones: class, gender and politics in England 1780–1850' in C. Steedman, C. Urwin and V. Walkerdine (eds.), *Language, Gender and Childhood*, London, 1985.

23. C. Hall 'The early formation of Victorian domestic ideology' in S. Burman (ed.), *Fit Work for Women*, London, 1979.

24. See J. Bentham, *An Introduction to the Principles of Morals and Legislation*, Oxford, 1839, particularly pp. 58–9, 268 and 280. See also the discussion in R.W. Krouse, 'Patriarchal Liberalism and beyond: from John Stuart Mill to Harriet Taylor'.

25. *Aris's Birmingham Gazette* 17/1/1831, 21/1/1833.

26. For example the Sunday Schools of the Anglican Christ Church in Birmingham. J.G. Breay, *The Faithful Pastor Delineated*, Birmingham, 1839.

27. Birmingham Brotherly Society, Minutes of the Meetings. Birmingham Reference Library. Mss no. 391175.

28. Birmingham Mechanics Institute, *Address of the Provisional Committee*, Birmingham, 1825.

29. R.Q. Gray, *The Labour Aristocracy in Victorian Edinburgh*, Oxford, 1976. Gray's study deals with the later nineteenth century. See also T. Tholfsen's discussion of middle-class hegemony in *Working Class Radicalism in Mid-Victorian England*; T.W. Laqueur's argument in *Religion and Respectability; Sunday Schools and Working Class Culture 1780–1850*, New Haven, 1976, that working-class people subverted middle-class intentions and made Sunday Schools into institutions of their own culture. For two sensitive accounts of the class-specific mediations which occur in cultural practice, see R. Colls, *The Collier's Rant. Song and Culture in the Industrial Village*, London, 1977; and M. Vitale 'The domesticated heroine in Byron's Corsair and William Hone's prose adaptation', *Literature and History*, vol. 10 no. 1, 1984.

30. D. Vincent, *Bread, Knowledge and Freedom*, especially chapter 7.

31. T. Tholfsen *Working Class Radicalism in Mid-Victorian England*, especially chapter 7.

32. There is a fascinating discussion of Cruikshank in L. James 'Cruikshank and early Victorian Caricature', *History Workshop Journal*, no. 6, 1978.

33. A Selection of Tracts and Handbills published in aid of the Temperance Reformation, Birmingham, 1839.

34. J. Smith *Speech at the Birmingham Temperance Meeting*, Birmingham, 1835.

35. S. Alexander, 'Women, Class and Sexual Differences in the 1830s and 1840s'. art cit.
36. For the best introduction to the literature on the family wage see H. Land, 'The Family Wage', *Feminist Review*, no. 6, 1980.
37. For a discussion of sex and its relation to skill, see A. Phillips and B. Taylor, 'Sex and Skill: notes towards a feminist economics', *Feminist Review* no. 6, 1980. For the development of a particular union and its restrictive practices, see J. Liddington and J. Norris, *'One hand tied behind us'. The rise of the Women's Suffrage Movement*, London, 1978.
38. A. John, *By the Sweat of their Brow. Women workers at Victorian coal mines*, London, 1984 and 'Colliery legislation and its consequences: 1842 and the Women Miners of Lancashire', *Bulletin of the John Rylands University Library of Manchester* vol. 61, no. 1, 1978. Tremenheere quoted p. 90. ·

5

David Cardiff and Paddy Scannell

'Good luck war workers!' Class, politics and entertainment in wartime broadcasting

Introduction

World War II produced dramatic changes in the cultural values of broadcasting. Between 1939 and 1945 the BBC's programmes became more popular in several senses of the term, as it adjusted to its wartime task of maintaining the nation's morale through all the vicissitudes of a modern, total war. We have argued elsewhere that more popular styles of broadcasting had begun to appear in the BBC's programmes before the war. Quizzes and parlour games, light drama serials, new kinds of variety and comedy programmes were introduced in the last few years of the 1930s. Greater attention was paid to the presentation of programmes and to the ways in which they were scheduled in order to fit more smoothly into the domestic routines and leisure-time of listeners.[1] The 1940 *BBC Handbook* was prepared to concede that 'rightly or wrongly, it was being urged a year or two ago that the BBC was aloof from its listening millions, offering programmes with a complacent air of "Take it or leave it".[2] But now, it was claimed, the ice, if ever it existed, had rapidly melted. New and friendlier methods had been established on the air.

In fact though, as we will show, the negotiation of friendlier contacts with the audience was a much more difficult and complex process — more a slow thaw than a rapid melting — in the years that followed. Nor was it a simple extension or acceleration of processes already in train before the war. Rather the general task of maintaining morale required a renegotiation of the social, political and cultural relations between the BBC and its listeners; a process which was intimately connected with the wider social and political changes that were taking place in wartime Britain.

In this article, we examine the changing social relations of broadcasting through three brief analyses of aspects of wartime programming which reveal the social, political and cultural realignments between the institution and its audiences. We do so, first, by tracing how the working class was foregrounded both in programmes and as a part of the audience which the BBC recognised and addressed in quite new ways. Second, we examine the BBC's handling of what emerged as perhaps the crucial issue in wartime

93

domestic politics: post-war reconstruction. Third, we consider the new programming strategies developed by the BBC for the presentation of popular entertainment. But before turning to these, we must first outline the broad characteristics of the changes in wartime broadcasting, the wider changes in the relations between the state and society and the central significance of morale both for the state and for the BBC.

The changes in radio

The popularisation of radio during the war is reflected in the changing proportion of serious to light fare when recorded as a percentage of total output. What follows are the BBC's own statistics, prepared in February 1942. In 1938 serious music made up 17.31 per cent of the total; in 1942 the figure was 8.84 per cent. Variety and revue rose from 5.76 per cent to 14.84 per cent, while, in the same years, dance music increased from 4.67 per cent to 9.97 per cent. Light music, a very broad category, shrank from 25 per cent in 1938 to 18 per cent by 1942. There was a slight increase in news and a slight decrease in drama, especially serious drama. Topical features, a non-existent category in 1938, made up 2.41 per cent of output by 1942.

Such quantitative shifts, though significant, do not begin to tell the whole story. Of prime importance was the reorganisation of the programme services. In the 1930s, the public had a choice between two channels: the National Programme and the Regional Programme. When war was declared in September 1939, the Regional Programme was suspended and the National Programme, renamed the Home Service, was for a few months the only channel available to the public. From 1940 to 1945 there were two programmes, the Home Service and the Forces Programme. As we shall see, these changes were initially forced on the BBC and met with less than universal enthusiasm. But the Forces Programme implied a whole new approach to the listening public, its tastes, needs and preferences. After 1945 the wartime arrangements were retained and extended. The Home Service continued, its character virtually unchanged. The Forces Programme shed its commitment to the troops and became the Light Programme. To these were added the Third Programme, broadcast only in the evenings and designed for 'serious' listeners. At the most general level, the rearrangement of the programme services implied a restructuring of the relations between broadcasters and audiences, whose significance we consider later in this article.

Changes between the state and society

World War II was, for the British, their first experience of total war — a war which directly affected all aspects of the lives of the whole population; a war in which the fighting front was not confined to engagements on foreign fields between opposing professional armies, but was brought home by German bombers to the major towns and cities of Britain; a war in which the factory front was as vitally important as the fighting fronts; a war in which Britain, in 1940, came closer to invasion by a foreign power than at any previous time in many centuries of its history. It was a moment of exceptional threat and crisis for the British state and for the society it represented; and it required a far greater degree of cooperation between government and people than had existed before.

In June, 1940, Churchill's newly formed coalition government shifted to a full-scale war economy. The Emergency Powers Act, passed on 22 June, gave the government complete control over all persons and all property and Ernest Bevin, Minister of Labour, was empowered to direct any person to perform any service he thought fit, and to set the wages, hours and conditions of the job. With Europe conquered by Germany, the British Expeditionary Force rescued from Dunkirk and invasion now imminent, the full extent of the underequipment of the British forces and of their inability to withstand an onslaught from Germany was starkly apparent to the government. With its new powers over industry, the most immediate task of the state, as Angus Calder has shown, was a massive and rapid increase in the manufacture of all the machinery of modern warfare in preparation for the coming Battle of Britain.[3]

In order to increase the number of people in production a range of interventions were made to improve working conditions and to ration equitably the necessities of life. For the first time, government departments paid close attention to improving working facilities in factories (wages, management–labour relations, on-site canteens and entertainment, medical facilities and day nurseries for the huge influx of female labour); to health and diet and, widely approved of, equal rationing of basic goods. The war brought about for the working class an increase in wages and an absolute rise in their standard of living. In stark contrast to the 1930s, it produced full employment, jobs for all.

These changes were instrumental necessities: that is, they were made as means to the end of first resisting, then defeating, Nazi Germany. They were determined by the pressures of immediate needs, with no long-term social or political objectives in mind. But as it became evident to many that the state could manage efficiently, on the whole, both the economy and the social needs of the population, the inevitable questions arose. Why hadn't it been done years ago? Would it continue after the war?

The answers to such questions had different but interlocking results in different sections of society. Among the major political parties and the trade union leadership there was a movement in the same general direction — a commitment to a managerial or welfare state as the regulator of the economy and of social needs. Articulate 'middle opinion' had moved in this direction a decade earlier. It now found itself in alliance with the politicians in drawing up the blue-prints for the post-war managerial state. Two key figures were John Maynard Keynes and William Beveridge. The former had shown how the state could manage the economy to stimulate demand and maintain high employment after the war. The latter's report on social security (December 1942) demonstrated how security for all (marriage and child allowances, unemployment and sickness benefits, old age pensions — social security 'from the cradle to the grave') might be implemented. Among the public at large there was a growing determination that there should be no return to the conditions of 1939 at the end of the war. In 1944 what most concerned them were the two key problems of employment and housing. They approved of the Beveridge Report. At the polls in 1945 they voted massively for the Labour Party as the more likely of the two parties to deliver these things.[4]

Morale, the Ministry of Information and the BBC

What has been described so far may be seen as the management of consent at a material level. The state, to an extent, equalised the war effort through a range of material concessions, mainly implemented in order to win the necessary labour and sacrifice from the population. But it was not that simple. World War II was the first war to be fought on all fronts at an ideological level, too. Not just the bomber, but radio, that other technical innovation of the inter-war years, carried a war of words to the enemy, neutrals, occupied countries, allies and the homes of all citizens of this country.

World War II was not, at the outset, a popular war. It inspired no surge of popular enthusiasm, unlike the First World War. The state could not unilaterally impose its will on the population. It needed to win their minds and hearts, to secure their will and consent to the business of beating Germany, to brace them against the expected horrors of modern warfare, to maintain their confidence in the leadership of government and the rightness of its cause. The instrument of these intentions was a new government department set up in 1938, the Ministry of Information, 'whose prime duty on the home front was to sustain civilian morale'.[5]

Nine months before the war began, it had been determined that maintaining public morale should be the principal aim of wartime programmes.[6] When war was declared, the BBC was linked to the state through the Ministry of Information whose responsibilities included the security and censorship of the press, cinema and broadcasting. The government had made it plain that it would not take over the BBC. It had also made it equally plain that it expected the BBC to work in close liaison with the Ministry of Information, and that in matters of national interest or such as affected the conduct of the war, it would be expected to act under the instructions of the government.[7]

Relations between the BBC, the Ministry of Information and other government departments were never easy. The new Ministry itself was in a state of chaos until Brendan Bracken took it over in 1941. Departments constantly tended not only to propose subjects for broadcast propaganda, but to prescribe their treatment even down to supplying complete scripts. The BBC's position, which, it complained, was seldom understood, was that while it would take advice and guidance from its many official clients on the key propaganda issues of the moment and on matters of fact relating to them, it always reserved to itself control of the forms and methods of presentation. In this way, it preserved a precarious measure of independence.

Ministry propaganda at first oscillated between cajoling, exhorting and bullying. It contained a veiled mistrust of the population, tinged with an element of fear. Could 'they' be trusted? As the war progressed, official attitudes changed. At first, propaganda was whistling in the blackout, for it was not based on any detailed knowledge of public opinion. What produced the change was the development of a systematic network of intelligence sources, organised by the Ministry of Information's Home Intelligence Unit, which constantly monitored the views and feelings in the country about all aspects of the war — from the great issues of the day to the minutiae of everyday life. As this information fed back into the system, there was a decline in exhortation and a more realistic assessment of the actual responses of people to wartime propaganda.

This movement was closely paralleled in wartime broadcasting. For most of the pre-war years the BBC had tended to presume that it knew what its audience required without making systematic efforts to enquire into what it might like. But through pressure from programme makers, a Listener Research Unit was set up in 1936.[8] This department, whose work was already influencing programming by 1939, grew in importance during the war and the scope of its activities greatly increased. Its reports were widely distributed in official circles as part of the general pool of intelligence about public opinion.

It was not easy for the BBC to readjust its attitudes to the audience. In many respects, it began its task of catering for the nation's morale sharing the same assumptions as the propagandists in the Ministry of Information. It lectured, cajoled or jollied along its audience. But when the war began in earnest, in the summer of 1940, the BBC found itself caught in a tug-of-war between the demands of official propaganda and the reactions of the public to such exhortations. The pressures on the institution from government and the public increased enormously, and showed a marked tendency to contradict each other. Senior management within the BBC shared the ruling assumptions and policies of Westminster and Whitehall. Programme makers, however, working 'out there' in the country, in much closer contact with the public, tended to align themselves with the attitudes of the audience. We shall see how, in the course of the war, official BBC policy on morale, propaganda and entertainment was increasingly modified in the light of greater knowledge of public opinion, audience attitudes and tastes.

Class, politics and entertainment

World War II was the People's War, and radio came to realign itself with the people in ways that were only tentatively present in pre-war programming. The working class had never been integrated into the National Programme before the war. Its presence, both as a subject in programmes and as the audience for whom programmes were made, was only fully established in Manchester's North Region, with its large working-class listening public. This changed dramatically with the crisis in the summer of 1940. Suddenly there was a spate of programmes about and for the working class. And, as with government, this recognition by the BBC of the work-force sprang from expedient need; from the realisation that the war emergency made labour the ultimate resource, the crucial factor, in the war effort. Without a massive reorganisation of the work-force and a massive increase in productivity, Britain would not survive. Radio's wartime task in this respect was twofold: to sustain the efficiency and morale of the work-force at work and at home, in the separated spheres of labour and of leisure. For the first time radio began to produce a range of programmes for workers in the factories. In the sphere of leisure the task of maintaining morale was of a more diffuse, societal nature. Programmes like *ITMA* appealed to all classes. Nevertheless, the increase in variety and in popular music, and the establishment of the Forces Programme aimed at *pleasing* the troops and, a little later, the civilian population, made radio more attractive and accessible to the working classes and more in line with their tastes and needs.

As the BBC attuned itself to the climate of public opinion, it sought to give expression to the emerging feeling in the population at large that the war was being fought not just to defeat Hitler, but to build a more just society in Britain after the war. This was a delicate matter for the BBC, confronting it with its own ambiguous position in relation to the government and its audience. Churchill simply wanted to suppress the issue of post-war reconstruction: 'everything for the war whether controversial or not, and nothing controversial that is not needed for the war'.[9] Debate about Britain *after* the war was, in this view, irrelevant and unnecessary. On the other hand, the BBC knew that, as the war progressed, the question was increasingly preoccupying the public. Its response to this dilemma — whether or not to ventilate the issue, and if so, how — posed the question of its own autonomy. Should it defer to the state, or respond to public opinion?

The creation of the Forces Programme was the clearest expression of the reversal of pre-war values in broadcasting. Cultural uplift and serious programmes were, as a matter of policy, excluded from the Forces Programme to the chagrin of, say, the Music or Drama Departments. Orchestral symphonies and classic plays were not what the troops or the work-force wanted, and must find their place in the Home Service. In the Forces Programme the tastes of the audience came first, and public service a long way second.

In the accounts that follow we show some of the ways in which the BBC searched for new popular styles and formats for the purposes of general morale, propaganda and political enlightenment. We try briefly to illustrate the form and content of the programmes and the processes that shaped their development. We pay close attention to the pressures upon the BBC: directives from government and official attitudes to propaganda on the one hand, and the gradual discovery of the attitudes of the general public on the other. We try at the same time to catch the tensions *within* the BBC between senior personnel aligned with official policies and attitudes, and junior staff more attuned to the audience. The interplay of all these forces reveals the continuing process of negotiation whereby the BBC sought to satisfy the often countervailing demands of government and audiences while maintaining its own claims to represent the interests of the nation as a whole.

Calling all workers

'Go to it!' was Herbert Morrison's famous slogan summoning the work-force to rally to the nation's cause in the critical summer months of 1940. Within weeks of the official call to work, the BBC's Feature Department, led by Lawrence Gilliam, had rushed out a series with the same title. The first programme — a kind of *Nationwide* survey of responses from individual workers up and down the country — began and ended with Herbert Morrison: 'Work is still the call. Work at war speed. Once again — till the war is ended — go to it!'. In the programmes that followed, the workers were heard to be hard at it in munitions, tank and aircraft production. The series set the tone for the work of broadcasting in helping to increase industrial efficiency and maintain the morale of the work-force inside and outside the factory.

'Calling All Workers' was the theme tune of *Music While You Work* which began on 23 June 1940, three weeks after Dunkirk. Its aim was to speed up factory production 'by so improving the morale of the workers that output will be stepped up during the whole of the work spell'. Exhaustive research showed that industrial music should be non-stop, without vocal numbers (they tended to distract workers who paused to listen to the words); and that it should be familiar, with a clearly defined melody, even tempo and consistent rhythm. Such music was found to be particularly suited to unskilled workers doing monotonous and repetitive tasks, and especially

99

effective for the huge influx of female labour, 'helping them to settle down to their new occupation'. By 1943, nearly 7,000 factories employing 4 million workers had installed loudspeaker systems to relay the programmes.[10]

The provision of entertainment in the factory soon became a routine feature of wartime radio. *Works Wonders*, which commenced on 5 October 1940, was an amateur talent show, performed by and for workers from a particular factory canteen during the dinner break. In the BBC, there were some doubts whether this show was altogether suitable for broadcasting since it scarcely measured up to professional standards, but it was tolerated as a useful contribution to morale. *Workers Playtime*, which commenced on 31 May 1941, used the same format but with the entertainment provided by well-known variety performers, and produced to the criteria of professionalism in the Variety Department. The original impetus for the show came from Ernest Bevin who particularly wanted entertainment to be provided for factories in out of the way places that were starved of such things. The Variety Department did not feel it was quite their job to do welfare work for the Ministry of Labour, but was content to do so if a good programme for the listening public could be produced at the same time. There were heavy pressures on the Department to include little pep talks to the workers in the programmes, but these were firmly resisted. The welfare aspect of the shows would be lost if they became the vehicles for unpopular uplift. 'There is nothing the British workman loathes more than having good done to him' (Head of Variety to Controller of Programmes, 20 October 1941). *Workers Playtime* was to be entertainment without strings.

These two shows, along with *Music While You Work* (twice or three times daily) ran throughout the war. They formed the stable basis of the BBC's continuing endeavour to maintain the productivity and morale of working people in the place of work itself. But along with them went a spate of programmes, mixing exhortation and uplift, addressed to the working class at home. The Schools Department produced *At the Armstrongs*, a domestic drama serial about an ordinary working family. It was full of good advice: don't stay up all hours listening to radio; get a good night's sleep and be fit and ready for the next day's work; don't panic about the air raids; think of your loved ones when the planes fly overhead and step up your work rate for their sakes, etc. But the most characteristic image produced was that of northern working-class community, a cheerful resilience to all the pressures of war and a determination to see it through and lick the Nazis. Typical of this approach was the work of the features producer, D.G. Bridson and his presenter Wilfred Pickles. Here's how *Lancashire Folk* (27 October 1940), the first in a series called *We Speak For Ourselves*, began. A local chorus sings 'I like to be there', and this is faded to applause and cheers from the Oldham audience, and Pickles:

Wilfred: Well done lads, well done. There's nowt caps a bit of a sing.
        It's good to hear folks sing these days now that Goering's

	doing his level best to shut us traps. All I can say is it takes a *lot* to keep Lancashire quiet, — aye, a lot more than we've had so far. The gradely folk aren't licked yet, — no, nor Merseyside neither . . . What about Oldham? Are you licked yet?
Everyone:	NOOOOOO!!!
Wilfred:	Nay I thought not! But it's funny y'know. You *ought* to be. The Germans think you are. Did you hear what [Haw Haw deleted from script] they said about you on t'wireless last week? They said there wasn't a smile to be seen in Lancashire; and that they weren't bothered about Oldham yet because there was nobody lived there but bald-headed bow-legged minders[11] and consumptive women! (Roars of laughter from everybody) . . .
Wilfred:	But what's Oldham got to say about t'war?
Mrs Truman:	Plenty! We ain't scared o' Hitler. We call him Tashy at home. He seems to think that if he can floor London he'll ha' floored all England. He seems to forget there's Lancashire. He won't floor us — any more than he's floored London (applause) . . .

In the production aims underlying this series was a tinge of fear that working-class morale might crack under the strain of bombing raids, or, worse still, become disaffected by German propaganda. To counter this the programme, and dozens like it, constructed that self-affirming image of 'the gradely folk' for consumption by the folk themselves; as an exercise in spontaneous free speech (though all were scripted and vetted for security reasons), as a communal knees-up in an atmosphere of cosy audience participation.

The style was transferred to programmes from the factories. Bridson invented the character of Billy Welcome for Pickles. Billy was everything the ordinary man should be in happier times — a friendly soul, generous and warm-hearted. But in his weekly radio travels Billy found few other ordinary folk in these times. For, as the *Radio Times* (8 May 1942) explained:

Ordinariness has dropped away from them in these hard warring days. There will be nothing ordinary, for instance, about the women munition workers Billy will meet and bring to the microphone from the Midlands on Thursday, in 'Billy Welcome's Day with the Women'.

A few months or a few years ago you [i.e. the middle-case listener] *might* have described all these people as Ordinary. But you can't say that of them today; upon their shoulders rests the future of civilisation.

The style of these programmes is illustrated and analysed in *Good Luck War Workers*, a cassette we made for the Open University's *Popular Culture* course. Their general aim was to prove to the listening public that behind the courage of our fighting forces lay the skill and dedication of the work-force, unstintingly turning out all the armoury and equipment necessary for the successful prosecution of the war. They sought to unite the home front, the work front and the fighting front in a common solidarity against the enemy. Bridson had no doubts about the value of such programmes.[12] But Pickles took a very different view of them in retrospect: 'Rank propaganda disguised as entertainment' he called them.[13] By 1942, evidence was beginning to accumulate in the BBC that that was how many working people saw such programmes too. It was becoming clear that the cosy image of a united industrial front hardly squared with the realities of working conditions in the factories.

This discovery was made not by the policy-makers and staff based in London, but by the producers who had to go to the factories in search of 'characters' for programmes like *From Factory to Front Line* or *Award For Industry*. The latter had started in June 1942 as a pat on the back for the workers, and singled out one individual as its 'worker of the week'. But it was none too easy finding suitable worker heroes for the series, as the producer Marjorie Banks soon found when she went to the factories approved by the various ministries. The Admiralty had suggested she go to BSA Guns Ltd. She wrote to Lawrence Gilliam on 27 July 1942:

> I went there yesterday morning and found that the Ministry of Labour had just stepped in to sack a number of hooligan shop stewards who were causing strikes every other week in the factory. There was no possibility of getting the shop stewards' agreement to a Worker of the Week as they were all up in arms and the whole place bordering on revolution. As the Manager pointed out, it was no time for a sunshine broadcast.

This was not an isolated incident and it seriously worried Gilliam. He wrote to A.P. Ryan, Controller of Programmes, urging that the policy on industrial programmes be immediately reconsidered. At the same time, the Head of Talks, Sir Richard Maconachie, was getting reports from the regional offices that workers were sick to death of the continual 'I was a nursemaid before I entered the factory' type of thing in talks and features. He advised Ryan of the feeling in most of the regions that London only took the Whitehall view of industry, and that the programmes were remote from the experience of the audiences to whom they were addressed (Maconachie to Ryan, 23 October 1942). Maconachie then asked Listener Research to discover how widespread this attitude was.

When this report came out a couple of months later, it confirmed every-thing the regions had been saying. Factory features were far more accept-able among those not in any way connected with industry. Only a minority of the workers appreciated them. For the rest, they were deeply disliked. The report quoted a range of comments from working people, all hostile. Such programmes were not genuine, sincere or truthful. They were obviously manipulative — 'put up jobs' with a strong smell of propaganda. Their style was pungently criticised: 'The people who take part in these programmes are badly chosen, and obviously reading tripe from a script. When the chaps in my works get a rotten job, or feel browned off, they often mimic these programmes. "Ho yes, I *love* my work". "Ho no, I never get fed up". "Ho yes, I would like to work longer hours", etc'.[14]

These programmes had begun in the summer of 1940 in response to the crisis. But by 1942, though the threat of invasion had long passed, the task of actually winning seemed still an immense, daunting and distant prospect. All the multiple inconveniences of war, its dislocations and disruptions, food shortages, clothes shortages, restricted travel, bombings, long hours of work, families split up and separated — all this was lived, daily, by the British people. The discontents in industry were not separable from that larger context. The BBC's industrial features, with never a hint of all this, appeared increasingly out of touch and it is not surprising that they were greeted with derision by the factory workers. They had even become the butt of the Variety Department. *ITMA* contained a satirical sketch of a Mr Prattle from the BBC interviewing Mr Faceache, the foreman of the ITMA factory, with interruptions from Tommy Handley, the manager:

Handley	You're keen on intensive production, aren't you? (*sotto*) Say yes.
Faceache	I ahm.
Prattle	Of course you're willing to tell listeners all about it.
Handley	Say no.
Faceache	Ahm nort.
Prattle	We're not getting very far. Are you nervous at the microphone?
Handley	Say no.
Faceache	I ahm.
Handley	And you're happy in your work? Say yes.
Faceache	Ahm nort.
Handley	That's funny, he knew his lines in the digs this morning.

Self-parody was never wholly absent in wartime broadcasting.

Faced with the evidence, Gilliam abandoned these industrial features. It is a clear example of how the decline in propaganda and exhortation was brought about by increasing knowledge of and responsiveness to public opinion. It is also important to note how, and from what sources, that knowledge was produced. It came from *below*; from producers taken aback by the realities of industrial relations, from regional staff out in the provinces in closer touch with the views of ordinary listeners, and from the evidence supplied by Listener Research. Meanwhile the BBC's top management was still plugging away at industrial propaganda in the news bulletins. In June 1943, the Director-General wrote to Brenden Bracken, Minister of Information, asking for more statistics and output figures from the supply and production ministries for inclusion in the bulletins. Bracken replied that he no longer felt productivity was an important news story. The Director-General expressed his astonishment. The BBC still felt the pressing importance of production as a means of keeping our people up to scratch, impressing the enemy with our strength, and of holding our own against the publicity given by the USA to her output. Bracken again refused to supply regular figures, not only on security grounds (information to the enemy), but more especially because any regular series of figures only underlined the overwhelming achievements of American production.

Thus official reasons for closing down on the issue were more concerned with external propaganda considerations than the climate of opinion in this country. They point, again, to divergent attitudes between ruling official circles, BBC senior management, programme makers and the general public. Thereafter the theme of the industrial front faded into silence. In the fourth year of the war its relevance had long been exhausted. There were other more critical issues touching on morale and the relationship between the people and their rulers, of which the question of post-war reconstruction was becoming the most significant.

Post-war reconstruction

One of the earliest and clearest statements on radio of the need to view the war not only as a struggle against Nazi terror but as an opportunity to end the poverty and inequalities of the pre-war years, came in a feature programme broadcast on 23 April 1940. A *New English Journey*, produced by D.G. Bridson, took J.B. Priestley back to the places he had visited and written about seven years earlier in this book *An English Journey*. In this classic of 1930s social documentation, Priestley had described three kinds of England: traditional Old England, industrial Britain ruined by unemployment and urban decay, and modern England with its new consumer culture of cars, cinema, radio, Woolworths, ribbon development, etc. In the radio programme, Priestley compared and contrasted the condition of England then with conditions in the changed circumstances of war:

> Clearly most of the places I visited have benefited economically from the war. What peace could not do war has done, bringing them regular work and wages. And it's about time we learned to plan and spend in peacetime as we do in wartime . . . There must be no attempt to turn back, to escape all responsibilities, the moment peace is signed . . . We'll soon be hearing much praise, as we always do in wartime, of the ordinary English folk. But there should go with that praise the most solemn promise that for folk so humorous, patient and fundamentally good, a nobler framework of life must

be constructed, and the vistas of mean little streets and ruined landscapes, the humiliations of bad housing, the heartbreaks of long unemployment, must vanish — as Hitler and his crooked cross must vanish — like an evil dream.

Priestley seems to assume that all the planning on behalf of ordinary folk will be undertaken by the progressive intelligentsia. The social engineers of the better society will be those academics, technical managers, planners, bureaucrats and writers who, troubled by the betrayals and failures of the 1930s, will now throw themselves with great energy into drawing up the blueprints for an efficient, planned society that will deliver the new social order.[15]

Such assumptions became more explicit in the efforts of the BBC Talks Department in early 1941 to shape up two series on post-war reconstruction. The first, an official series on peace aims, was planned by senior BBC staff with the Ministry of Information, and required the approval of the cabinet. To complement this, Christopher Salmon of the Talks Department suggested a second series expressing the hopes and fears of ordinary working people:

> I am not proposing that we should ask working men and women what social legislation they would like to see implemented after the war, for actual legislative proposals, even of the kind which bear directly on working-class conditions, are better discussed by people with administrative experience and a knowledge wider than working people can hope to have of the whole political and economic fabric within which the changes have got to be made. But what we cannot get from the expert or the administrator is a knowledge of what I have called our social 'treasure' . . . If we can persuade our [working-class] speakers to tell us, with the warmth of remembered experience, what they have striven after and where and how they have been disappointed we shall begin to know under what sort of conditions they could live a fuller and more satisfactory life (Salmon to Maconachie, July 18, 1941).

The official plans had other objectives in mind: to impress both the Axis powers and America that Britain *was* a democracy fighting for democracy. The initial idea for the series on peace aims was based on three assumptions: that the talks should be based on a method that could not be tolerated in Germany and Italy, free discussion; they should deal only with the general principles of peace aims, since their details had not yet been worked out; they should appeal to the United States who, the more it saw Britain's willingness to tackle the issue with energy and a new spirit, the more it would be willing to support our cause. The series should be presented as a weekly 'Radio Forum' called *Democracy Thinking Aloud*. The Head of Talks forwarded the proposal to the Ministry as an Aunt Sally to be knocked into better shape in discussion with ministerial staff. Maconachie preferred to

105

call the series *Where Are We Going*, but had doubts about both titles and the general method of approach: 'Though the main object would be to demonstrate the extent to which freedom of discussion was possible in this country, it would be necessary in practice to impose definite restrictions on the choice of speakers, subjects and methods of treatment.' All speakers must support democracy and the prosecution of the war and thus communists, fascists and 'active' pacifists would be excluded. There would be no extempore speech, and scripts must be routinely vetted and strictly adhered to by speakers. Thus to call the series *Democracy Thinking Aloud* seemed misleading and unsuitable. On the other hand *Where Are We Going* was equally problematic since the likely answer was 'still further towards socialism'. Whether this would go down well with the home audience was debatable, but to give that impression to the Americans might well defeat a major point of the exercise. 'We understand', said Maconachie, 'that the individualist feeling is strong in the USA' (Maconachie to Harold Nicholson, March 16, 1941).

The series was seen in the BBC as a test of the amount of freedom the government would grant the Corporation in wartime for the presentation of politically controversial issues. They soon found out. Though the idea had the initial support of the Ministry of Information, there were fears that Churchill would dislike it and so it was shelved.[16] Some months later a much diluted version was produced called *Making Plans* along with *The Working Man Looks at Reconstruction* derived from Salmon's proposals. Listener Research wanted to investigate responses to the series but this was vetoed by the Ministry of Information. Nevertheless, the BBC got some feedback through its Forces Listening Groups. Here are some of their responses:

> By far the greatest part of the classes were imbued with pronounced left wing ideas and many were confessed Marxists. To them the chief interest in the series lay in its bearing on nationalization and collectivization, with the emphasis on political implications rather than practical economics (RAF station — Education Officer's report).

> When men do listen, they get the impression that high brows of the left and right are arranging their future, possibly to their detriment, behind their backs. Their unspoken thought is that they are not going to be pushed around by such people, who could be taught their place by a whiff of direct action (Army Education Officer).

After that the issue lay dormant on radio until it surfaced again with renewed vigour in response to the Beveridge Report (1 December 1942). To gauge public response to Beveridge, the Ministry of Information had commissioned, from its own Home Intelligence Unit and from BBC Listener Research, inquiries into the general state of opinion in the country on post-war Britain. The Ministry's report indicated that while the vast majority had no clear views about the morrow, there was a 'thoughtful minority' cutting across all classes who had very definite opinions. Listener Research addressed itself to this minority the week before the report, and found overwhelming interest in the issue and equally strong support for a continuing public debate on the matter. The most urgent issues which *must* be faced were unemployment (93 per cent), equal educational opportunities for all (80 per cent), housing (77 per cent) and an international authority capable of keeping the peace (73 per cent).

The Report was launched with a fanfare of publicity by the Ministry of Information but then, just as quickly, that support was withdrawn. From dawn on 1 December, the BBC broadcast details of Beveridge in 22 languages: it was yet another piece of propaganda directed at enemies, allies and occupied countries to prove that democracy was alive and flourishing in Britain. Beveridge himself gave a short talk to the home audience on the same day and there was a feature programme about his life and work a few days later. But thereafter there was silence. The Army Bureau of Current Affairs was ordered not to publicise the report among the troops, and the government said nothing for two months. The ultimate strategy adopted by the cabinet was to welcome as much of it as possible in principle while affirming that no commitments could be given to it. The public saw this as a foretaste of what they might expect when the war ended. The lack of any positive response from the government to the report marks the point at which a gulf began to appear between rulers and ruled.

The Listener Research report (24 November 1942) had noted that 'the BBC will, at the appropriate time, clearly have an important part to play in focusing public attention upon reconstruction'. It was to be some time before the appropriate moment arrived. But in 1944 the BBC ran two major series on the twin issues uppermost in the minds of the public as the end of the war approached — housing and employment.

The Corporation attached great importance to *Homes For All* (March–April 1944) and *Jobs For All* (December 1944). Much thought was given to their planning and presentation and Listener Research produced detailed analyses of audience response to both series. *Jobs For All* did not propose 'to examine any particular published plan or to pursue the problem in political terms, but to discuss the economic conditions of full employment in language which anyone and everyone could understand.' The series was deliberately addressed to those nearest the base of 'the social pyramid' who were felt to be most practically and directly concerned with the issue, since they were most threatened by unemployment. While the programmes should be educative, while the speakers should be as authoritative as possible, and while the series should do the BBC credit in intellectual circles, none of these considerations should interfere with the main objective. The essential quality required of speakers was their ability to give the 'unlearned listener' the feeling that the subject was both practical and not beyond his comprehension (Maconachie to Salmon, 2 September 1944).

Jobs For All tried a number of strategies to bridge the gap between the expert and the ordinary person. The first programme was given over to scripted recollections by ordinary people of their experience of unemployment before the war. In the second programme the expert, Noel Worswick of Nuffield College, Oxford, was to be questioned by an invited studio audience of 'ordinary people' played by actors from Unity Theatre speaking more or less impromptu. The sixth of the eight programmes had Worswick on the topic of full employment in the world economy. He was to develop his theme with the aid of a farmer, an artisan, a consumer and a Mr Sykes from Yorkshire whom the BBC had supplied with a hammer. He was to bang on the table with this instrument whenever he didn't understand the expert. Things got off to an unintentionally comic start when Mr Sykes dropped his hammer almost fusing the microphone, but after the programme progressed smoothly enough.

The awkwardnesses of the programmes, their hesitancies and uncertainties in the quest for a popular idiom can only be fully appreciated by listening to them. It seems to us that for all the effort that went into bridging the gap between expert and citizen the effect was the reverse. The differences of language and idiom widened rather than narrowed the distance between them.

The series drew quite good-sized audiences, but Listener Research noted three factors that worked against it; lack of interest, the difficulty of the subject and cynicism. This last response had been noted equally in *Homes For All*.

> A good many people, relatively more working class than middle class, are apparently so sceptical about the sincerity of post-war intentions by the powers that be, that they regard any public discussion of plans as, at best a waste of time and, at worst, as an attempt to allay public anxiety on the part of high-ups who have no real intention of taking adequate action.[17]

This attitude was directed against the state not the BBC, but it did tend further to undermine the good intentions of the broadcasters.

These programmes were part of the BBC's own post-war plans for its future survival, which partly explains why they were so carefully prepared and exhaustively analysed. With the end in sight, the Corporation did not want to emerge from the war looking like an agency of the state. It wanted to reclaim its own independence which it had largely lost in the first few years of the war, and it signalled this intention by resuming the discussion of major social and political issues, though in a non-controversial style. Taking up the concerns of the majority audience with housing and employment was one assertion of its own claims to freedom.

Entertainment

My attention has been drawn several times to the way soldiers 'guy' the presentation of some items by the BBC. At lunch time in many places, as soon as the announcer says, 'Workers' Playtime!' someone anticipates the inevitable 'roar of spontaneous applause' by breaking into ironical cheers . . . In the long pause before the Prime Minister begins an important speech, men say, 'Come on, we're impressed enough' . . . The acuteness and critical faculties of comparatively uneducated soldiers are always surprising me (Report to the BBC from observer in the forces, 4 April 1942).

It was an encounter with listeners in khaki that forced the BBC to rethink its pre-war programme strategy. On 7 January 1940, the corporation began an experimental service to supply cheerful, undemanding programmes for the soldiers of the British Expeditionary Force (BEF), stationed in France. Within weeks, a general was complaining that the programmes were by no means what the men wanted. They had preferred Radio Fécamp, an English-language commercial station which had recently been closed down by the allies. This verdict was on the whole supported by a report on 'Listening by the BEF', prepared by a former BBC official, A.P. Ryan.

Ryan stressed one fact about military listening which had profound consequences for programme policy. Very few men had their own radio sets and the bulk of listening was in groups. This meant two things. First, concentrated listening became impossible and background listening became the rule. Secondly, the majority decided what to hear and when to switch off. Ryan claimed: 'The troops won't mind if a proportion of good serious stuff is included in their programme out of deference to policy views as to what constitutes good balance. They won't mind — *and they won't listen.'* Before the war, the output of both National and Regional programmes had been organised on a principle of 'mixed programming'. Listeners were offered a varied cultural diet and were encouraged to be selective in their choice of items. In this way, the BBC hoped to broaden the cultural horizons of its public. But many had found the policy patronising and numerous pressures had persuaded BBC planners in the late 1930s to consider introducing a popular alternative programme.[18] Ryan's report clinched the argument, but although the alternative programme was now in being, the BBC would have to work hard to make it popular. He concluded:

> There is a chance for the BBC to get beyond its present position of public respect and to win also public affection. It can only do this if it establishes for itself a self-denying ordinance against the more austere kind of programmes and by experimenting frankly in the difficult technique of approaching simple men without boring them, and at the same time without talking down to them (A.P. Ryan, 23 January 1940).

The Forces Programme was at first broadcast only in the evenings. The first transmission included the BBC Salon Orchestra, a song recital from Peter Dawson, Mantovani and one dance band. This was very much in the BBC's tradition of defining light music as light orchestral or palm court, interspersed with song recitals tending towards the nostalgic. It was an essentially middlebrow idea of a popular programme. Dance music and 'crooning', long known to have wide appeal, were rationed sparingly. But in February the pattern changed. The day started at 6.30 a.m. with a lively record show. There followed dance music, cinema organ and more records, with an occasional military band or more nostalgic items. At midday and in the early evening there was usually a variety show. The most striking break with BBC custom was to be heard on Sundays. Before the war, Sunday broadcasting meant heavy doses of church services, austere music and talks and the audience responded by tuning in to Radio Luxembourg in droves. But now, not only was religious material kept to a minimum, but the surrounding matter was much as on weekdays. When the BEF returned to Britain in June 1940, the Forces Programme soon established itself as a popular alternative programme for the whole population, attracting 65 per cent of the civilian audience. With its introduction, the proportion of listeners who were satisfied with the performance of the BBC in general rose from 66 per cent to 80 per cent. In accounting for this popularisation, two tendencies in programme policy deserve particular mention. The first was towards an assimilation of the techniques of American commercial radio which the BBC had always shunned. The second was towards a democratisation of the content of entertainment, with more audience participation, a nurturing of performers who would be accepted as the representatives of ordinary men and women and the creation of more topical, mildly subversive forms of comedy.

Asa Briggs has stated that 'fear of commercial interests played a real though very minor part in the BBC's efforts to develop its own service for the BEF'.[19] But the Director of Variety did take Radio Fécamp as a model for the Forces Programme, though arguing that the BBC could do infinitely better, and he did hire producers from commercial radio, like Howard Thomas who created two of the most successful wartime programmes, *Sincerely Yours*, with Vera Lynn, and *The Brains Trust*. Fear of future commercial rivals undoubtedly influenced BBC policy. The Controller of Programmes realised that the new service appealed to those who had listened to the commercial stations in the 1930s. Since these stations would 'crop up like mushrooms again' when peace came, it should be 'a cardinal point of BBC policy to retain its hold on this popular audience, both now and after the war' (B.E. Nicolls, 1 January 1942).

American radio shows were first imported by the BBC to reduce the strain on its own Variety Department which, besides having to increase its output, was suffering from the effects of evacuation, first to Bristol and later to Bangor in North Wales. Then, as now, American shows came cheap. A programme that had cost the sponsors $12,000 was available to the BBC for as little as £15. Soon Bob Hope, Jack Benny and the like were proving popular with British audiences. When US troops began to arrive in Britain it was felt that the BBC should try to entertain them in the manner to which they were accustomed. As one BBC producer put it, 'generally speaking the ordinary American does not like British radio. It is going to be a very hard job to make him like it, but the attempt should be well worth making as it might result in the British listener liking British radio!' (Gilliam, 10 August 1942). When the US military introduced their own American Forces Network, however, the BBC was anxious to restrict the range of its transmitters, fearing that those in Britain who favoured the introduction of commercial radio might 'point to the American Forces Network as an example of a normal commercial chain, with accompanying disparagement of BBC output' (Director of Programme Planning, 24 July 1943). In 1944, worried that American shows might 'become a Frankenstein', the Director-General of the BBC urged their withdrawal. One of the few criticisms of the new Light Programme revealed by Listener Research in 1945 was that 'the demise of popular wartime American Variety left a gap which British Variety stars could not fill'.[20]

An enduring American influence was felt in new styles of presentation and continuity and in the routinisation of schedules. Before the war, in order to discourage 'tap' listening and to prevent jarring contrasts between items, the BBC had separated programmes by intervals of silence which sometimes lasted as long as five minutes. Once 'tap' listening was accepted as a fact of life, new methods were called for. A BBC committee which met in 1940 looked to American radio which 'owes its great reputation largely to the beautiful timing and precision of its presentation' (Forces Programme Committee, 30 September 1940). Besides calling for slicker continuity, the committee encouraged announcers to adopt a more personal and friendly manner. The Controller of Programmes could see no point in imposing continuity between disparate items and resisted the personal touch. 'Every time an announcer says 'I' he ceases to be the voice of the BBC' (Report by the Controller of Programmes on Presentation, 3 April 1941). But changes were made and, in 1942, even the Home Service introduced a system of continuity with a single announcer presenting the whole evening's programmes in the role of 'voice of the station'.

In the 1930s the BBC had rejected 'a rigid programme on the American principle, in which for the greater part of the week, precisely the same artists appear at precisely the same time, in programmes advertising precisely the same products'.[21] Though the policy was beginning to change in the late 1930s, there was still a resistance to the regular weekly series. The streamlined and repetitive style of programming which characterised the Light Programme in 1945 was developed not so much in the domestic services as in the North American Service of the BBC. Its slogan was

'British in content, American in appeal' and it hired American producers to advise on presentation. The first two Controllers of the Light Programme had worked for this service and brought to home listeners not just slick presentation but a cast-iron rigidity of scheduling which, as they soon realised, attracted a growing audience.[22]

These developments can be seen as the starting point in British broadcasting of what Raymond Williams has described as 'a significant shift from the concept of sequence as *programming* to the concept of sequence as *flow*'.[23] In devising a service for background listeners it was natural that the BBC should borrow from the US techniques which were developed to capture and retain audiences in the face of competition. Regularity of scheduling too had definite advantages for Variety producers. The series format enabled performers to perfect their characterisations without repeating their acts, enabled writers, once they had established a stock situation, to explore its permutations, develop running gags and catchphrases and at the same time introduce a wide range of social and topical references.

BBC Variety producers had always avoided topicality for fear of stirring political controversy but in wartime it was impossible to ignore current events and social upheaval. There was always a tension in the treatment of wartime themes. Different sections of the audience had to be considered. For example, the changing role of women was reflected in a number of ways. To encourage women in the factories, established radio characters like the cockney housewives, Gert and Daisy, were transformed into irrepressibly cheery munitions workers, joking about the difference between gunpowder and face powder ('one goes off with a bang, the other goes on with a puff'). Housewives at home had to be encouraged to 'up and at 'em' and on the radio there was the comedian Clarkson Rose to jolly them into salvaging scrap metal.

> Get together all your junk and hand it to the man
> Who'll call for it and take it out and bung it in the van.
> They'll turn it into armaments and you can say with pride
> The metal in your old suspenders helped to turn the tide.

Meanwhile, Vera Lynn, in her weekly 'letter' to the forces, *Sincerely Yours*, reassured the menfolk that in spite of all the commotion the girl they left behind retained her essential passivity: 'You'll disappoint her, you'll hurt her, you'll make a fool of her. But she'll stand by you, she'll take the kicks, she'll be proud to call you ''my man''.'

Entertainment was used as a vehicle for propaganda which itself became a source of entertainment. The *ITMA* version of a factory programme has already been cited. Another *ITMA* target was official bureaucracy. The show was set for a time in the 'Ministry of Aggravation and Twerps', a veiled reference to the Ministry of Information, and the dithering 'man from the ministry' who could never quite come to the point, was one of the regular cast of characters.[24]

The way in which service life enforced contact between different social classes proved a fertile source of humour. Although a BBC programme directive of 1942 had stated that representations of the military 'should avoid ''Blimp'' colonels, alcoholic majors, languid subalterns and troops who invariably drop their aitches', the successful series *Much-Binding-In-The-Marsh* traded on the relationship between the vague and idiotic officers and the downtrodden but wily other ranks. The producer thought that the show's appeal lay in the fact that while the other ranks could laugh *at* the stupidity of the officers, the commissioned ranks could laugh *with* them.[25] This cocking of snooks at authority survived the war and became a staple of radio and television comedy.

The cult of 'ordinary people', already noted in the factory shows and in serials like *At The Armstrongs*, was reflected in all kinds of entertainment. It was the very ordinariness, the 'girl next door' qualities of Vera Lynn, which qualified her for the title of 'Forces' Sweetheart'. By broadcasting camp concerts, performed by the troops themselves, the BBC discovered new performers with the 'common touch', like Max Bygraves, and it clung on to them after the war. 'Listener participation' became a key formula, applied most liberally to a show called *Ack Ack Beer Beer*. This was designed to provide isolated anti-aircraft units with a sense of belonging. It was largely produced by the men themselves who supplied not only much of the entertainment but also snippets of news from 'divisional journalists'. This kind of thing did not survive the war. The appeal was parochial and certain items, such as the regular 'comedy quiz', offended the sensibilities of BBC administrators. The Director of Programme Planning found the sound of a soldier singing 'Roll Out the Barrel' in the guise of a duck, a cuckoo and two other birds 'particularly nauseating'.

The administrators' attitude towards the Forces Programme was one of weary resignation. When the Director of Music suggested that some classical music would be of spiritual value to the troops, the Controller of Programmes assured him that they wanted only dance music and variety, adding 'this may be a melancholy example of herd habits . . .' (Nicolls to Boult, 29 January 1940). The Controller could only justify the new service in instrumental terms. It was 'a programme of a particular kind with a particular purpose, which provides a great many programmes of a low cultural level (Variety, etc.) or culturally negative (e.g., light music)' (Nicholls, 1 January 1942). Variety producers were given their head but were subjected to niggling rebukes if their work was thought to exceed the bounds of propriety. It is not surprising that the morale of the Variety Department had plummeted by the war's end.

Although the values of commercial entertainment penetrated the BBC during the war, their post-war influence was carefully confined to the Light Programme. Even the Light was not supposed to try to attract more than

60 per cent of the public and just how uncommercialised the values of BBC planners remained may be gauged from the distribution of programme budgets in 1946. The Light Programme, with 60 per cent of the audience, was allocated £11,000 per week; the Home Service, with 40 per cent, got £11,500 while the Third Programme, which was heard by barely 1 per cent of listeners and which was only on the air after 6 p.m., got £5,000. In 1948 the Director General, William Haley, sought to reassert pre-war policy by arguing that as the education and culture of the community rose, so listeners would be seduced from Light to Home and eventually to the pinnacle of the Third.[26] But Listener Research soon found that both the size and social composition of the respective audiences remained static. Just as post-war governments had to respect public demands for a retention of many of the social benefits which were a by-product of the war, so the BBC had to retain its popular programmes. The new division between services was a compromise, but it was the price that the BBC had to pay for the preservation of its monopoly.

Conclusions

In condensed accounts such as these it is not easy to catch all the nuances of the complex processes whereby socio-political authority and leadership is sought for and resisted, is worked at, for and against. The factory programmes, for instance, were instrumental and manipulative and were seen as such. But stripped of their obvious propaganda content they had an appeal to the mass of ordinary listeners. *Workers Playtime* and *Music While You Work* continued in the Light Programme for many years after the war, while the style of the industrial features was taken over and reworked by Wilfred Pickles as the basis for *Have a Go!*, the most popular single show on radio in the 1950s. This programme fitted exactly, indeed was part of that working-class culture described in *The Uses of Literacy*; a culture which was, and knew itself to be, incorporated within a dominant culture, the world of 'them' rather than 'us'.[27] Post-war radio provided spaces for the popular pleasures of the majority which had been very largely excluded before the war. In so doing the BBC had discarded its earlier assumption of cultural leadership for a more pragmatic assessment of what its audiences wanted from radio. An integral part of this process was the negotiation of consent, the winning of popular support, and the fluctuating compromises and realignments that were arrived at. In the course of the war, the BBC gradually shifted from being more oriented towards government at the outset to being more oriented towards its audience at the close. That is the theme running through the various changes in the direction of more popular styles of programming described above.

What were the wider implications of this change? It seems to us to have involved a revision of the concept of democracy. The original ideal of public service broadcasting had rested on the intention of democratising politics and culture by offering a new mass audience access to forms and processes from which it had previously been excluded. It aimed to raise the levels of information, knowledge and taste and so to make all members of society more actively responsive to, and responsible for, the nation's culture and the nation's politics. This prescriptive intention, with its roots in late nineteenth-century liberalism, cannot be crudely dismissed as élitist or manipulative. Its major contradiction lay in the fact that it separated culture, knowledge and political attitudes from their basis in the differing material economic and social circumstances of the population. It idealised both culture and politics and the national community, and required for its sustenance a utopian position of genuine autonomy for broadcasting as a social institution. If, before the war, the BBC had had to learn the extent to which its continued existence depended upon the tolerance of its political masters, during the war it came to understand more fully the extent to which it depended on the good will of its audience.

World War II made huge demands on the collective will and efforts of the British people. In so doing it eroded older patterns of social and political deference and the ready acceptance of decisions imposed from above. The new role for central government, of managing the economy and the social needs of the population, was the product in part of the new need to satisfy the demands of an electorate that now expected it to improve the material conditions of life through full employment, rising incomes and better social security. Both government and party politics were to be more and more concerned with managing and responding to public opinion and demand in the post-war era. So the changes in wartime broadcasting appear to us as one aspect of a gradual, but significant, change in the nature of political, social and cultural relations in Britain — a movement away from the exercise of direct leadership and rule by dominant political and cultural alignments, towards negotiated agreements in which the apex of the social pyramid must win the consent and agreement of the base for its actions. Just as there could be no return to government in 1945 to the politics of the 1930s, so there could be no going back for the BBC to the role it had assumed before the war.

Notes

[The main source for material in this article is the BBC Written Archive Centre, Caversham, Reading.]

1. See P. Scannell and D. Cardiff, 'Serving the Nation: Public Service Broadcasting Before the War' in B. Waites, T. Bennett and G. Martin (eds.), *Popular Culture: Past and Present*, Croom Helm, London, 1982.
2. *BBC Handbook*, BBC Publications, London, 1940, p. 83.
3. See A. Calder, *The People's War*, Panther, London, 1971, pp. 121–36.

4. See K. Middlemas, *Politics in Industrial Society*, André Deutsch, London, 1980.
5. I. McLaine, *Ministry of Morale*, Allen & Unwin, London, 1979, pp. 94–5.
6. See A. Briggs, *The War of Words. The History of Broadcasting in the United Kingdom*, vol. III, Oxford University Press, 1970, p. 91 and I. McLaine, *Ministry of Morale*, pp. 230–1.
7. See Briggs, *The War of Words*, p. 91 and McLaine, *Ministry of Morale*, pp. 230–1.
8. See A. Briggs, *The Golden Age of Wireless. The History of Broadcasting in the United Kingdom*, vol. II, Oxford University Press, 1965, pp. 265–80.
9. Cited in K. Middlemas, *Politics in Industrial Society*, p. 273.
10. See A. Briggs, *The War of Words*, p. 756.
11. Machine minders.
12. See D.G. Bridson, *Prospero and Ariel*, Victor Gollancz, London, 1971, p. 77.
13. W. Pickles, *Between You and Me*, Werner Laurie, London, 1949, p. 126.
14. Listener Report, no. 1458, December 1942.
15. See P. Addison, *The Road to 1945*, Quartet Books, London, 1977, pp. 64–90.
16. See I. McLaine, *Ministry of Morale*, pp. 173–4.
17. Listener Report, no. 2553, 22 April 1944.
18. See D. Cardiff, 'Time, Money and Culture: BBC Programme Finances, 1927–1939'. *Media, Culture and Society*, vol. 5, no. 3–4, 1983.
19. A. Briggs, *The War of Words*, p. 127.
20. A. Briggs, *Sound and Vision. The History of Broadcasting in the United Kingdom*, vol. IV, Oxford University Press, 1979, p. 60.
21. Editorial in *The Listener*, 30 September 1936.
22. See M. Gorham, *Broadcasting and Television since 1900*, Dakers, London, 1952, p. 215.
23. R. Williams, *Television, Technology and Cultural Form*, Fontana, London, 1949, p. 114.
24. See T. Kavanagh, *Tommy Handley*, Hodder and Stoughton, London, 1949, p. 114.
25. See L. Bridmont, *Leslie Bridmont Presents*, Falcon Press, London, 1949, p. 58.
26. See W. Haley, *The Responsibilities of Broadcasting*, BBC Publications, London 1948, p. 11.
27. See R. Hoggart, *The Uses of Literacy*, Pelican, Harmondsworth, 1965, pp. 72–101.

6

Colin McArthur

The dialectic of national identity: The Glasgow Empire Exhibition of 1938

'Tir nam Beann, Dachaidh Mo Ghaoil' [Land of the mountains, my beloved home]
Inscription above the entrance to the Clachan, Glasgow Empire Exhibition, 1938

In the summer of 1983 the Scottish Development Agency entered into a promotional exercise with Selfridges, the London department store. Over a substantial area of floor-space a Scottish village was constructed (see Figure 1), the shape of the papier mâché walls reprising Scottish rural vernacular architecture, the square containing a (by all appearances) genuine parish pump and trees, and the backdrops consisting of painted hills and castles. Attached to the walls at various places were enamelled signs, of the type common between the wars, for products such as Wild Woodbine and Richmond Gem cigarettes and leaning against the various trees and walls were milk churns, wagon wheels and a grocery boy's delivery bike of the kind generations born between the wars can recall from their childhood. The names over the buildings included Flora Macdonald's China Gifts, The Balmoral Shop (crystal and glass), The Laird's Shop (knitwear), The Sweetie Shop, and The Gamekeeper's Inn. The interior of the latter was panelled in wood, had sheep and stags' heads on the wall, stuffed grouse and salmon in glass cases, and an old copper kettle on top of the iron stove which nestled in a homely papier mâché hearth. The only potentially discordant note was the handful of LP discs scattered on the rough hewn table outside the inn, but the titles of the discs were entirely in keeping with the overall milieu — *The Gathering of the Clans, Caledonian Heritage* and *The Crags of Tumbledown Mountain*, the latter with the pipes and drums and regimental band of the Scots Guards celebrating the regiment's exploits in the Malvinas War.

The central contradiction which the Selfridges Scottish village (needless to say, unconsciously) poses is that a country five-sixths of whose population live in cities and are oriented towards industrial production (in transition, of course, from traditional coal- and steel-based heavy industry

Figure 1

towards electronic industries) should be constructed — not by poets and artists, but by the central agency concerned with national economic regeneration — exclusively in rural highland terms. It is a complex issue of the historical construction of national identity and the reasons why such constructions were and are necessary.

It is often assumed (perhaps most markedly in nationalist rhetorics) that national identity is an essence, a given, a timeless fact of nature, rather than the product of concrete historical forces. Tom Nairn explores nationalism as a general European phenomenon of a specific historical period and comes to a very different conclusion:

> How may we describe the general outlines of nationalist development, seen as 'general historical process'? Here, by far the most important point is that nationalism is *as a whole* quite incomprehensible outside the context of that process's *uneven* development. The subjective point of nationalist ideology is, of course, always the suggestion that one nationality is as good as another. But the *real* point has always lain in the objective fact that, manifestly, one nationality has never been even remotely as good as, or equal to, the others which figure in its world-view. Indeed, the purpose of the subjectivity (nationalist myths) can never be anything but protest against the brutal fact: it is mobilization *against* the unpalatable, humanly unacceptable, truth of grossly uneven development.
>
> Nationalism in general is (in Ernest Gellner's words) 'a phenomenon connected not so much with industrialization or modernization as such, but with its uneven diffusion'. It first arose as a *general* fact (a determining general condition of the European body politic) after this 'uneven diffusion' had made its first huge and irreversible impact upon the historical process. That is, after the combined shocks engendered by the French Revolution, the Napoleonic conquests, the English industrial revolution, and the war between the two super-states of the day, England and France.
>
> This English-French 'dual revolution' impinged upon the rest of Europe like a tidal wave, what Gellner calls the 'tidal wave of modernization'. Through it the advancing capitalism of the more bourgeois societies bore down upon the societies surrounding them — societies which predominantly appear until the 1790s as buried in feudal and absolutist slumber.
>
> Nationalism was one result of this rude awakening. For what did these societies — which now discovered themselves to be intolerably 'backward' — awaken into? A situation where polite universalist visions of progress had turned into means of domination. The Universal Republic of Anacharsis Cloots had turned into a French empire; the spread of free commerce from which so much had been hoped was turning (as Friedrich List pointed out) into the domination of English manufactures — the tyranny of the English 'City' over the European 'Country'. In short, there was a sort of imperialism built into 'development'. And it had become a prime necessity to resist *this* aspect of development.[1]

Nationalism, then, is a response to the phenomenon, much discussed in the modern world, of the *core–periphery* relationship, the process whereby economically strong core countries draw weaker contiguous countries (or more accurately, regions) into a satellite relationship across the entire range of the forms of social life. The core–periphery phenomenon has been extensively discussed with regard to economics and politics, less extensively with regard to culture and ideology.[2] While the emphasis, with regard to economics and politics, has been correctly on the extent to which the core regions use and benefit from those on the periphery and that, to a certain extent, the area of culture and ideology can be discussed in the same terms, the exploration of the opposition in relation to culture and ideology has to be much more dialectical for, in the very act of equipping themselves ideologically to be core countries and to sustain the undoubted strains of so becoming, the core countries at the same time defined the Other, the regions they themselves were not — i.e., the peripheral regions.

This raises a second strand of Nairn's argument that nationalism is pre-eminently a bourgeois form and that a particular class fraction of the bourgeoisie — the intellectuals and artists — was central in the process of mobilisation of the masses necessary to make particular nationalisms potent politically and, in certain cases, militarily. As Nairn points out, the cultural mode within which this mobilisation took place was Romanticism. It is within the categories of Romanticism that the process (whereby the core and its Other, the periphery, were simultaneously defined) takes place. The process was and is a complex one with contradictions within and between cores and peripheries, but the central, inescapable fact is that the point of utterance of the categories, the site of definition of the ideological and cultural contours of the core and its Other, the periphery, lay with the core countries. Thus it was that, in the period beginning in the mid-eighteenth century, a particular kind of person and society came to be defined in the core countries, largely by posing their opposites and finding them in peripheral or distant societies. It was part of the dialectical complexity that — as the darker side of the new core societies became more apparent — the ideological architects, the intellectuals and artists, began to identify more and more with the Other they had themselves constructed. The ideological construction both of the core and the periphery can be illustrated by a table of oppositions:

core	*periphery*
city/town	country
civilisation	barbarism
rationality	emotion
individual	community
dressed	undressed
barbered	unbarbered
culture	nature

masculine   feminine
ambitious   shiftless

This system of oppositions (which is by no means exhaustive) comes into play whenever a core culture has dealings with a peripheral one, for example in European encounters with the South Seas in the eighteenth century and Africa in the nineteenth century or, within national borders, in the relationship between, on the one hand, immigrants of European stock in the USA and, on the other, the Red Indians or Negroès. However, the same process of definition by structural opposition was at work within Europe itself, most notably in the defining of the Celtic fringe as Other to the dynamic core societies of England and France. As Malcolm Chapman says in his exemplary book *The Gaelic Vision in Scottish Culture*:

> Since the eighteenth century, the Celtic fringes have posed for the urban intellectual as a location of the wild, the natural, the creative and the insecure. We can often find it said, with warm approval, that the Celts are impetuous, natural, spiritual and naive . . . Such an approval is drawing on the same system of structural oppositions as is the accusation that the Celt is violent (impetuous), animal (natural), devoid of any sense of property (spiritual), or without manners (naive) the bracketed terms [being] effective synonyms of the words that precede them, that we would use to praise rather than to deride . . . We are dealing here with a rich verbal and metaphorical complex . . . [It is not] important to distinguish between those who find a favourable opinion of the Gael within this complex, and those who dip into it to find the materials for derision. In both cases the coherence of the statements can only be found at their point of origin, the urban intellectual discourse of the English language, and not at their point of application, the Celt, the Gael, the primitive who is ever-departing, whether his exit be made to jeers or to tears.[3]

Apparently complimentary descriptions of the Other ('natural', 'sensitive', 'spiritual', etc.) constitute a discourse which exploited peoples the world over know to their cost. Ostensibly flattering to them, it is in reality the ideological dimension of economic and political expropriation, a discourse formulated by the oppressor within which the oppressed are allocated their place in terms congenial to the needs and fears of the oppressor. One of the more chilling revelations of Chapman's book is the extent to which Gaels (and indeed Scots as a whole) come to live within the mental universe fashioned by their oppressors and to define their own identities accordingly. This phenomenon is a general feature of diverse kinds of colonialism and imperialism and has been pointed to by, among others, Franz Fanon, Anthony Wilden and Edward Said.[4]

The effect of such historically pervasive discourses is to produce serious problems of identity for the oppressed and to establish traditions of representation which lay down rules by which particular races and terrains will be represented within the entire range of available discourses and sign systems.[5] This is decidedly a handicap (but, by the nature of the phenomenon, rarely recognised) for indigenous artists seeking to represent their own cultures or even, at a more workaday level, for exhibition organisers seeking to construct a Scottish village in Selfridges.

However, there is a fundamental instability in the process which can be clarified by reference back to the Nairn–Gellner assertion that nationalism is the product of uneven economic development and the motor for mobilising social forces to achieve modernisation. Even the most 'backward' of regions is under compulsion to develop economically and that factor very often, at the ideological level, throws into crisis, destabilises the identity assigned the 'backward' region or race, initially by their oppressors but subsequently (through the coming to dominance of established discourses) by themselves. This moment of crisis in its diverse concrete instances is worthy of attention and can be seen at work in, for example, Figure 2, where copywriter's rhetoric struggles to reconcile incompatible constructions of the American South in its bid for modernisation. This is not, of course, to evaporate the real historical distinctions between the American South and, say, Scotland; rather to point to the extent to which quite diverse core–periphery relationships produce similar dialectics of national–regional identity.

A recurrent site of this contradiction is the national exhibition, a mechanism evolved by core countries such as England and France to bind up the wounds of civil strife at home and celebrate their industrial or colonial triumphs but, by the compulsive nature of the developmental process, adopted by peripheral countries and regions in their own striving for modernity.[6] For such a pervasive and ideologically replete mechanism (there were in excess of 50 exhibitions in the UK alone in the period from 1890 to 1939), it has been remarkably scantily researched. Scotland has figured quite substantially among these, both as a nation in its own right and as a component of the United Kingdom and Empire, from the Glasgow Exhibition of 1901, through the Highland and Jacobite and Scottish Home Industries Exhibitions of 1903, the Scottish National Exhibition of 1908, the Coronation Exhibition of 1911, and the British Empire Exhibition of 1924, to the Empire Exhibition of 1938 which was itself held in Glasgow and, as such, was the site of multiple contradictions.[7]

Before proceeding to an examination of the Empire Exhibition of 1938 from the point of view of its negotiation of the contradiction of Scotland as a historically assigned terrain of the imagination and Scotland as a dynamic, modern industrial nation, it is necessary to reassert the complexity and instability of the concept of national identity. It is not an *essence* but a *process* constantly open to change and development according to the needs of the moment. This can be graphically illustrated by the mechanism whereby the core countries such as France and England, through their control over discourse, created the Other, the peripheral or distant terrains which — with the development of travel and tourism — were to become the

Figure 2

Two Hearts That Beat As One

The South has two hearts.

One is filled with the romantic charm and cherished tradition of bygone days . . . yet it's still young and gay.

The other is the Southland's new, strong, industrial heart . . . daring, courageous, optimistic . . . beating with high hopes for the future.

In thousands of modern factories it is pulsing with activity . . . throbbing with growth and vitality . . . absorbing nourish-ment from the boundless resources of a fertile land . . . pumping endless streams of goods to all parts of the country.

All along the 8,000-mile Southern Railway System, these "two hearts that beat as one" offer the old-time warmth of a Southern welcome . . . and unlimited opportunity for all industries.

"Look Ahead—Look South!"

Ernest E. Norris

President

SOUTHERN RAILWAY SYSTEM
The Southern Serves the South

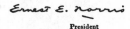

Figure 3

Irish Section, Glendalough,
Coronation Exhibition, London, 1911.

playgrounds within which the core countries' *homo oeconomicus* would replenish his soul. This mechanism proved insufficient for the spiritual/ideological needs of *homo oeconomicus* as the dream of infinite progress soured and (with the horrors of industrialisation) the landscape he himself inhabited darkened. What was required was the creation of a spiritual/ideological Other on his own terrain, for the English *homo oeconomicus* a timeless England of the imagination, different from though serving the same spiritual/ideological needs as the peripheral Others fashioned by the ideologues of *homo oeconomicus*. By the time of the Coronation Exhibition of 1911, not only was there being constructed an Ireland and a Scotland of the imagination, but an England, too (see Figures 3, 4 and 5).

The Selfridges conception of Scotland as a lowland, rural village set against a highland backdrop is a conception with 250 years of dominant discourse underpinning it. It represents an amalgam of the two hegemonic literary discourses within which Scotland has been represented — Tartanry and Kailyard. The former, a world of Romantic grandeur, embodied initially in the works of Sir Walter Scott, the latter, representing 'a Scotland of parochial insularity, of poor, humble, puritanical folk living out dour lives lightened only by a dark and forbidding religious dogmatism', embodied initially in the works of Sir James Matthew Barrie though both have reproduced themselves across the entire range of available sign-systems including easel painting, photography, advertising, postcards, film and television.[8] It is not that the organisers of the various exhibitions in this century and the last set out deliberately to construct

Figure 4

Scene in Scottish Section,
Coronation Exhibition, London. 1911.

Figure 5

English Village,
Coronation Exhibition, London, 1911.

Scotland in terms of the Selfridges village, rather that history had bequeathed no alternative models of representing Scotland. It comes as no surprise therefore to find the village (or ruralised town) as a key motif in every exhibition in which Scotland has been represented (see Figures 6, 7, 8 and 9. However, such is the force of the dialectic between uneven economic

Figure 6

Figure 7

development and the assigned identity of Scotland as 'natural' and rural,
that the discourse of the village (or ruralised town) has to enter into
constant collision with the idea of Scotland as a dynamic, thrusting,
modern industrial nation. This collision can be followed through virtually
every aspect of the 1938 Glasgow Empire Exhibition and the meta-

Figure 8

discourses (guide books, special issues of local newspapers, newsreels) which surround it.[9]

To a great extent the Exhibition was conceived and developed primarily within an economic discourse. It arose as an idea within the Scottish Development Council in the summer of 1936 and the preparatory work was done by the Finance and General Purposes Committee of the Council. The Council itself had been set up in 1931 to encourage industrial development and it operated throughout the early 1930s in a context of sharp debate about the chronic unemployment and social deprivation of (particularly the West of) Scotland. That social experience and those debates shaped profoundly the nature of the economic discourse within which the Exhibition was conceived and developed and were a strong determining factor on the themes (e.g., public health) within which Scotland as a modern, industrial nation was presented.[10] By the time the Exhibition actually occurred the West of Scotland, under pressure principally of naval rearmament, was emerging from the Depression, but the economic discourse of the Exhibition constantly throws glances over its shoulder to the bleak conditions within which the Exhibition was conceived. However, the modern thrusting economic discourse must constantly negotiate the other, historically hegemonic, discourse which conceives of Scotland in different terms. The dialectic is evident within particular contemporary statements about the exhibition:

> Behind an event of this kind there must, of course, be an industrial motive
> . . . It is fairly obvious that an exhibition which contains a Palace of

Figure 9

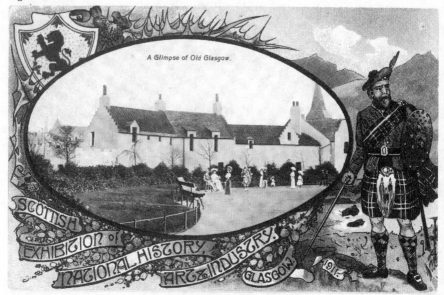

A Glimpse of Old Glasgow.

SCOTTISH EXHIBITION of NATIONAL HISTORY ART & INDUSTRY GLASGOW 1911

Figure 10

A SMALL SCOTCH FRAE THE CLACHAN EMPIRE EXHIBITION

Engineering . . . two great Palaces of General Industry; . . . a Palace of Travel, Transport and Industry; a Coal Utilisation Pavilion and an Agricultural Pavilion is comprehensive, measured by any standard, but when there is added to that an immense number of Dominion, Colonial, and private pavilions it is clear that the whole industrial structure of the British

Empire and its potentialities will be on view . . . . . . The Highland
Clachan, if not new in conception, is exceptionally well done and mirrors the
environment in which lie the roots of our race, a race which thrived on
hardship and which, however widely it has spread itself over the world's
surface, clings to its essential characteristics'.[11]

It is also evident in the layout of the Exhibition itself and of the contents
of the *Glasgow Herald's* special Exhibition issue with articles on 'Britain's
Shop Windows: the Palaces of Industry' and 'British Craftsmanship:
Palace of Engineering' lying cheek by jowl with articles on 'Building the
Empire: Great Part Played by Scotsmen' and several pieces on Scotland's
past. The two Scottish pavilions effectively convey the Jekyll and Hyde
quality of Scottish identity caught within the dialectic of urban/modern
against rural/ancient, the one pavilion concerned with the health of
modern Scotland, the other containing tableaux of Scotland's past.

However, the 'purest' expression of the Scotland of the imagination is
unquestionably the Clachan as described in the *Glasgow Herald*'s account of
the visit of the King and Queen to it. The account is deeply informed by the
dialectic and, in the particular incident it recounts, is reminiscent of the
tributes of Indian princes at a nineteenth-century imperial durbar,
recalling the descriptions which have been offered of Scotland as 'a Third
World country' and its relationship with England as constituting 'internal
colonialism':[12]

From the base of the Tower the King and Queen were taken through the
country house and modern flats erected by the Scottish Committee of the
Council for Art and Industry, and then they stepped out of the Exhibition's
modernistic atmosphere of severely designed and gaily coloured pavilions
into the homely setting of the Clachan's thatched cottages, calm lochan and
stony paths.

It was a memorable picture and an unusual experience for the royal
couple, as it will be for thousands of visitors to the Exhibition. A piper played
stirring marches and reels on the banks of the lochan, into which tumbled a
laughing burn, and from some of the cottages came the gentle lilt of Gaelic
singing.

The Queen stopped first at the Highland post office and listened for a
moment to clarsach playing in an adjacent cottage, but the most touching
incident of the tour came in the St Kilda Cottage. The King and the Queen
were received by 75-year-old Finlay McQueen — regarded as 'king' of St
Kilda before the evacuation of the island — who greeted them with 'God
bless you both and your family' in Gaelic — his only language — and then he
dropped on one knee to kiss the hands of their Majesties.[13]

In one of the representations of the Clachan (Figures 10, 11, 12 and 13)
there can be glimpsed an oddly discordant feature. Looming over The
Clachan is the Tower of Empire (Figure 14). The very essence of

Figure 11

THE CLACHAN, EMPIRE EXHIBITION, SCOTLAND, 1938.

Figure 12

THE CLACHAN, EMPIRE, EXHIBITION, SCOTLAND 1938

modernity, it seems to have been inspired in equal measure by Le Corbusier, MGM and the Flash Gordon serials. The Clachan and the Tower of Empire are the polar points of the dialectic which threatens to render individual Scots schizoid and which, in an uncanny prefiguring of the rhetoric of the Southern Railway System advert (see Figure 2) — and

Figure 13

THE CLACHAN, EMPIRE EXHIBITION, SCOTLAND, 1938.   X.37.

Figure 14

THE TOWER OF EMPIRE BY NIGHT.
EMPIRE EXHIBITION SCOTLAND 1938.   X.160.

131

illustrating the generality of the ideological struggle between cores and peripheries — runs through the address of welcome to the 1938 Exhibition by its president, the Earl of Elgin and Kincardine:

> Scotland as the home of the Exhibition has at once a unique privilege and a magnificent opportunity.
>
> She will be 'At Home' . . . For her visitors from far and near she will display her manufactures and her wares; she will disclose and emphasise her opportunities for trade and commerce and she will "discover" her heart.
>
> In Bellahouston Park there will be gathered comprehensive and constructive proof of Industry, Science, Art, Engineering, Social Progress and Recreation. It will be a great meeting-place and in its widest sense a University of Empire. But the Exhibition will also be for many a stepping-stone to a more intimate knowledge of Scotland's history and romance, and to a fuller enjoyment of her opportunities for sport and pleasure.[14]

For nearly 200 years Scotland had lived within a classic peripheral identity assigned it by the artists and ideologues of the great European core cultures through the mode of Romanticism and through their control of the means of (intellectual) production. However, the brute fact of uneven economic development compelled the Scots to bring into collision with that assigned identity a new fashioned identity more appropriate to a dynamic, modern nation. Great national moments of self-presentation, such as the Glasgow Empire Exhibition of 1938, were the occasions when the ongoing dialectic of modern/urban against rural/ancient emerged in its most public and delirious form. Such occasions hold a *political* lesson. The process of speaking with two voices; the fissures; the uncertainties; the grating shifts of gear from one discourse to another assert, once more, the fluid, unstable character of national identity. Such occasions proclaim that national identity is not a set of inborn, natural characteristics in a people, but the product of that people's history. With the realisation of instability comes the realisation of the possibility of change. National identity comes to be seen, therefore, not as a set of eternal, mosaic tablets, but as a terrain of struggle where, to be sure, certain regressive and politically disabling discourses may currently be in hegemony but which require constant reutterance and rearticulation to sustain that hegemony. Crucially, that hegemony is open to challenge by a counter-hegemony offering new definitions of national identity.

Clearly such a task is massive in the Scottish context so heavy is the weight of inherited discourse about what it means to be a Scot and to inhabit the peculiar terrain that is Scotland. As with the transformation of identity wrought on the Scots, through the discourse of Romanticism, in the period 1790–1830, the role of artists and intellectuals — the producers of discourse — in effecting and sustaining another transformation will be central. The level of consciousness of the problem and of the task to be accomplished is not high among Scottish artists and intellectuals. Scottish cinema and television, from *Local Hero* to the Hogmanay Specials of the various channels, are deeply complicit with the regressive discourses of Tartanry and Kailyard while literature and the visual arts in Scotland seem substantially preoccupied with the less productive formalist aspects of cosmpolitan modernism. The most hopeful growth points on the Scottish scene are those figures and mechanisms who have identified the regressive discourses within which most of the work produced in Scotland is shaped and who have made the starting point of their work the confronting and dismembering of those discourses. The film-maker Murray Grigor in *Scotch Myths*, for example, takes apart the major historical figures from 'Ossian' Macpherson to Harry Lauder who have constructed Scotland in regressive terms; the print maker and ceramicist Eric Marwick pricks venerable Scottish institutions and reflects on Scotland's relationship with the outside world; and the cultural journal *Cencrastus* interrogates (somewhat unevenly) the whole spectrum of art and media practice from a left nationalist perspective. However, these piecemeal interventions will be for naught unless the question of Scottish culture is made a central area of concern in Scottish political institutions. Scottish left and/or nationalist political institutions have in common with similar British institutions a fundamentally depoliticised view of art. To be sure they are different from more ostensibly conservative political institutions in calling for more money for the arts but their ideology of art is virtually indistinguishable from that of the right — i.e. a belief in the artist as expressive fount and in works of art as discrete objects wholly explicable in terms of their creators' 'talent' or 'genius'. An arts and education policy which rejected this conception of art and defined art rather as the site of ideology, as one of the central processes whereby individuals are encapsulated into positions from which they make a wide range of judgements about the society they live in, would require the major Scottish 'discourse' institutions — the Scottish Education Department, the National Trust for Scotland, the Scottish Arts Council, the Scottish Film Council, and the Scottish universities — to address the question of Scottish culture more urgently than currently they do and in a much more debate-centred way.

Within such a policy it is just possible to imagine a Scottish National Exhibition in which the discourses of Scotland as prelapsarian Eden and as bustling capitalist nation have, at the very least, got to struggle to maintain their current hegemony.

Notes

1. T. Nairn, *The Break-up of Britain*, New Left Books, London, 1977, pp. 96–97.
2. The politico-economic dimension is discussed most notably in I. Wallerstein, *The Modern World System*, 2 vols, Academic Press, New York, 1974. An important exception to the absence of cultural/ideological discussion is the essay by Cairns

Craig, 'Peripheries' in *Cencrastus*, no. 9, Summer 1982, pp. 3–9. I am indebted to Cairns Craig for drawing my attention to the extensive socio-economic literature on the core—periphery question.

3. M. Chapman, *The Gaelic Vision in Scottish Culture*, Croom Helm, London, 1978, p. 18.

4. In, amongst other works, F. Fanon, *Black Skin, White Masks*, Paladin, London, 1968; A. Wilden, *The Imaginary Canadian* Pulp Press, Vancouver, 1979; and E. Said, *Orientalism*, Routledge and Kegan Paul, London, 1978. But see Homi K. Bhabha, 'The Other Question — the Stereoptye and Colonial Discourse', *Screen*, vol. 24. No. 6 November–December 1983, pp. 18–36, for the complexity and instability of stereotypes.

5. For an account of how Scotland and the Scots have been and, regrettably, continue to be represented in the cinema and on television, see C. McArthur (ed.) *Scotch Reels: Scotland in Cinema and Television*, British Film Institute, London, 1982.

6. For an excellent discussion of the ideological meanings of the Paris Exhibition of 1889 — 'reconciliation, rehabilitation at home, and imperial supremacy abroad' — see Debora L. Silverman, 'The 1889 Exhibition: The Crisis of Bourgeois Individualism', *Oppositions: a Journal of Ideas and Criticism in Architecture*, Spring 1977, pp. 71–91.

7. The remainder of this essay deals only with *one* of the contradictions of the 1938 Exhibition, that relating to Scottish identity in terms of rural/regressive against urban/modern. A full account of the Exhibition would have to discuss the articulation of these dicourses with the central organising discourse of the Exhibition — imperialism.

8. See Cairns Craig, 'Myths Against History: Tartanry and Kailyard in Nineteenth Century Scottish Literature' in C. McArthur (ed.), *Scotch Reels*.

9. It is a collision which recurs thereafter in recent Scottish history. It is present in the half-dozen or so documentary films specially made for the 1938 Exhibition through Films of Scotland and in the 20-year output of the post-war version of the same body set up in 1954. For a fuller discussion of this see C. McArthur (ed.), *Scotch Reels*, pp. 58–63.

10. See R.H. Campbell 'The Scottish Office and the Special Areas in the 1930s', *The Historical Journal*, March 1979.

11. *Glasgow Herald*, special Exhibition issue, pp. 15, 61.

12. M. Hechter, *Internal Colonialism: The Celtic Fringe in British National Development 1536-1966*, Routledge, London, 1975.

13. *Glasgow Herald*, special Exhibition issue, pp. 13–14.

14. *Scotland's Welcome*, Collins, Glasgow, 1938, pp. 17–18.

7

Tony Bennett

Hegemony, ideology, pleasure: Blackpool

When the Eiffel Tower created its *furore* among the Parisians, Blackpool showed its enterprise by being the first place in the United Kingdom to put up a similar erection! When the Great Wheel at Earl's Court, London, tickled the Cockneys with its novelty, Blackpool was the only town in the United Kingdom to erect one of its own![1]

Thus the 1897 Blackpool Town Guide, typical in its claims to outdo every other town in Britain, the capital city included. In 1924, the standard of comparison Blackpool constructed for itself, only in order to exceed it, was imperial Rome:

Just south of the Victorian Pier is Blackpool's latest attraction acknowledged by all the swimming authorities to be the largest and finest enclosed open-air swimming bath in the world. We can go the world over and back into the days of the older civilizations, but we cannot find anything more wonderful than this magnificent new bath, not even the Coliseum of Rome in the height of its glory.[2]

Throughout its history as a popular holiday resort, Blackpool has represented itself as a town operating on the very threshhold of modernity, exploring and pushing back the outer limits of progress. The claims, moreover, have typically had a distinctively northern, and especially Lancashire, articulation. Never slow to cock a snook at the metropolis — cockneys being idly tickled by the Great Wheel whilst the people of Blackpool go ahead and build one — Blackpool has, at various times, imaginarily placed itself at the centre of the nation and, even more grandiosely, of the Empire, thus disputing London's claims to pre-eminence. In this respect, the 'discourse of modernity' which has governed the forms in which Blackpool has represented itself has been connected, at various moments, to a distinctive brand of northern populism, the two jointly forging an image of 'the people of the North' as sharing a no-nonsense, down-to-earth, practical regional spirit, best exemplified in the triumphal achievements of northern industrial capitalists, constructed in opposition to the all-talk, no-action pretensions of the South. A true case of 'second city firsts', Blackpool has, I want to argue, thus furnished the site for the enunciation of a distinctively regional claim to cultural leadership, albeit one heard only within the confines of northern, and particularly Lancashire, culture.[3] At the same time, this discourse of modernity has also occasionally pointed in other directions, dismantling opposing discourses by articulating their claims to itself. Current publicity posters for the revolution — a loop-the-loop ride at the Pleasure Beach — thus declare: 'Join the Revolution — Only Here at Blackpool's Pleasure Beach'. This not only puts London in its place but is as effective and economical an instance of the containment of oppositional discourses as Marcuse could have ever hoped to find.[4]

My purpose in this essay is to consider the operation of this discourse of modernity and the varying ideologies and sets of values that have been drawn into association with and expressed by means of it at different moments in Blackpool's history. In doing so, I shall be partly concerned with such representational forms as town guides and publicity brochures. However, I shall focus rather more on the popular entertainments which, at different times, have predominated in the town, considering these from the point of view of the discourses embodied in the sedimented forms of their architectural styles or, more pliably, in their characteristic themes and modes of address. My particular concern, in relation to these, will be to elucidate the part that the regimes of pleasure embodied in such popular entertainments — that is, not merely the forms of pleasure on offer but the systems of signs and associated ideologies under which they are constructed and offered as pleasures — play in relation to the processes of hegemony more broadly conceived.

Elements of a history[5]

Although Blackpool has long boasted that it was the world's first working-class holiday resort, it became so very much against its will and better inclinations. The commercial development of the town as a holiday resort dates from the 1790s with the opening of a railway line between Preston and the Fylde coast. Throughout the greater part of the next century, however, Blackpool remained, and struggled hard to remain, a dignified holiday resort catering principally for the respectable middle classes and upper strata of artisan workers from the northern manufacturing towns. The town's political machinery, dominated by local tradesmen catering for this market until more or less the turn of the century, provided the necessary infrastructure (piped water, street lighting, the promenade, etc.), to support the commercial development of recreational facilities within the town. The capital which funded these projects — public and private — came from two main sources. Many ventures, such as the North Pier (1865), were financed by local subscription. Others were capitalised by Lancashire and Yorkshire businessmen. Very little London capital, or, indeed, capital from anywhere outside the northern counties was attracted to Blackpool until towards the end of the century.

The forms of recreation provided in this period, especially from the mid-century on, were of an excessively 'rational' and improving kind. The North Pier, utterly lacking in commercial embellishment, offered little more than the opportunity for dignified perambulation over the ocean. The Winter Gardens (1878) epitomised the town's claims to culture and elegance. Constructed with the declared intention of making Blackpool a major European cultural centre — rivalling London — its opening was celebrated with a degree of civic pride and pomp that now seems scarcely credible: the mayors of 68 towns were invited to process through the town, led by the Lord Mayor of London in his ceremonial carriage. Whilst, of course, the actual practice may have been different, a Blackpool holiday was both represented and organised as a refined and cultivated affair. John Walton paints the following picture of Blackpool holiday-makers in the period prior to the 1880s:

> Whether they were manufacturers, professional men, shopkeepers, clerks or working men in skilled or supervisory grades, whatever the differences between them in other respects, they generally accepted common standards of propriety and decorum. They gave due weight to the code of moral responsibility which went hand in hand with the pursuit of economic independence, and they sought at least to keep up appearances. The working men among them were self selecting, for only the relatively thrifty and aspiring could afford to come to the seaside for more than the odd day before the great price fall of the late nineteenth century. They saved carefully and spent, according to their lights, 'rationally', on items of long-term practical utility; and they saw their seaside holiday in these terms. They eschewed frivolity or excess, cultivating regular habits and an earnest demeanour. They took their pleasures seriously, and a seaside holiday was the occasion for rest, recuperation and edification. Health was pursued by judicious and carefully-regulated bathing, and by gentle exercise where the medical ozone could be inhaled. Improving recreations were permissible, and the pursuit of 'useful knowledge' was expressed in conchology and fossil-hunting. Such visitors desired little in the way of commercial entertainment, although their preoccupations were reflected in increasingly lavish aquaria and winter gardens at the larger resorts by the 'seventies, and there was a steady demand for concerts, plays and even well-conducted dances. But the main *desiderata* were good natural amenities, quietness and decorum, for there were sensibilities here to be protected.[6]

Respectable middle-class and artisan holiday-makers were not, however, the only people to visit Blackpool during this period. From as early as 1781, when a road was opened up between Preston and Blackpool, agricultural labourers from northern Lancashire had made their way to

Blackpool at weekends or on special festivals. In 1840, the opening of a rail link between Preston and Fleetwood put Blackpool within easy day-trip reach of the northern spinning and weaving towns and, from 1842, special excursion trains regularly plied the line, dropping Blackpool passengers off at Poulton until a direct line to Blackpool was opened in 1846. The initial impetus behind the development of excursion trains was largely of a 'rational' and improving kind. Organised by temperance and religious bodies, and sometimes directly by employers, their purpose was to expose the working classes, if only for a day, to the improving physical and moral climate then prevailing in Blackpool. However, where voluntary organisations led, workers' co-operative associations and straightforwardly commercial ventures could follow. By the 1850s, Blackpool was subject to a regular flood of day-trip visitors — as many as 10,000 a day coming in by train alone — both at weekends and in the wakes holidays of the northern industrial towns; that is, virtually right through the summer.[7]

And with the people came tradesmen catering for their tastes in food, drink and popular entertainments. Freak shows, small side-shows and competitions, waxworks, monstrosities, quack medicine, popular dramas, small mechancial rides — such were the popular entertainments which followed the popular classes to Blackpool. Combining elements of both traditional wakes celebrations and the newer urban fairs which, by the mid-nineteenth century, were increasingly taking the place of the former,[8] they also anticipated aspects of the fixed-site mechanical fun-fairs of the 1880s and 1890s. And the primary zone of their operation was the beach, traditionally unregulated land, outside the control of the local political machinery. From mid-century, the organisation of pleasure at Blackpool thus exhibited a Janus face. The improving, civilising recreations aimed at the middle class and upper artisan holiday trade dominated the promenade and town centre whilst the beach was occupied by the messy and variagated sprawl of countless side-shows competing for the working class day-trip market. In effect, both the traditional and newer urban forms of popular recreation, under considerable attack in the inland towns at the time, had been displaced to Blackpool beach where they were able to thrive in an excess of unbridled vulgarity.[9]

Not surprisingly, the citizens of Blackpool, especially those who had invested in the middle-class holiday market, sought to resist and to turn the tide of this working-class invasion which threatened to drive away the respectable trade. The beach, moreover, had become an ideological scandal, an affront of the town's carefully constructed image as the embodiment of a unique blend of respectability, progress and modernity, a triumphal hymn to the hard-headed verve and practicality of the northern bourgeoisie. Initially, an attempt was made to exclude day-trippers by petitioning the railway companies not to run excursion trains to the town. When this failed, attention concentrated on bringing the piers and the beach within the scope of the town's regulatory capacities. In 1868, Central

Pier — or, as it was colloquially known, 'the People's Pier' — was opened. Catering specifically for the working-class trade (entry was free and unimpeded compared with the penny entrance fee charged at the North Pier), Central Pier became a major centre for popular entertainments, particularly drinking and dancing, both of which were free from the restrictions prevailing in the town. One of the corporation's first acts, when Blackpool became an incorporated borough in 1876, was to extend its licensing and policing authority to include the piers. The beach, however, was the site of the longest struggle between the 'respectable' and the 'popular' within Blackpool leading, in 1897, to an attempt to prohibit all trading on the beach. The outcry which greeted this forced the corporation to relent to the degree of allowing food and drink stalls to operate on the beach but drawing the line at 'Phrenologists, Quack Doctors, Mock Auctioneers and Cheap-Jacks'.

This attempt to exclude the popular tradition from Blackpool backfired owing to the peculiar structure of landownership prevailing in the town which enabled showmen evicted from the beach to set up shop in the forecourts of houses on the promenade.[10] Instead of being exiled from the town, popular entertainments deriving from the wakes and urban fairs thus gained a more scandalously prominent position within it, elevated from the beach to the promenade, thus laying the foundations for the Golden Mile — a vast stretch of stalls, side-shows, freak shows, curiosities and the like which dominated Blackpool's frontage south of the Tower until the early 1960s.

This direct attack on the beach, however, was the product of rather different interests and alliances from those which had fuelled earlier attempts to regulate the forms of pleasure permissible in the town. By the 1880s and 1890s, principally as a consequence of the rise in disposable family income in Lancashire's cotton towns, Blackpool was attracting a considerable volume of working-class *holiday*, as distinct from *day-trip*, trade. Population statistics attest to the significance of this period within Blackpools' development. In 1861, Blackpools' resident population was 3,707. By 1891, it had grown to 23,846 and, by 1901, to 47,348. Similarly, the period witnessed a quantum leap in the number of registered landladies — who provided residential and catering facilities geared specifically to the working-class market — from 400 in 1871 to 4,000 in 1911.[11] The middle-class holiday trade declined in the same period, partly because middle-class visitors began to go elsewhere to escape the 'degraded' tone of Blackpool and partly because falling prices brought about a relative reduction in middle-class spending power. The consequent increase in the ratio of working-class to middle-class holiday-makers, and in the relative value of their custom, resulted in the development of a significant entertainment industry aimed at a mass working-class market. The high capital requirements of this industry attracted to Blackpool a new type of entrepreneur and a new breed of impresario. It also, and for the first time, led to a significant amount of London capital, especially from sources associated with the music hall, being invested in the town.

In a useful survey of the development of the seaside towns of north-west Lancashire, Harold Perkin has argued:

> Each resort has its own peculiar history and evolution, but in general the most important factor in determining the social tone was the competition for domination of the resort by large, wealthy residents, hotel keepers and providers of 'genteel' entertainments such as concert halls and bathing establishments; by small property owners, boarding-house keepers and purveyors of cheap amusements; and, later in the century, by large capitalist enterprises, usually financed from outside, providing cheap, spectacular entertainment for a mass public.[12]

By the late nineteenth century, as a consequence of these developments, the terms of the struggle over popular recreations in Blackpool and the patterns of alliance associated with it had changed. No longer one between entrepreneurs catering for the 'respectable' market and small showmen catering for the 'vulgar' tastes of the popular classes, the attack on the latter now came from an alliance between the 'respectable' interests in the town and the new entrepreneurs and impresarios who wished to develop the working-class market, rather than to eliminate or reform it, with this latter group playing very much the active, leading role.

However, this is not to suggest that the terms within which this struggle was conducted were purely commercial in orientation. There were considerable ideological interests at stake, too. Most historians are agreed that the commercially provided forms of mass entertainment which typified the later nineteenth century — the music hall, spectator sports and the popular press, for example — proved considerably more successful in promoting the cultural hegemony of the ruling classes than had earlier attempts at morally reforming the people by promoting the spread of 'rational recreations'. Whilst this is true, the suggestion which sometimes accompanies this argument — that the shift from the one strategy to the other was a shift from a struggle for hegemony conducted by ideological and cultural means to one conducted purely by commercial means — is misleading. The popular entertainments promoted on a highly capitalised basis in the late nineteenth-century embodied a programme of ideological and cultural re-formation just as much as had the earlier 'rational recreations', albeit that the means whereby popular values and attitudes were to be 're-formed' had changed significantly. The 'rational recreations' movements, in seeking both to oppose and repress traditional and developing forms of working-class recreation, had aimed to re-form the popular classes by filling their lives with a different cultural content. The later, commercially provided forms of mass entertainment, by contrast, sought less to oppose the given forms of working-class recreation

140

than to reorder their ideological and cultural articulations. They transformed working-class culture not by taking issue with it as a monolithic entity and seeking to install in its place another monolithic entity (the 'rational' culture of the middle classes) but by breaking it down into its elements — its taste, preferences and characteristic activities — and hooking these and, with them, the people, into an association with hegemonic ideological formations.

At Blackpool the shift from the one strategy to the other was aptly symbolized by the appointment of Billy Holland as manager of the Winter Gardens in 1887. As I have noted, the Winter Gardens were founded with the express ambition of bringing culture to Blackpool. The aim, in the words of a founding shareholder, was to provide 'high class entertainment which no lady or gentleman would object to see'. Within a few years of its opening, however, declining revenues forced the controlling company to sacrifice culture for profit. Billy Holland, earlier a manager of a music hall in the London suburbs where he had gained a certain notoriety for his slogan, 'Come and Spit on Bill Holland's Hundred Guinea Carpet', effectively reversed the Winter Gardens' policy of cultural improvement in implementing, as his catch-phrase, the motto 'Give 'em what they want'.

But, in 'giving 'em what they wanted', such impresarios at the same time transformed the tastes, preferences and practices of the people, inscribing them in new sets of cultural and ideological relations. Virtually all the forms of mass entertainment developed in Blackpool in this period, in catering for the people's tastes also relocated their recreations, wrenching them away from their traditional associations and selectively reconstructing them in an association with new sets of values and ideologies. In the main, two sets of themes predominated. Perhaps most influential initially, imperialist motifs were strongly present in both the architectural styles and characteristic themes of a wide range of popular entertainments; Nigger (*sic*) minstrel shows at the Winter Gardens; the construction of an Indian façade to the South Pier; the 1913 design of the Casino, the main frontispiece to the Pleasure Beach, in the style of an Indian palace, the staging of mock naval battles out at sea including, on one occasion, the mock invasion (successfully repulsed!) of the town by Afghan hordes; penny slot machines which, when activated, depicted white men shooting 'natives': in these ways, the thematics and architecture of pleasure inveigled the pleasure-seeker in relations of complicity with imperialist values and sentiments.

More influential in the longer term, however, was the rearticulation of the discourse of modernity which, initially a complement to the image of respectability the town had constructed for itself, assumed an increasingly brash countenance. In their very material form, many of the popular entertainments developed in this period stood as a triumphant testimony to the powers of northern industrialism. The Tower, the centrepiece of the town's phallic boasting ever since its — as the 1897 Town Guide put it —

'erection' in 1894, displayed the prowess of 'the workshop of the world' in the sphere of pleasure. More generally, the harnessing of machinery for pleasure embodied in the development of mechanical rides — especially, in the early twentieth century, at the Pleasure Beach — constituted a modernization of pleasure which, had it been allowed to, might have spoken for itself as a sufficiently eloquent testimony to the virtues of progress. But it was not allowed to. Persistently, as the increasingly dominant form of hailing in operation at Blackpool, impresarios claimed to be offering 'the latest', 'the most up to the minute' forms of popular entertainment, often 'direct from America'. Dick Hebdige has argued that, throughout the twentieth century, American influence on British popular culture has largely been regarded as a threat to indigenous forms of hegemony and, as such, something which conservative critics have universally deplored and resisted.[13] This has not been true of Blackpool where the discourse of modernity came to assume an increasingly Americanised form, working with the town's previous image rather than against it, resulting in the construction of the town as being in advance of the rest of Britain in anticipating, implementing ahead of its time, America as the very image of the modern. A little America in Lancashire: it was in the terms of this newer and brasher northern populism that the image of Blackpool was re-formed, although less in its official versions of itself than in the commercially provided forms of popular entertainment predominating in the streets.

In order to appreciate the broader cultural significance of these transformations in the forms of Blackpool's self-presentation, however, it is necessary to shift our attention away from Blackpool and toward the characteristics which most specifically distinguished Lancashire working-class culture in the late-nineteenth and early twentieth centuries.

A 'regional popular'

In his *Work, Society and Politics*, a study of the culture of the work-place in the Lancashire factory system, Patrick Joyce takes issue with accounts which construe the stability of late nineteenth-century Britain as the result of the 'ideological capture' of a labour aristocracy effected by the promulgation of a bourgeois ethic of respectability. In the case of Lancashire, he argues, such approaches fail to account for the degree to which the vast mass of the proletariat, and not just the upper strata of skilled operatives, was accommodated to the status quo. Moreover, he suggests, they tend to present a one-sided, over-intellectualised picture of the processes whereby hegemony is fought for, won and lost. The labour aristocracy thesis, in the stress it places on the nexus of ideas defined by the terms 'respectability' and 'self-improvement', is a version of what Joyce calls 'ideological hegemony' in which analysis focuses on the degree to which a common stock of ideas is able to mediate the relations between ruling and subordinate classes. Against this view, he argues that the hegemony of the owning classes in mid- to late-nineteenth-century Lancashire was achieved by more distinctively social and cultural means, chiefly attributable to the way the system of factory paternalism — and the dense web of social and cultural relations which radiated out from the factory — permeated the very tissue of daily life for the Lancashire working classes. Their accommodation to the factory system and, through that, to the Lancashire bourgeoisie, he writes, 'occurred not so much at the level of ideas and values, but at the centre of people's daily concerns, in terms of their sense of personal and communal identity'.[14]

Joyce also takes issue with the view, mainly associated with the work of Perry Anderson, that the industrial bourgeoisie failed to become a genuinely hegemonic class in the nineteenth century, sacrificing political power and its ambition to exert intellectual and moral authority over society as a whole to the political and intellectual representatives of the landed classes for the sake of consolidating its economic power.[15] To the contrary, Joyce argues, by the mid-century the Lancashire industrial bourgeoisie had every cause for self-satisfaction and little reason to consider itself merely a poor relation to the élites prevailing at the national level. It had consolidated the basis of its economic power in the factory system and, through the mechanisms of employer paternalism, had established a set of social and cultural relations which yoked working-class life, in all its dimensions, into a close orbit around and dependency on the factory. It wielded effective political power at the local and regional levels via its control over the machinery of local government, and played an increasingly prominent role in civic life, both corporately, through its funding of museums, parks, libraries and the like, and privately, by means of the wide range of cultural activities — sports, brass bands, day-trips to the seaside — supported by individual employers on a voluntary basis. The result, Joyce concludes, was a distictively regional form of hegemony which functioned, on all levels of social and cultural life, to check the political power of the central state apparatuses and to limit the purchase, within Lancashire, of national styles of political, moral and intellectual leadership. Not merely a regional 'exception to the rule', Joyce contends, but one which should induce a more qualified appraisal of the situation prevailing nationally:

> When the mentality of the industrial bourgeoisie in these years is correctly understood, there is cause for looking again at the national scene through the eyes of Marx, and seeing England as the most bourgeois of nations, the industrial bourgeoisie going from strength to strength and consolidating its economic power in political terms despite the aristocratic appearances of national government.[16]

The important point to stress here is that the regional hegemony of the Lancashire bourgeoisie was, to a considerable extent, directly dependent on its displacement of and opposition to the forms of hegemony which prevailed at the national level. It constituted an identifiably distinct system of culturally organized class relationships which, in part, worked because it was constructed against the aristocratic appearances of national government. In gridding the opposition bourgeois–aristocratic onto the opposition North–South so that the latter, regionally organised perception of cultural differences overrode class-based perceptions of cultural differences, it grouped 'the people of the North' into a putatively undifferentiated unity against those of the South.

The history of the forms and organisation of pleasure at Blackpool, and above all of its ideological articulation, lends some degree of support to this contention. The discourse of modernity, varying in form but always the articulating centre of Blackpool's constructed self-image, was most effectively condensed not as an abstracted set of ideas — although it was active in this form, too — but in the sedimented forms of the town's architecture and its pleasures, made concrete, as Gramsci insisted an enduring hegemony must be, at the level of the mundane and the particular, a set of lived ideological relations which the visitor inescapably entered into and breathed in with the ozone. Moreover, at least until recently, it was a discourse which possessed a distinctively regional edge, connected, historically, to the system of employer hegemony Joyce describes by a multitude of strands. It is worth recalling that the typical context in which the northern working classes visited Blackpool was not as individuals or families but as members of work-based communities — moving there in whole streets and towns during wakes weeks, or visiting for a day on the occasion of annual outings which were frequently factory-based and organised and paid for by employers. (Joyce records that the Preston firm of Horrockses and Miller sent 1,570 members of its work-force to Blackpool as early as 1850). To visit Blackpool, in this context, meant to encounter a discourse that had slipped sideways, uncoupled from its usual association with work and harnessed to the mechanisms and machinery of pleasure. Furthermore, it meant to encounter a discourse that had been, to a degree, delocalised, shorn of its associations with a particular town, a particular industry or a particular employer and given a regional and, by the end of the nineteenth century, a popular voice and presence in contrast to the sombre pretentiousness of, say, Manchester and Liverpool city centres.

Hugh Cunningham has argued that, by the end of the nineteenth century, the people's culture, compared with the hey-day of Chartism, had been massively depoliticized, bolted back into a safely residual niche within the national culture.[17] The history of popular entertainments in Blackpool, whilst exemplifying this tendency, also suggests that it is mistaken to regard the struggle in which ruling groups engage to win the hearts and minds of the people as a unitary one, without contradictions, enunciated exclusively at the national level. The struggle for the popular in Blackpool formed part of a specifically regionally based system of cultural and intellectual leadership constructed in a degree of opposition to that prevailing at the national level. The blended combination of the discourse of modernity and northern populism which, toward the end of the nineteenth century, came to characterise the forms of 'hailing' predominating in Blackpool's popular entertainments worked to dismantle traditional forms of popular recreation more directly linked to and emerging from the popular classes and to substitute in their place commercially provided forms of popular entertainment in which regionally popular traditions and values, particularly those of northern chauvinism, whilst surviving, were also articulated to the cultural claims and pretensions of northern industrial capitalists. In effect, Blackpool and all that it was made to stand for within the regional culture, compacted 'the people of the North' into a unity constructed in an opposition to the metropolitan élites. In this respect, it constituted the site for the operation of a putatively hegemonic discourse — admittedly limited in its reach — enunciated at a regional level, a 'regional-popular' organised in a relationship of partial opposition to or partial collusion with the national-popular. This is emphatically not to suggest that this contradiction was the site, even remotely, of a significant cultural or ideological 'rupture'. But it is to suggest that regionally specific inflections of the organisation of cultural and ideological class relationships will repay closer attention.

Nor is this to suggest that the discourse of modernity has been the only one in evidence at Blackpool — of which more later — or that it has been unitary in its functioning and effects. To the contrary, it has been profoundly multi-accentual, capable of being inflected in different directions and of articulating different values at different points in time and for different publics. Initially a complement to the aura of respectability which characterised the early development of the resort, the town's motto of progress has consistently retained its responsible, improving, rational connotations. This has been particularly true of the official images of the town put into circulation by the corporation, images which, at times, have assumed positively visionary proportions. One of the clearest examples of this is provided by the 1924 Town Guide in which the discourse of modernity is articulated to a rhetoric of planning to conjure up an image of Blackpool as a future arcadia to be produced by enlightened rulers:

> Blackpools' pioneers, though they were possessed of the virile spirit of 'Progress', which has become the Borough's official motto and very real watchword, did not know the ultimate size of the great city of health and happiness they were well and truly laying. The result was that up to a few years ago Blackpool was practically parkless and singularly devoid of trees, greenery and flowers . . . Blackpool's modern rulers have a vision which

they mean to realize. It is that of a vast, beautiful and balanced Borough stretching at least from the borders of Fleetwood to those of Lytham, with parks and trees and broad, airy thoroughfares everywhere, and it is by no means impossible that the whole Fylde coast-line from the Wyre to the Ribble will become one vast health resort under unified government.[18]

However, in its more characteristic forms, as enunciated at street level in the claims and practices of the major entertainments industries operating in the town, the discourse of modernity, at least since the beginning of the twentieth century, has had a more abrasive, more populist edge, undercutting the more outlandish pretensions of the town's civic leaders. It has also, in more recent years, bent that rhetoric back on itself, disconnecting its specifically regional associations, appealing above the heads of the Lancashire bourgeoisie to a broader, more updated vision of progress in its anticipatory Americanisation of pleasure. This has been particularly true of the post-war period. With the decline of the cotton industry, the demise of the factory system and the virtual disappearance of the whole set of social and communal relations associated with it, the themes of modernity and progress — still massively in evidence — have split in their functioning. On the one hand, they have assumed an increasingly self-referential character. In this respect, Blackpool, these days, represents nothing so much as itself — an isolated pool of modernity surrounded by a ravaged industrial hinterland which has singularly failed to keep up with the times. On the other hand, Blackpool increasingly seeks to associate itself with the modernity of an abstracted international capitalism shorn of any specifically regional associations. The role of Lancashire and of Lancashire culture in mediating between and connecting the two, making Blackpool, as representative of Lancashire, by the same token the representative of a modernising capitalism is, these days, and for obvious reasons, conspicuously absent.

Blackpool's bid for modernity, in other words, is nowadays constructed in spite of, rather than because of, its being in Lancashire. Its 'modern' past, increasingly appearing as the product of an antiquated history, constitutes, in this respect, something of a problem in that the town is littered with the archaic relics of earlier, once advanced but now outmoded technologies (the Tower). The pressures which this creates are keenly felt. It is clear from recent Town Guides that, even in its official forms, Blackpool is once again trying to update its image. In an attempt to secure a larger share of the middle-class holiday market, the resort now increasingly represents itself as a cosmopolitan leisure centre — the Las Vegas of the North — whilst simultaneously distancing itself from its traditional Lancastrian and working-class associations. Even the traditional aspects of a Blackpool holiday — such as a stroll along the piers — have been updated (they all have 'super-modern frontages'). At Blackpool, everything is new no matter how old it is.

Text and performance

The functioning of this discourse of modernity, however, can only be properly understood when placed in the context of the opposing discourses it has worked against and helped to dismantle. The vaunting claims through which it has sought to undermine and rival the cultural centripetalism of the metropolis have constituted merely one of the discourse's cutting edges in this respect. It has also faced in the other direction, operating against the mutated echoes of the carnivalesque, a transgressive discourse embodied in the practices of the popular classes and their preferred entertainments which, from the mid-nineteenth century, has constituted the unofficial Blackpool, the underbelly beneath its constructed image of progress, respectability and modernity.

The spirit of carnival, of course, has never been as strong in Britain as in Europe, particularly France where, as Mikhail Bakhtin has shown, the tradition of popular carnival fuelled the development of Renaissance humanism and where, as Le Roy Ladurie has demonstrated, carnival celebrations could, at times, spill over into directly political forms of social protest.[19] None the less, the carnival tradition in Britain was never entirely vanquished by the 'triumph of Lent'. Christopher Hill has detailed the respects in which the subversive and transgressive aspects of carnival informed the messianic vision of a wide range of radical sects during the English Revolution.[20] Although shorn of any connection with developed political philosophies, elements of the carnivalesque continued to inform the popular festivals which periodically interrupted the annual cycle of agricultural labour in the eighteenth century. In a recent discussion, Douglas Reid has argued that many of the elements of carnival — excessive eating and drinking, the suspension of sexual prohibitions, the subversion and transgression of normal rules of behaviour, the symbolic inversion of dominant ideological values — remained central aspects of the wakes celebrations of early nineteenth-century workers:

> 'goose-riding', horse-racing, foot-racing in *déshabillé*, all through the main streets of the town, bizarre competition and great feasting, were certainly reversals of everyday norms, even for the chief participants. To most of the crowd the extraordinary concentration of unfamiliar amusements and familiar acitivities taken to excess must have constituted wakes as 'rituals of disorder'.[21]

This is not to suggest that, in itself, the carnival tradition should be construed as progressive or that rituals of transgression should be counted as oppositional in their own right. Nor did Bakhtin ever advance such a view, although this is often how his work has been appropriated. What Bakhtin celebrated in his study of Rabelais was not the carnival tradition as such but the direction in which that tradition was made to point, the

147

specific way in which its cultural and ideological meaning was inflected, in being articulated to the progressive currents of Renaissance humanism.[22] It was the *fusion* of these two traditions and the new meanings which accrued to the carnivalesque as a consequence, rather than the mere brute fact of carnival, that Bakhtin regarded as valuable. Whereas most theorists of carnival stress only its negative aspects, construing it as merely a compendium of transgressive rituals, Bakhtin placed a quite exceptional emphasis on its positive aspects. The value of excess associated with carnival eating, drinking and sexuality, he argued, formed part of an image of the people as a boundless, unstoppable material force, a vast self-regenerating and undifferentiated body surmounting all obstacles placed in its path. For Bakhtin, the unique significance of the Renaissance consisted in the respects in which the transgressive aspects of carnival were connected to Renaissance criticisms of medieval ideology whilst its positive aspects were simultaneously connected to progressive humanist currents of thought, the body of the people serving as the very image of and prototype for a secular and humanist philosophy of history as a continuously unfolding process of human self-creation. In Rabelais, he argues, 'the destruction of the old picture of the world and the positive construction of a new picture are indissolubly interwoven with each other'.[23]

In sum, Bakhtin's concern was not with carnival but with the *discursive rearticulation* of elements of the carnivalesque in the culture and ideology of the Renaissance. It is thus the *transformative* aspects of Rabelais' work that he constantly stressed: 'Rabelais by no means advocated crude gluttony and drunkenness. But he does affirm the lofty importance of eating and drinking in human life, and strives to justify them ideologically, to make them respectable, to erect a culture for them.'[24] In other contexts, deprived of these specific ideological and cultural articulations, he judged the various elements of the carnivalesque quite censoriously. It is thus that he contrasted the way Rabelais connects the stress placed within carnival on material and bodily processes to a humanist view of the body as a harmonious combination of corporeal and mental functions, to be developed through physical and intellectual exercise, to 'the licentiousness and coarseness of medieval practice'.[25] Similarly, he spoke of the subsequent degeneration of carnival language and its functioning: 'To this very day, the unofficial (male) side of speech reflects a Rabelaisian degree of indecency in it, of words concerning drunkenness and defecation and so forth, but all this is by now clichéd and no longer creative.'[26]

There can be no question, then, of any uncritical celebration of carnival as if the practices which comprised it somehow spoke their own meaning, voicing the authentic spirit of the people independently of the prevailing social and cultural relationships in which they are inscribed. Carnival may be, as Terry Eagleton has suggested, no more than a 'popular blow-off'.[27] It may also be, as Reid makes clear in his discussion of wakes celebrations, connected with customs that are wantonly cruel and sexist. For all that, the

148

residue of the carnivalesque which survived in the nineteenth-century wakes and, later, urban fairs constituted a discourse which refused to be placed, which rejected the subalterned niche preserved for the working classes within bourgeois culture and which effected, however inarticulately and temporarily, a periodic overthrowing, a *bouleversement* of the bourgeois values of 'sobriety, orderliness, "rationality" and the pursuit of progress'.[28] It is for this reason, Reid suggests, that in the late eighteenth and early nineteenth centuries, local élites withdrew their support and patronage from wakes celebrations and, with the backing of the upper strata of skilled artisans, began to hem them in with restrictions. Urban fairs were similarly persecuted in the mid-century only, as Hugh Cunningham observes, to be actively promoted by both central government and local authorities toward the end of the century, presented as an aid rather than a threat to public order. Cunningham advances three reasons for this change. First, the values and norms of showmen changed as they became 'respectable and wealthy entrepeneurs of leisure, patronized by Royalty'.[29] Second, the mechanisation of fairs meant that fairground entertainments were increasingly brought into line with the values of industrial civilization, a testimony to the virtues of progress. Third, and in good part as a consequence of these changes, the habits of fairgoers changed; by the end of the century, he argues, 'fairgoing had become a relatively routine ingredient in an accepted world of leisure' as 'fairs became tolerated, safe, and in due course a subject for nostalgia and revival'.[30]

The struggles surrounding the history of popular recreation in Blackpool rehearsed these more general developments, giving them a peculiarly condensed expression owing to the exceptional concentration of popular entertainments within the town. At the same time, the struggles were more protracted as a consequence of the longer-term and more permanent sites that, first, the beach and, later, the promenade afforded elements of the carnivalesque placed under pressure in the inland towns. As late as the 1930s, Tom Harrison pointed to the general pervasiveness of carnival elements in Blackpool.[31] Indeed, remnants of the carnivalesque can still be found in Blackpool, although they are now exceedingly marginalised, located only within the interstices of the town's pleasure economy — in the back-street shops selling masks, willy-warmers and a whole range of incredible phallic objects — or, in a massively incorporated form, in the multiple references to the world of carnival at the Pleasure Beach, references which keep alive the discourse of carnival only in an always-already recuperated, Disneyfied form.[32] And, as elsewhere, the carnivalesque was opposed and dismantled by a combination of tactics — initially, by means of attempted legal regulation and prohibition and, subsequently, by means of breaking it up into its constituent elements and culturally re-forming those elements, modifying their meaning, by drawing them into the orbit of, and making them complicit with, the discourse of modernity.

The history of the Pleasure Beach illustrates both these processes. Located at the southern edge of the town, the Pleasure Beach occupies what used to be, in the mid-nineteenth century, a gipsy encampment where both resident families and itinerant entertainers offered a variety of traditional entertainments — astrology, fortune-telling, palmistry, phrenology and so on. Mechanical rides were first developed on this site — originally just a vast area of sand stretching back from and continuous with the beach — in the late 1880s. During the same period, the site was also occupied by exhibitions derived from the wakes fairs — peep-shows, fat ladies and the like. Whereas initially the corporation had opposed these developments, it lent its support to two entrepeneurs who, in 1895, bought the tract of land on which these entertainments were located with the express purpose of developing it into an integrated open-air pleasure complex on the model of American amusement parks. At this time, the site was occupied by a jumble of independently owned and operated mechanical rides existing side-by-side with gipsy amusements and side-shows characteristic of the urban fairs of the period. Its transformation into the Pleasure Beach — a huge, walled-in entertainments complex, run as a single entity by a private company still in the hands of the family of one of its co-founders — was accomplished by a variety of strategies, all of which were well in place by the 1930s. Taken together, these resulted in a modernising streamlining of pleasure which early achieved a degree of unity unobtainable elsewhere in Blackpool where the fragmented structure of land ownership permitted — and, to a degree, still permits — the coexistence of different regimes of pleasure.

First, by means of legal powers secured from the corporation, gipsies were prohibited from operating on the site and, by 1910, were finally evicted. This not only made the Pleasure Beach more respectable; it dislodged from the site the traditional Romany entertainments which jarred with the model of pleasure embodied in the importation of increasingly sophisticated mechanical and theme rides from Amercian amusement parks. This has been perhaps the most distinctive of the Pleasure Beach's techniques of modernisation. Beginning with the introduction of dodgems in 1910 — billed as 'The first in Europe direct from America' — the Pleasure Beach has periodically updated itself by importing a series of ride innovations from America, constantly weaving these into its rhetoric of self-representation as offering the biggest, the best, the only one of its kind, the unique, the latest, the most up-to-the-minute range of thrills, spills and popular entertainments. Related to this, independent side-show operators were transformed into concessionaries, allowed to operate on the site (in return for a portion of their take) only if they conformed with the requirements of company policy. This entailed, very early on, the exclusion from the site of all elements of the grotesque and the modernisation of such traditional side-show entertainments as remained. The net result of these tendencies is a peculiar contradiction. The forms of machinery in use at the Pleasure Beach today operate to suspend the normal restraints which hem in and limit the body, but all of this takes place within a system of signs operative in the themes of the rides, their architectural design and the predominant forms of hailing in use which is solidly compacted with an unabashed ideology of progress. The body may be whirled upside down, hurled this way and that by the machinery of the rides, but, in the coding of these pleasures for consumption, the dominant symbolic order remains unwaveringly the right way up.

However, to consider only the discourses embodied in the sedimented forms of the town's major popular entertainments would give a misleadingly one-sided impression of the cultural 'feel' of Blackpool. This is not merely to suggest that there are elements which contradict or differ from the dominant ideological coding of pleasure in the town such as I have described it, although this is true. Paradoxically, contemporary Blackpool is also the site for the enunciation of a simply massive discourse of nostalgia, of a longing for selectively preserved and romanticised pasts, although I would argue that this discourse is ultimately contained within the discourse of modernity in the form of the claims the town makes to be the only holiday resort sufficiently forward-looking to keep the remnants of its past — the Tower and the piers, for example — in good working order. Rather more to the point is the consideration that if, as I have argued, the ideological coding of pleasure at Blackpool has certain textual properties, then, just as is the case with the relations between any text and its readers, so the 'text of pleasure' prevailing at Blackpool does not itself automatically produce or guarantee the way it will be responded to or negotiated by the pleasure-seeker. This is to take issue somewhat with Louis Marin's analysis of Disneyland; or, at least, it is to suggest that it is a model which should not be uncritically extended elsewhere. According to Marin, the system of ideas and values given concrete form in the thematics of Disneyland constitute a 'representation realised in geographical space of the imaginary relationship which the dominant groups of American society maintain with their real conditions of existence or, more precisely, with the real history of the United States and with the space outside of its borders'.[33]

He further contends that the way the geographical space of Disneyland is organised — its division into various sections (Adventureland, Frontierland, Fantasyland, Tomorrowland, Mainstreet USA) and the ordering of the relations between them — constitute a narrative and one, moreover, which entirely constrains the narrative performance (the tour) of the visitor. In order to construct his or her tour into a narrative — a sequence of events with meaning — the visitor is forced to rely on the representations of America and its imaginary history which totally pervade the park as an entirely self-enclosed environment.

In other words, Disneyland is an example of a *langue* reduced to a univocal code, without *parole*, even though its visitors have the feeling of living a personal and unique adventure on their tour. And since this *langue* is a stereotyped fantasy, the visitor is caught in it, without any opportunity to escape.[34]

Blackpool, even the Pleasure Beach, the most consummate expression of its discourse of modernity, differs from this in at least two respects. First, the town lacks a singular narrative organisation. Unlike Disneyland, it was not constructed in accordance with a preconceived plan but has rather been progressively constructed and selectively reconstructed, in partial and piecemeal fashion, thereby making for a series of discourse clashes and different narrative possibilities at any given point in time. Second, the visitor to Blackpool is not always already narrativised in the manner of the visitor to Disneyland, a subject already placed within Disney ideology, before he or she gets there, by the output of the Disney film industry. In effect, to visit Disneyland is to complete a process of narrativisation inaugurated elsewhere. No such broader narrative system bears on the visitor to Blackpool. Instead, the visitor is able to deploy a wide range of cultural resources in constructing his or her pleasure-route through the, in any case, more uneven and contradictory 'text of pleasure' prevailing in the town. And among these resources are elements of the carnivalesque. For Bakhtin, it is important to recall, carnival was, above all, a practice of the people and its theatre was the street. To the degree that it still exists in Blackpool, the carnivalesque takes this form — the never-ending excess of eating and drinking, the disruption of conventional temporal rhythms, the transgression of normal rules of dress and behaviour by the wearing of funny hats and the like. In themselves, of course, such practices are of no special value or political significance. But they point to a residue, a utopian excess which spills over the ability of the discourse of modernity to frame and contain, interpret and make intelligible the visitor's experience, a residue which could be made to point in fruitful directions.

Tom Harrison recorded that imitation bosses once figured prominently as targets at the Pleasure Beach and noted that there used to be a dummy policeman in a stationary car on the dodgems which had to be removed as the figure became damaged too quickly and too repeatedly. In 1981, street sellers were offering dartboards printed over with a full-face picture of Margaret Thatcher. A couple of years previously, giant Charles ears were the feature of the season. Not much to go on, but pointers as to the ways in which the same set of pleasures might, in being ideologically recoded, give rise to different meanings with different political effects. At least, such an orientation to popular entertainments, seeking to reorder their cultural and ideological articulations and, thereby, to hook popular practices into an association with critical or progressive values is preferable to one which opposes such practices in the name of some higher, abstracted ideal.

Notes

1. Official Town Guide, 1897, p. 33 (I am indebted to Grahame Thompson of the Open University for making copies of Blackpool Town Guides available to me and for pointing out their considerable value and interest).

2. Official Town Guide, 1924, p. 34.

3. Southern visitors are, and always have been, a statistical rarity at Blackpool. An English Tourist Board survey conducted in 1972 revealed that Blackpool relied overwhelmingly on the northern counties, Scotland and, to a lesser extent, the Midlands for its business.

4. See H. Marcuse, *One Dimensional Man: The Ideology of Industrial Society*, Sphere Books, London, 1968.

5. Many of the perspectives in this section are derived from B.Turner and S. Palmer, *The Blackpool Story*, Palmer and Turner, Clevelys, 1981. Unattributed quotations are also taken from this source.

6. J.K. Walton, *The Blackpool Landlady: a social history*, Manchester University Press, 1978, pp. 137–8.

7. Wakes holidays were derived from rush-bearing festivals, usually held in the summer to celebrate the anniversary of the dedication of a local church. As such, their dates were variable — August in Middleton, June in Oldham. See J.K. Walton and R. Poole, 'The Lancashire Wakes in the Nineteenth Century' in R.D. Storch (ed.), *Popular Culture and Custom in Nineteenth Century England*, Croom Helm, London, 1982.

8. Walton and Poole argue that the decline of traditional wakes celebrations has been exaggerated, but do not dispute that this was the general tendency.

9. For a useful survey of the mid-century attacks on fairs, see H. Cunningham, 'The Metropolitan Fairs: A Case-Study in the Social Control of Leisure', in A.P. Donajgrodzki (ed.), *Social Control in Nineteenth Century Britain*, Croom Helm, London, 1977.

10. J.K. Walton has convincingly argued that many of Blackpool's peculiar characteristics can be attributed to the extremely fragmented structure of land ownership which prevailed in the town from towards the end of the eighteenth century. This enabled small tradesmen to establish themselves in the town in a way that was not possible in Southport, for example, where a much more highly concentrated structure of land ownership facilitated the exclusion of commercial activities which might detract from the 'respectable' tone of the town; see J.K. Walton, 'Residential Amenity, Respectable Morality and the Rise of the Entertainment Industry: The Case of Blackpool, 1860–1914', *Literature and History*, vol. 1, 1975.

11. I am indebted to John Golby of the Open University for these figures.

12. H.J. Perkin, 'The "Social Tone" of Victorian Seaside Resorts in the North-West', *Northern History*, vol. XI, 1975–6.

13. See D. Hebdige, 'Towards a Cartography of Taste, 1935–1962', *Block*, no. 4, 1981.

14. P. Joyce, *Work, Society and Politics, The Culture of the Factory in later Victorian England*, Rutgers University Press, New Jersey, 1980, p. xv.

15. See P. Anderson, 'Origins of the Present Crisis', *New Left Review*, no. 23, 1964.

16. P. Joyce, *Work, Society and Politics*, p. 3.

17. See H. Cunningham, 'Class and Leisure in Mid-Victorian England' in B. Waites,

T. Bennett and G. Martin (eds), *Popular Culture: Past and Present*, Croom Helm, London, 1982.

18. Official Town guide, 1924, p. 42.

19. See M. M. Bakhtin, *Rabelais and His World*, MIT Press, Cambridge, Mass. 1968; and E. Le Roy Ladurie, *Carnival in Romans*, George Brazillier, New York, 1979.

20. See C. Hill, *The World Turned Upside Down: Radical Ideas During the English Revolution*, Penguin, Harmondsworth, 1975.

21. D.A. Reid 'Interpreting the Festival Calender: Wakes and Fairs as Carnivals', in R.D. Storch (ed.) *Popular Culture and Custom*, p. 129.

22. For a fuller discussion of this aspect of Bakhtin's work, see T. Bennett, *Formalism and Marxism*, Methuen, London, 1979, pp. 82–92.

23. M.M. Bakhtin, *The Dialogic Imagination*, University of Texas Press, Austin and London, 1981, p. 169.

24. Ibid., p. 185.

25. Ibid., p. 171.

26. Ibid., p. 238.

27. T. Eagleton, *Walter Benjamin, or Towards a Revolutionary Criticism*, New Left Books, London, 1981, p. 148.

28. D.A. Reid, 'Interpreting the Festival Calendar', p. 125.

29. H. Cunningham, 'Class and Leisure', p. 163.

30. Ibid., p. 164.

31. T. Harrison, 'The fifty-second week: Impressions of Blackpool', *The Geographical Magazine*, April, 1938.

32. I have discussed this aspect of the Pleasure Beach elsewhere. See T. Bennett, 'A thousand and one troubles: Blackpool Pleasure Beach' in *Formations of Pleasure*, Routledge and Kegan Paul, 1983.

33. L. Marin, 'Disneyland: A Degenerate Utopia', *Glyph* I, p. 54.

34. Ibid., p. 59.

Section three

Form and ideology in popular culture

Introduction

'. . . we consider the objects solely in relation to their meaning, without
bringing in, at least not prematurely, at least not before the system be recon-
stituted as far as possible, the other determinants (psychological, sociological
or physical) of these objects, we must certainly not deny these other determinants, which each depend upon another relevancy, but we must treat
them also in semiological terms, that situate their place and function in the
system of meaning . . . The principle of relevancy obviously requires of the
analyst a situation of 'immanence', we observe the given system from
within.

Roland Barthes[1]

The clear merit of the structuralist strategies of textual analysis on which
Barthes dwells, lay in the extent to which structuralists sought to avoid
reductionist treatments of a whole range of texts, consciously avoiding
treating the texts of popular culture, for example, as the epiphenomenal
reflections of a real world, either in common-sense terms or in terms of the
economic base, the conditions and relations of production in Marxist
theories. Instead, structuralist studies granted to such texts a real
autonomy and directed attention at the systems of meaning through which
they worked. At the same time, there were undoubtedly problems with the
structuralist concern with the 'text in itself', a theoretical impetus which
carried with it a tendency to produce ahistorical and formalist readings of
texts, ignoring, for example, the moments or occasions of both production
and consumption of texts and laying down the ideological 'meaning' of
such texts on the basis of a single reading, carried out by the structuralist.
In some structuralist accounts the popular text and its ideological meaning
were conceived of as 'fixed', closed; the subjectivity of its reader or viewer
moulded by the internal mechanisms of the text; hence the advocacy of
avante garde forms by structuralists who perceived such texts as inherently
more open.

All four of the following essays attempt to come to terms with the heritage
of structuralism in the analysis of texts, but also to move the terms of the
debates around textual analysis to a rather different terrain. Colin
Mercer's account of the field of entertainment attempts to review and displace the controversies surrounding the concept of realism. Rather

156

than focusing upon the central tenets of the realism debate in which representation is judged by epistemological criteria, truth or ideological effect this article attempts to consider the conditions of legibility and of effectivity of popular forms of entertainment. In rethinking Brecht's part in the realism debate, Mercer suggests that Brecht's 'realist' strategies require attention less for their 'realism', than for the way in which they undercut and revealed other 'realisms' as a series of techniques and technologies. Crucially, Mercer goes on to identify how popular entertainment addresses and forms entities such as 'the people' and 'the nation' indicating how vitally important the social organisation and technologies of entertainment and 'occasions of reading' are. The field of technologies through which popular entertainment works cannot according to Mercer be reduced to questions of formal textual analysis but has to be understood in terms of the way in which popular entertainments at particular moments operate rhetorically to invest individuals, peoples, communities and nations in complex relationships.

Richard Middleton's essay takes up the question of the pleasures of popular music in a somewhat neglected area, that of musical syntax, examining the role of repetition in the dialectics of musical pleasure. Mass-culture theorists such as Adorno suggest that repetition or standardisation is an effect of the commercial music industry under capitalism and functions in terms of social control. Middleton, however, takes issue with this and with its common-sense variant, arguing that different types of repetition have characterised different forms of popular music and pointing to some historical interactions between different types. Moreover, Middleton takes his analysis much further in considering the way in which musical repetition has its basis in the aural relationship of child and mother, marked by highly repetitive sounds, and pre-dating the formation of the subject in language. Using the work of Freud and Barthes, Middleton radically rethinks the operation of repetition in popular music, to indicate how it can act ideologically both in the region of social control and in terms of producing broader and more open psychological effects.

The last two articles focus on specific textual practices. The second of these, Alan Clarke's account of the changes within the television police series in Britain from the 1950s to the 1970s, provides both an overview of the genre and a more detailed account of specific shifts in the genre in relation to the texts of *Dixon of Dock Green* and *The Sweeney*. Just as importantly, Clarke is also concerned to examine the political and ideological significance of these shifts in the crime series. Clarke identifies the influence of the American crime series and points to the movement away from the television police acting within a well-established public community, being involved in a happy family life and operating towards the criminal world with a social conscience, which characterised Dixon and the more cynical 'This is not the boy scouts, you know' attitude of Regan, the hero of *The Sweeney*. Clarke locates the differences between Dixon and Regan and the organisation of the crime series in the shifting ideological configurations of the period in which the government under Heath increasingly moved to treat a wide range of issues from student protest to industrial action under the banner of 'law and order'. Effectively eschewing the view that the television crime series simply reflected changes in contemporary police practice, Clarke points to the way in which the television crime series both was implicated in a more general debate about 'law and order' and worked through quite specific generic conventions.

Finally, Janet Woollacott's essay examines a television genre which was popular at the same time as the crime series, that of situation comedy. Here, the concern is both to establish the generic specificity of situation comedies, their use of particular comic and narrative strategies, for example, and to consider some of the more general theoretical and political questions raised by the study of popular genres. In particular the article stresses the complexity of the relationships between popular genres of fiction and other ideologies, arguing that the notion of hegemony provides no simple answers but a key to understanding the complex and shifting relationships between a dominating articulating principle such as that of 'law and order' in the 1970s in Britain and the fictional field.

Notes

1.   R. Barthes, *Elements of Semiology*, Jonathan Cape, London, 1967, p. 95.

8

Richard Middleton

In the groove, or blowing your mind? The pleasures of musical repetition[1]

In recent years the question of the pleasure of popular music has been placed firmly on the agenda for discussion. Partly this has been the result of a spillover from work on the pleasures of literary and film texts; partly it was the result of a realisation that existing sociological, sub-cultural and musicological studies of popular music had neglected this vital area: the area, after all, which would appear to do most to legitimate the existence of the music from the listener's point of view. The important early studies are Frith and McRobbie[2] and Laing and Taylor.[3] Both devote most of their attention to the *performer*: singing styles, singers' images, performance gestures, etc., the former through a broadly sociological account of rock music's part in the expression and organisation of sexual roles, the latter through a basically structuralist approach to the ways in which subject-positions are constructed within the codes of rock singing. What is largely lacking so far is any sustained examination of the pleasures produced by musical syntaxes themselves.

Laing and Taylor introduce into their argument Roland Barthes' conception of the 'grain of the voice'. Barthes contrasts the physical materiality of singing (its 'grain') with its communicative power and relates this to his distinction between *jouissance* and *plaisir* as types of pleasure. He too, then, is most interested in the voice — though he carefully points out that the same approach can be applied to instrumental playing.[4] Now, I am certainly not arguing here for any ontological distinction between 'performance' and 'text': musical syntaxes are not formal abstractions but structures of relationships set up by and in physical bodies; as Henri Lefèbvre puts it, 'musicality communicates corporeality. It renders the body into social practice . . . deploying their resources, music binds bodies together (socialises them)'.[5] If, for *analytical* reasons, this essay puts the 'grain' of performance on one side in order to focus on the underlying structures of musical syntax, this is in the hope that subsequent work will put the two back together again.

The most widely applicable aspect of popular musical syntaxes — thus the most suitable for an initial study — is that of repetition; and this in turn bears closely, in all its manifestations, on questions of like and dislike, boredom and excitement, tension and relaxation: in short the dialectics of musical pleasure. Almost all popular songs, to a greater or lesser extent, fall under the power of repetition. Why is this, and what are the effects?

Repetition in popular music

'It's monotonous'; 'it's all the same'; 'it's predictable': such 'popular common-sense' reactions to popular music have probably filtered down from the discussions of mass culture theorists. From this point of view, repetition (within a song) can be assimilated to the same category as what Adorno termed standardisation (as between songs). Of course, the significance of the role played by such techniques in the operations of the music industry — their efficacy in helping to define and hold markets, to channel types of consumption, to preform response and to make listening easy — can hardly be denied; it is, however, equally difficult to reduce the function of repetition simply to an analysis of the 'political economy' of popular music production and its ideological effects. Despite Adorno's critical assault,[6] despite later twists to the theory by, for instance, Fredric Jameson,[7] who argues that rather than being a negative quality of mass culture, repetition is simply a fundamental characteristic of *all* cultural production under contemporary capitalism, the question of repetition refuses to go away. Why *do* listeners find interest and pleasure in hearing the same thing over again? To be able to answer this question, which has troubled not only mass-cultural theory but also traditional philosophical aesthetics, as well as more recent approaches such as psychoanalysis and information theory, would tell us more about the nature of popular music, and hence, *mutatis mutandis*, about music in general, than almost anything else.

Common-sense criticisms of the prevalence of repetition in popular music usually derive from a specific analytical error: a particular conventionalised proportion of repetition to non-repetition is naturalised (I say 'conventional' because, considering music world-wide, the extent to which repetition is characteristic of particular musical syntaxes varies enormously); most popular music is then said to transgress this norm. As already suggested, this view mostly trickles down from mass-culture theories such as Adorno's which sees repetition in popular music as a function of a specific mode of production and its associated social relations. But *all* music contains repetition — though of an enormous variety of types. I would like to see the extent and nature of repetition in a given music as produced by and located at the point where several sets of determinations intersect: the 'political economy' of production; the 'psychic economy' of individuals (the metaphor derives from Freud); the musico-technological media of production and reproduction (oral/written/electric); and the effects of music-historical traditions (the syntactic conventions of which have a certain inertia and a certain relative autonomy, overdetermining the socially and historically specific configurations resulting from the operations of the previous factors).

Adorno seems, as a matter of fact, to have had little to say about repetition *per se* in popular music; his comments on this subject come in his work on twentieth-century 'art' music, notably his study of Stravinsky,[8] which, interestingly, is psychoanalytically inflected. There are some problems with this 'psychoanalysis'. For example: it treats all 'returns of the repressed' as necessarily 'regressive' ('archaic impulses cannot be reconciled with civilization')[9]; it tends to discount the instinctual structure of individuals, its 'irreducible biological base', as Marcuse called it, in favour of an apparently totalising effect of the social conditions of mass culture; and, in a way familiar in psychoanalytic interpretations of art, it reads content straight across from psyche to artistic object, paying little regard to the specificities of signifying form, and their significance for the structure of the psyche itself. Adorno sees the 'infantilism' of early Stravinsky (*c.* 1911–18) as psychotic, and describes the prevalence of repetition as a symptom of catatonia. Commonplace dismissals of repetitive effects in pop music as 'childish', 'primitive' or 'hysterical' clearly have the same roots. But behind the vulgar self-preservation of the virtuously civilised lies something which we can hang on to: Adorno's recognition that repetition has to do with the operation of the primary processes of the psyche. This is something we must return to.

Adorno, of course, had very much in mind an attack on 'civilisation' as he understood it. Hence his attitude to what he regarded as the 'pseudo-primitivism' of Afro-American derived popular music forms. The importance of repetition in Afro-American musics hardly needs establishing: riffs, call-and-response structures and unchanging rhythmic patterns are everywhere. But before we can understand the significance of this fact, and of the *kind* of repetition involved, we need to locate repetition itself, as a syntactic variable, within an overall theory of musical syntax.

Repetition in musical syntax

Analytically, we can posit two (ideal) structural types: the *monad* (the circular, the 'mythic', the blank space — most nearly approached by silence or by a single, unchanging, unending sound); and the *infinite set*[10] (the linear, the 'narrative'; most nearly approached by pieces whose aim is that nothing be heard twice). One might argue — still on a strictly theoretical level — that whereas natural language, because of its denotative function, 'tends towards' an extreme of total differentiation, music, because of its self-reflexive character, 'tends towards' an extreme of total sameness. Such an argument would base itself on the observation that, considered as sets of coded conventions, musical syntaxes are marked by an unusual degree of predictability: indeed, music's basic materials, rhythm and pitch, are actually 'cut out' from the natural spectra by the workings of periodic repetition. At the (theoretical) ultimate, then, music reduces to infinite repetition. In reality, however, one would have to fix these two extremes not to particular signifying systems but to tendencies or dispositions within signifying practice as a whole — to which language and music, respectively, are abnormally prevalent. Thus, in practice, different musics and different language-systems are located at different points on the line between the extremes.[11] Roman Jakobson, whose distinction between the modes of *metaphor* (similarity, selection: the paradigmatic axis) and of *metonymy* (combination, contiguity: the syntagmatic axis) is somewhat analogous to my distinction, points out that prose and poetry may be contrasted precisely by their tendencies towards metonymy on the one hand, and metaphor (together with other manifestations of similarity, such as metre and rhyme) on the other.[12] The tendency of musical codes is like that of poetry *but more so*.

Nevertheless, within musical practice we can envisage a scale stretching between *monad* and *infinite set* on which actual syntaxes are positioned at a variety of points (see Figure 1). Some important sub-markers are shown here. Binary switching reduces the non-monadic to simple either/or choices (e.g., same or different, A or B); many syntactic moves are of this type. From this point of view, repetition represents a binary question which always receives the same answer (A, A, A . . .); clearly, as repetition of a single element proceeds, the question becomes weaker, and the music moves towards monadic plenitude. Digital selection extends binary switching somewhat, retaining, however, the principle of limited series containing restricted sets of discrete quantities (e.g., scale steps, durations, related to each other in simple arithmetical ways: one plus one plus two plus one, etc.). Analogue selection makes available infinite ranges of choices along continuous spectra (how much to repeat, how loud, how great a pitch or rhythmic inflection, etc.).[13]

Since music is a multiple parameter system (pitch, duration, timbre, etc.) and, almost always, a multiple layer system (melody, bass, accompaniment, riffs, rhythm section, backing vocals, call-and-response, etc.), particular syntaxes do not sit neatly at one particular point on the spectrum. Rather, different syntactic processes are mixed up together; moreover, in the mixing, they do not remain wholly themselves: they are articulated together, each mediating the other (thus, a binary switch chord-oscillation — say, a tonic-subdominant riff — can be 'worked into' a melody digitally organised as to pitch relationships (major scale, let us say), the whole being given a gradual (analogue-based) crescendo. Moreover, since music is a temporal system, different syntactic processes can operate simultaneously on different structural levels (thus, a digitally organised set of notes can, at the next level up, be subjected to repetition, forming a riff, and, at the next level, this whole riff-based section can be juxtaposed with different music, say, a 'middle eight', to form a binary switch).

Within a particular music, or individual song, the existence, role and nature of repetition is a major distinguishing tool for analysis, helping to indicate synchronically existing differences, in relation to other musics and songs, and also helping to mark out historical changes in musical styles. But to do the distinguishing is no easy matter. The significance of repetition is closely bound up with its role in the total syntactic structure, that is, with the nature of what is repeated, and with the relationship of the repetition to the other processes that are present (how dominant it is, its place in the texture, whether it is linked into the operation of another technique: thus, for example, a repeated unit can be worked into a relatively highly differentiated 'narrative' flow through the device of sequence).[14]

The variety of ways in which repetition can be used is potentially infinite. Again, however — and once more strictly on the level of theory — we can distinguish certain basic models. First of all, I would like to differentiate between what I shall call *musematic* repetition and *discursive* repetition. (I take the term 'museme' — by analogy to the linguists, 'morpheme', a 'minimal unit of expression' — from Tagg).[15] Musematic repetition is the repetition of short units; the most immediately familiar examples — riffs — are found in Afro-American musics and in rock. Discursive repetition is the repetition of longer units, at the level of the phrase (defined as a unit roughly equivalent to a verbal clause or short sentence, not too long to be apprehended 'in the present,'[16] the sentence or even the complete section.) The effects of the two types are usually very different, largely because the units differ widely in the amount of information and the amount of self-contained 'sense' they contain, and in their degree of involvement with other syntactic processes. Moreover, musematic repetition is far more likely to be prolonged and unvaried, discursive repetition to be mixed in with contrasting units of various types (as in the AABA structure of the classic Tin Pan Alley ballad form). The former therefore tends towards a one-levelled structural effect, the latter to a hierarchically ordered discourse. They may be tentatively characterised as 'epic-recursive' and 'narrative-lyric', respectively. Formulaic or repetitive recursive frameworks are often combined with a 'surface' displaying complex, minutely inflected (i.e. analogue-tending), often improvised variation; while the narrative-lyric model tends towards the 'developmental' type, most strikingly developed in the European 'art' tradition, in which the underlying form is a 'one-off' while the 'surface' is in many ways relatively crude and impoverished.

The basic models outlined here are often correlated with oral and literate modes of composition respectively; and to the extent that popular music production in the 'electric age' shares some characteristics with the methods of oral creation, these relationships might be pursued into the musical cultures of the highly developed societies. However, it would be better to see these modes of production not as crudely technologically

163

determined but as actively summoned into development and strongly mediated by the needs of distinct socio-economic configurations. For instance, the association of literate, particularly printed, musical compositions with the development of bourgeois society is too well established to need further comment. The principles of musematic repetition and recursive structures are certainly suited to the methods of oral composition (because of the limits of human memory and the usefulness of a 'given', one-levelled framework); similarly, discursive repetition and hierarchically organised structures can be more easily worked out on paper. But there are plenty of examples of discursive repetition in orally created music and of musematic repetition in written pieces.

Considered as social-historical categories, rather than technologically-determined norms, the two basic models proposed here can be related to those described by the musicologist János Maróthy. He distinguishes the (usually oral) 'collective variative' types of pre-capitalist societies (in which 'individualisation comes about through a continuous approach to the typical . . . a short time . . . [reaching] full expression through countless repetitions and variations') and the 'bourgeois solo song', appearing in the Middle Ages and reaching its maturity in the eighteenth and nineteenth centuries (with its single-point-of-view, hierarchical ordering of an overall, self-contained symmetry, longer units, and impoverished binary choices on the 'surface').[17] It is important to see that these two types are historically not *entirely* mutually exclusive — indeed, to some extent they interact to form a variety of sub-types. Even more significantly for us, the influence of 'collective variative' techniques has revived in the twentieth century, notably through the impact of Afro-American musics.

Repetition in Afro-American musics is most often musematic (riffs; call-and-response structures; short, unchanging rhythmic patterns). Even when one aspect evolves in a mildly 'developmental' way, such as the chord sequence of twelve-bar blues, derived from European hymn tunes, there is often a substratum of riffs and other repetitive devices, and in blues phrase structure turns out to be organised in binary parallelisms and antiphonies.[18] By contrast, European popular song forms (before Afro-American influence) mostly use discursive repetition, usually worked into hierarchical structures marked by a use of phrase-contrast and development, by a stress on symmetry (out-and-back, away–home patterns, complete with a sense of 'narrative closure'), and by an important role for harmonic progressions (which, as the chord changes pull the listener along, again contribute to 'narrativity'). In other words, in Afro-American genres, compared to traditional European song forms, the whole centre of the overall structural assumptions moves leftwards along the scale, away from the analogue/hierarchical and towards the binary/repetitive. The coincidence of the rising influence of these genres with the replacement of literate by oral-electronic composition methods may well be one factor in the way twentieth-century popular music has developed. In the next section I want to discuss some of the effects of the resulting typological contrast.

Some examples

Complete coverage of repetition practice in popular music is well beyond the scope of a short essay. What I want to do here is illustrate a few basic types, some interactions between them, and an overall historical change. I shall draw my examples from three sources: nineteenth-century British popular music; Tin Pan Alley song (*c*.1900–39); rhythm and blues, and rock music.

In nineteenth-century music hall song, repetition is usually discursive — at the level of the phrase. Quite often the repeated phrase is slightly altered for harmonic reasons. As a rule, indeed, varied repetition, when it occurs, does not play off a relationship between recursive framework and variative detail (as in much musematically organised music) so much as it approaches the technique of sequence (that is, it is provoked by a need to fit changing harmonies rather than an interest in variation itself), or the technique of 'phrase-*structure* repetition'. In the latter, the surface details change but there is a kind of 'parallelism' or 'analogical repetition' between phrases on the level of harmonic-rhythmic structure and basic melodic shape. Maróthy had identified this type of symmetrical parallelism, or repetition by analogy, as a prime characteristic of bourgeois song as a whole.[19] Perhaps the most typical repetition technique in music hall song is that of sequence — typical because it is at the same time repetitive and non-repetitive: the unit of repetition is *worked into* a larger unit of 'narrative' flow or lyrical symmetry. Even when shorter units — approaching musemes — are repeated in music hall song, they are almost always drawn out into a longer line through sequence. In bourgeois song in general, sequence is a way of holding on to at least some of the power of repetition while as it were, *cutting it down* to size, and *stitching it into* other structural processes. Sequence *composes* time (rather than marking time or obliterating it, as straight repetition, especially if musematic, seems to do); it makes us aware of rise and fall, a discursive hierarchy, and thus refers us to irreversible experiences.

The prevalence of sequence in this kind of song confirms a general tendency there to absorb repetition into more complex structures. It is a tendency which can be traced back easily to the bourgeois song styles of the eighteenth and nineteenth centuries; all the techniques mentioned above, for instance, can be found in such early nineteenth-century songs as Henry Bishop's 'Home Sweet Home' and 'The Mistletoe Bough', Joseph Knight's 'Rocked in the Cradle of the Deep' or Henry Russell's 'Woodman, Spare That Tree'. There too — as in the later music-hall repertory — one notices that repetition is confined to the melodic level: at the extreme, it strikes one as an icing on the cake, the cake itself being mixed from narrative-harmonic ingredients.

The influence of Afro-American music can already be heard in a few nineteenth-century popular songs, particularly in America; and with this influence came musematic repetition. When ragtime hit Tin Pan Alley, this influence became a flood. Musically, however, there was no clean break: the techniques of phrase-repetition, phrase-structure repetition and sequence remained important, and indeed Tin Pan Alley song, from 1900 to 1939, can, from the point of view of repetition practice, be seen as involved in a constant struggle between the two traditions.

Classic early examples of Tin Pan Alley incorporation of musematic repetition are Irving Berlin's 'Alexander's Ragtime Band' of 1911 and Lewis Muir's 'Waiting for the Robert E. Lee', written the following year. By the 'jazz age', the technique was endemic. However, musematic repetition was still generally worked in with older-established techniques — phrase-building and sequence. Often, musemes are treated sequentially in a traditional way. Sometimes they are coupled with longer units, which are sequentially repeated. The further we move from Tin Pan Alley towards theatre song, and from the 1920s into the 1930s (there are two relationships here, historically intertwined), the more musematic repetition tends to be worked into complex analogue-based structures. In the hands of the Broadway masters — George Gershwin, for example — quite complex fusions can result. At the same time as incorporating some musematic repetition, Tin Pan Alley songs retained the use of discursive techniques: indeed, the classic ballad form of the period (a 32-bar AABA) relies upon them for its overall structure. Moreover, repetition is still almost totally confined to melody — though the occasional song hints at the use of short harmonic 'cells' (a two-, three- or four-chord unit, treated as a museme and repeated).

Musematic techniques, as a primary structuring device, first broke through in a big way, in mass-audience popular music, in the work of the 1930s swing bands (in the form of riffs). Where exactly in music history this technique originated is difficult to say; but in the end it is less important to identify particular sources than to locate the technique in general everyday (oral) practice in black culture: this of course is what recordings, out of marketing and other considerations, have always under-represented. Thus black bands in the 1930s often made up 'head' arrangements based on simple riffs, for dancing; only afterwards, if successful, were they sometimes given lyrics and worked out 'properly'. However, musematic techniques, while undoubtedly suited to the oral composition methods common in rhythm and blues and rock, should not be simply correlated with 'folk spontaneity'. Elaborate studio-created pieces based on riffs are not uncommon (the Beach Boys would be a classic case here — for example, 'God Only Knows' and 'Good Vibrations'); and, after all, it is the new electro-mechanical media which have made possible the fade-out (the ultimate form of repetition, since it actually does fulfil itself in monadic silence).

Lionel Hampton's celebrated 'Flyin' Home' can serve as a classic example of riff technique (actually a *collection* of short melodic-rhythmic riffs, heard together and successively), on its way from swing to rhythm and blues. For examples of the technique's assimilation by jump and rhythm and blues bands in the 1940s, almost any of Louis Jordan's recordings are excellent sources — or, for instance, Roy Milton's 'Do The Hucklebuck'. In all these cases, the relationship between riff framework and variative detail (improvised solos, inflected instrumental playing) is important. From this point, riff techniques spread through almost all black popular music. Riffs can comprise more or less the whole piece; alternatively, they can be a framework underneath vocal and/or instrumental variative elaboration. They can be continuous, or worked into an antiphonal call-and-response (i.e. binary) pattern. They can be unchanging in pitch level, or be 'pitch-layered' (a better term than 'sequence' in this context) against an (often 12-bar blues) chord progression. They can be melodically memorable, or chiefly rhythmic in impact (a method leading to funk and disco styles). Always their effect, to a greater or lesser extent, is to level out the temporal flow, challenge any 'narrative' functionality attaching to chord patterns and verse sequences, and 'open up' the syntactic field for *rhythmic* elements (again, often short repeated patterns) to dominate (for instance, Bo Diddley's well-known 'shuffle' rhythm). The shorter and more insistently repeated the riffs, the more powerful these effects.

From rhythm and blues, these techniques permeated rock 'n' roll and from there spread widely within rock. Again, the variety of usage is considerable.[20] For instance, combinations of riffs can be worked into chord patterns, as often happens in, say, Rolling Stones songs. Or the riff(s) can be virtually the whole framework, with perhaps an important role for surface variative detail; a classic example is Led Zeppelin's 'Whole Lotta Love'. Some musicians combine musematic riff repetition with aspects of other repetition techniques (cf. the earlier Tin Pan Alley 'compromise'). In Bob Dylan's 'Masters of War', for example, a discursively constructed vocal — derived from white 'folk' traditions — with phrase repetition, sequence and phrase-structure repetition, is accompanied by a relentlessly repeated guitar riff.

Of more general importance to a study of musematic repetition in Afro-American and rock music is the fact that it encompasses not only melody but also rhythm and harmony. Developments in rhythm are too extensive and various to be covered properly here; but it is worth noting that rhythm — treated basically as an aspect of harmonic narrativity in nineteenth-century and Tin Pan Alley song — emerges as a distinct 'layer' in jazz and rhythm and blues, notably through the use of identifiable (repeated, musematic) syntactic units by drummers: 'back beat' and eight-to-the-bar patterns, etc. This usage has established both the role of rhythmic units in the

167

formation of structural frameworks and the familiar relationship between such frameworks and variative (in this case rhythmic) detail. The latter is more important in jazz-rock and various styles of 'progressive' rock, less so in rhythm and blues, mainstream rock, teenybopper pop and disco.

Just as melodic musematic repetition stems from Afro-American musical practice, so the harmonic equivalent — short chord sequences, usually two or three chords, repeated — clearly has its origins in black music. This technique appears in early gospel music; from there it passes into the work of secular vocal groups and early soul singers (1950s James Brown and Ray Charles, for example), and becomes a staple ingredient of black music from the 1960s on. One route whereby it reached rock may have been through the influence of black singers and groups on the Beatles and other early 1960s British groups; at any rate, it soon became a primary rock technique. The immense significance of this is obvious, for its effect is to cut back the *differentiation* of harmonies, the 'narrativity' of harmonic syntax, to a minimum. The Who's 'My Generation', in which a continuous two-chord oscillation is supplemented by a melodic riff, illustrates one common type of application. Often, as there, the riff is worked into an antiphonal structure.

Once again, some of the most interesting examples are 'compromises'; the classic source here is the work of the Beatles, a large proportion of Lennon–McCartney songs being based on the working of harmonic riffs into a discursive structure, usually derived from AABA ballad form. As the Beatles, and many other groups, realised the potential offered by the studio-made LP, even more complex examples became possible. Such tracks as Jefferson Airplane's 'The Ballad of You and Me and Pooneil' and 'We Can Be Together'/'Volunteers' are lengthy multi-sectional pieces in which many of the sections are built on melodic, rhythmic and harmonic riffs, but at a higher structural level (where the sections are put together) the range of choices (which section to repeat, how long to continue it, etc.) is quite large.

Effects of repetition

In the previous section I sketched out a basic contrast within the practice of repetition together with a few examples of specific manifestations and syntheses. In this final section, I want to try to relate this differentiation within the syntax to differences in *effects*. That, however, presupposes a general approach to the effects of repetition *per se*.

Popular common sense not only tends to see repetition as an aspect of commercial manipulation (see p. 160 above) but often also associates it with the phenomenon of being 'sent', particularly in relation to 'hypnotic' rhythmic repetitions and 'primitive' audience trance: a collective 'loss of the subject' in a state, perhaps, of what has been called *jouissance*. How can we square the two? How is it possible to square a psychology of repetition, with its biological aspects and generalising ambition, and the historically specific Adornian notions of repetition as a function of social control? Maybe it is not squaring that is needed so much as a certain relaxation of the analytical strangle-hold to allow a space in which multiple determinations can be seen to operate. The psychoanalytical interpretation of repetition is itself not univocal, as we shall see; indeed, taking up Freud's metaphoric construction of the psyche as an *economy*, we may compare 'good' and 'bad' readings of repetition there with the ambiguity in the 'real' economy between repetition seen as an organic process (that is, in ecological processes) and as a manifestation of 'Fordism' (mass production and the standardised series). I would like to be able to rescue repetition both from the abstracted, intra-linguistic readings of formalists and from those cultural theorists who would reduce it to a mere correlate of the social relations of monopoly capitalism. In reality, it is situated — or rather, it is *worked*, and *does its work* — precisely on the terrain where social determinations, linguistic conventions and what Peter Fuller[21] has termed the 'relative constants' of the human condition intersect. Jameson has argued that repetition in mass culture is *quite* different from repetition (generic conventions, stereotypes, etc.) in pre-capitalist forms[22] (this in self-contradiction, since he also suggests that in certain other aspects, mass cultural products can transcend their specific socio-historical conditions of production). But popular music — which, as he himself explains, is now blurring the distinction between the individual song and the musical field, by virtue of the repetitive processes inherent in mass culture — actually provides a striking model for the ways in which repetition techniques *can* overreach the needs of capitalist practice; for its reliance on repetition internally to the syntax as well as externally, as between constituents of the genre, acts to conjoin (not always harmoniously, to be sure) narrow socially functional effects and broader, psychologically more open meanings.

First let us return to Barthes' typology of pleasure, which he develops in relation to a distinction within signifying practice between signification and *signifiance*. *Signifiance* arises

> when the text is read (or written) as a moving play of signifiers, without any possible references to one or some fixed signifieds . . . *Signifiance* is a *process* in the course of which the 'subject' of the text, escaping the logic of the *ego-cogito* and engaging in other logics (of the signifier, of contradiction), struggles with meaning and is deconstructed ('lost') . . . Contrary to signification, *signifiance* cannot be reduced, therefore, to communication, representation, expression: it places the subject (of writer, reader) in the text not as a projection . . . but as a 'loss', a 'disappearance'. Hence its identification with the pleasure of *jouissance* . . .[23]

Plaisir, on the other hand, is for Barthes, 'a pleasure . . . linked to cultural enjoyment and identity, to the cultural enjoyment of identity, to a homogenising movement of the ego'.[24] *Plaisir* results from the operation of signification, the working of the coded syntactic conventions out of which the text in question is formed, through which the subject knows him/herself; it 'is linked to a *comfortable* practice of reading'. *Jouissance* results from the fracturing of this system, bringing 'to a crisis his [the reader's] relation with language'.[25]

Barthes goes to some trouble to stress that the line of division is hazy, 'the distinction will not be the source of absolute classifications'.[26] Nevertheless, there is a tendency for Barthesian approaches to slip too easily into a dichotomy of 'message' and 'material', *plaisir* being connected with the formal relations within the signifying system, *jouissance* with the material presence of the signifier itself, which breaks the code; indeed, Barthes' restriction of the deepest pleasures to instances of the deconstruction of meaning — and his resulting interest in the discontinuous, 'schizophrenic' methods of many post-modernist texts — can be regarded as continuing the traditional romantic-modernist response to the predictability and standardisation characteristic of mass culture, by privileging innovation and refusal of any code.[27] But can 'message' and 'material' be demarcated quite so easily — especially in music, where the working of the signifying system is tied less to concrete external referents than to the materiality of the signifiers themselves and the correlation of that materiality with the structure of the body? It can be argued that music is the *primary* art because, within the process of psychological development, its origins lie in the aural relationship of baby and mother, which, together with the tactile relationship, pre-dates the significance of visual (still more, verbal) signs (dependent as that is on an apprehension of the external world as *other*)[28]. The initial connotations of sound-structures (the origins of which may go back beyond the repetitive 'coos' of the mother even into the womb: the (equally repetitive) sound and feel of maternal breathing and heartbeat) are prior to any emergence of a subject, in opposition to external reality; for this reason the basic pleasure of music may be thought of as narcissistic — just as its basic technique was earlier described as infinite repetition, or, in terms of psychological development, as the 'primal metaphor', in which everything is combined in a 'great similarity'. If these connotations and pleasures remain available in the unconscious after formation of the subject, and if, as Lacan[29] argues, the unconscious (site of *jouissance*) is not the formless jumble of vulgar pseudo-Freudianism but is structured, there is no need to limit *jouissance* in music to a level somehow beyond structure, to an assertion of materiality against form.[30]

Guy Rosolato has argued that the predictability of a known musical system can be ruptured not only by the presence within it of something unknown, unexpected, untranslatable (Barthes' theory) but also 'by opening it up through variation, or by carrying it to the limit'.[31] To the extent that repetition is defined, precisely, as carrying predictability to the limit (see p. 161 above), it becomes possible to link repetition not (not only?) with the *plaisir* of signification (the most obvious extrapolation from Barthes) but (also?) with the possibility of *jouissance*. In this case, 'if the drive[32] can be considered like the metaphoric play of music, the latter becomes the metaphoric representation of the drive substituted for the subject'.[33]

The ambiguity over the meaning of repetition — is it an aspect of the ego-function *vis-à-vis* mastering reality or is it the representant of a primary drive which may 'substitute for the subject'? — is not a purely musical problem; it informs all branches of human experience, and may be found in the work of Freud himself. According to Freud, all the drives are governed by a constancy or inertia principle; they all 'tend towards the restoration of an earlier state of things',[34] attempting to reduce excitation to a minimum or at least to a state of equilibrium. Thus the operation of the 'pleasure principle' is defined precisely as the search for a diminution in the tension of desire. But it is only in his *Beyond the Pleasure Principle* (written in 1920) that this view is connected with the problem of repetition, in the context of a fully worked-out theory. The famous *fort–da* game, in which a little boy dramatises the absence and reappearance ('gone' . . . 'there') of his mother by means of the repetitive manipulation of a wooden reel, gives rise to two possible explanations. First, it could be seen as a way of mastering reality, controlling the pain of renunciation — hence, in terms of ego-functioning, as a particular channelling of the pleasure principle; this interpretation could be carried not only into the area of social relations but also into that of symbol-making: if 'symbolisation . . . is the counterpart of dissatisfaction, [if] desire . . . gives rise to speech', then the working out of tension and detension within signifying systems, by means of repetition/non-repetition structures, could be regarded as a technique of 'mastery over . . . absence and loss'.[35] Clearly, it is in this area that the roots of *plaisir* are to be found.

Freud's second explanation is more radical. He posits a new instinctual formulation, in which repetition represents a drive 'more primitive, more elementary, more instinctual than the pleasure principle which it overrides'; this drive, whose task is the 'binding' of free psychic energy prior to the pleasure principle getting to work on it, and whose nature is an 'expression of the inertia inherent in [all] organic life', was christened the death instinct — death being the ultimate state of inertia.[36] Since death represents, so to speak, a definitive 'loss of the subject' (the monadic silence of the grave), since repetition, on this reading, originates on very deep pre-subjective levels, it is presumably available not only for conservative functions of control but also moments of *jouissance*.

However, against Thanatos, the death instincts, Freud erects a protagonist: Eros, the life instincts, represented through sexuality, and the only drives to resist the tendency towards dissolution. And Eros is characterised in terms of 'clamour', against the 'muteness' of the death instincts; 'that which escapes the principle of constancy is Eros . . ., the disturber of sleep, the "breaker of the peace" '.[37] As Freud's argument develops, he

171

discovers the possibility of new kinds of pleasure, not tied to the constancy principle: 'it cannot be doubted that there are pleasurable tensions and unpleasurable relaxations of tension'.[38] It is here, presumably, in the operations of Eros, that the Barthesian *jouissance*, based as it is on disturbance and contradiction, has its roots. Are we back, then, to a simple dualism?

The answer is given in Freud's own work, for the implication is clear that Life and Death are not a mutually exclusive pair, working in a simple correlative structure (Death–repetition–ego–control–*plaisir*; Life–distruption–sexuality–*jouissance*), but that the various terms of the psyche are articulated together in various ways. In the first place, the dualism appears as an 'overlapping of roles . . . of two coextensive domains . . . In a sense, everything is death, since self-preservation is the circuitous path on which each living substance pursues its own death. In another sense, everything is life, since . . . the self-preservation of the individual derives from mutual attachment of the cells . . . Sexuality is at work wherever death is at work.' In the second place, the dualism is located not on the level of concrete aims and objects but of undifferentiated *forces*, and these *cut across* the various functions of the psyche (ego-functions, sexual functions).[39] The energies of the two basic drives are available to be channelled in different directions. Thus, Thanatos — in the form of repetition, for instance — can serve both ego-instincts (*plaisir*), and, in the form of narcissism, sexual desire (*jouissance*); (cf. the implications of Avron's theory, above p. 170: no doubt the concept of narcissism can be extended to include collective forms, which seem characteristic of many kinds of musical response). Moreover, it would be surprising to find that the more physically involving forms of musematic repetition in music (boogie woogie rhythms, for instance) have nothing to do with sexuality. As Freud himself pointed out, copulative *jouissance* (the pleasure of sexual climax, one of the original meanings of the French word), though originating in the tension of erotic desire, is made possible by repetitive stimulation, and is actually felt, and often described, as a kind of *dying*.[40] Here repetition pursues a trajectory through tension to final 'loss'. It seems likely, in fact, that *all* activities represent a complex mixture of forces, and any temptation to an either/or, *plaisir/jouissance* dichotomy must be abandoned, in favour of a conception of tension, struggle, mediation, a pleasure-*field*.

Within the psychic economy, then, repetition appears to us only in complex mediated forms. Within signifying systems, too, repetition does not represent itself as 'natural', nor purely as instrumental (under the function of control). Instead, we can say that its forms represent a cultural *work* — or rather they exist and are worked out at the point where socially constructed cultural codes and the structure of the subject meet. As Lacan puts it, repetition, or

> the game of the cotton-reel is the subject's answer to what the mother's absence has created on the frontier of his domain — the edge of his cradle —

namely a *ditch*, around which one can only play at jumping . . . The activity as a whole symbolises . . . the repetition of the mother's departure as cause of a *Spaltung* [split] in the subject — overcome by the alternating game, *fort–da* . . . whose aim, in its alternation, is simply that of being the *fort* of a *da*, and the *da* of a *fort* . . .[41]

Repetition, at its simplest, is the minimum step into the game of language and culture.

What this conception opens up for us is a space within which specific manifestations of repetition-practice in popular music can be located as manifestations of a complex cultural game, into which play a variety of social and pyschic forces. The clarity, periodicity and importance of repetition in a particular syntax, then, can be related to the force and proximity of the death instinct, its precise effects to the nature of what is repeated and the extent to which it is mixed up with other elements (channelling repetition in particular directions). It is a question of the nature and complexity of the cultural apparatus that is constructed out of the primary energies. Thus, musematic repetition would seem *per se* to be more 'basic', discursive repetition to involve more ego functions. (Maróthy describes the form of bourgeois song as connected with the construction of the bourgeois ego, in its self-preservative little world). At the same time, the musematic repetition of a short harmonic ostinato (in the Beatles, say) will have different effects from the musematic repetition of a physically involving, primarily rhythmic riff (in the Rolling Stones, for example), even if from a formalistic viewpoint the role of musematic repetition in the two cases is about equal. The idea that 'the Stones give us energy, the Beatles take energy', a personalised form of a quite commonly felt distinction within popular music, probably refers to the ability of music with a greater reliance on musematic repetition to achieve a *resonance* with primary psychic energy flow, setting it in motion, while more discursive forms, even including repetition, demand a greater *investment* of ego-energy. Similarly, the 'constricting' effect of musematic repetition in a Bob-Dylan protest song such as 'Masters of War' and its 'liberating' effect in his rhythm-and-blues influenced songs, 'It Take A Lot to Laugh' for instance, is explained musically by differences in syntactic context, psychologically by a difference in drive-channelling into the ego instincts on the one hand, into the sexual instincts on the other.

The game can of course be disrupted, the subject 'lost'. For instance, the very force of repetition can, as it were, obliterate the significance of content; as continuous repetition approaches that point where we *know* that change is ruled out, the point of monadic unity, then the game effectively ceases. A good deal of popular music privileges this 'rhythmic obstinacy, reiteration to excess, and obliterates organisation and variety; a hypnotic abandon to this energy is also the expression of an energy'.[42] It would be a mistake, however, to limit *jouissance* to this level, still more to separate rigidly the *plaisir* of the game from the *jouissance* of its disruption. The

173

relationships between repetition-*jouissance* and Barthesian *jouissance* can perhaps be explained as resulting from differing proportions of Life/Death drives within the particular function: a high proportion of Eros directs the sexual instincts into desire-for-the-other (for the signifier, in the case of music), resulting in the pleasure of the physical 'grain', as Barthes calls it; a high proportion of Thanatos channels sexuality, via repetition, towards narcissism, resulting in the pleasure of 'collective dying' — and providing the grain of truth behind the jibes about the masturbatory solipsistic nature of the pleasure of much contemporary pop music. More generally, it seems likely that *plaisir* and *jouissance* are actually dialectically intermingled processes (thus *jouissance* is not conceivable outside a context in which *plaisir* operates — just as the unconscious, as Lacan makes clear, is not prior to the subject but comes into being as a function of the creation of subjectivity); they are continually active, in listening as in life, forever teasing and slipping. One example is Rosolato's conception of the disruption of a code (or better, the pulling aside of the curtain of predictability) 'by opening it up through variation', of which the relationship between repetitive frame- work and variative detail, discussed earlier, would provide many instances. Perhaps what is needed, theoretically, is a meta-pleasure prin- ciple, which *organises* the relations of its two subordinates within the pleasure-field. It might be that this could be found by looking to the notion of *suture*, developed in Lacanian psychoanalysis and subsequently in film theory; suture there is taken to refer to an operation of *binding*, a *placing* of the subject in relation to the discourse in which it figures, but at the same time it continuously maintains the possibility that the stitching will open, revealing the gap, the *edge*, where, according to Lacan, the unconscious is to be located.[43]

It should by now be clear — in general terms — how the ensemble of social determinations breaks upon the pleasure-field. 'Pleasure' is a social term; similarly, people and syntaxes repeat themselves in socially deter- minate ways. Psychological subjects do not stand over against social reality but take their specific forms as the result of its working of their resources. To pursue this in a more detailed way would require the application to 'repetition theory' of a *historicised* theory of psychoanalysis, taking account of the operations of specific ideological formations; this is impossible here. One example must suffice. It is directed towards the mass-culture critique of late capitalist cultural products — for surely the explanation of the ideo- logical role of repetition there is that its 'natural' use as an ego-control function has been generalised socially as a political power; the associated *plaisir* presumably then turns masochistic, the pleasure of control sliding into that of being controlled.

There is no need, however, to see this process as monolithic, or uni- determined. It is open to struggle. Certainly the various pleasures of musical effects are not like bran-tub goodies, freely or randomly available; they come ideologically sorted, shaped and wrapped. But the ensemble of forces in the field is too complex and too dynamic to be regarded as a completely homogeneous totality; how can, say, a thumping rhythm and blues riff be turned *simply* into a collective rubber-stamp? The production of musical syntaxes involves active choice, conflict, redefinition; at the same time, their understanding and enjoyment take place in the theatre of self-definition, as part of the general struggle among listeners for control of meaning and pleasure.

Notes

1. Parts of this essay also appear in ' "Play it again, Sam" ': some notes on the productivity of repetition in popular music', *Popular Music*, vol. 3, 1983. I am grateful to Cambridge University Press for permission to reuse them here.
2. S. Frith and A. McRobbie, 'Rock and sexuality', *Screen Education*, vol. 29, 1978–9.
3. D. Laing and J. Taylor, 'Disco-pleasure-discourse: on "Rock and sexuality" ', *Screen Education*, vol. 31, 1979.
4. R. Barthes, *Image-Music-Text*, trans. Stephen Heath, Fontana London, 1977.
5. H. Lefèbvre, 'Musique et sémiologie', *Musique en Jeu*, vol. 4, 1971.
6. See T.W. Adorno, 'On popular music', *Studies in Philosophy and Social Sciences*, vol. 9, 1941, pp. 17–48.
7. F. Jameson, 'Reification and utopia', *Social Text*, vol. 1, no. 1, 1981, pp. 130–48.
8. T.W. Adorno, *Philosophy of Modern Music*, trans. Anne G. Mitchell and Wesley V. Bloomster, Sheed and Ward London, 1973.
9. Ibid., p. 168.
10. The term is taken from mathematical set theory.
11. Nevertheless, the fact that the points occupied by language and by music tend towards opposite ends of the spectrum is of importance for analysis when the two are combined, as in songs.
12. R. Jakobson, 'Two aspects of language and two types of aphasic disturbances' in *Selected Writings*. vol. II, Mouton, The Hague, 1971, pp. 239–59.
13. The terms 'digital' and 'analogue' are adapted from their use in computer design. Digital computers translate information into quantities on a numerical scale, generally (although not necessarily) the binary scale; analogue computers represent a unit of information by means of a precisely analogous (hence any size) electrical voltage.
14. Sequence in music is the technique of repeating a melodic unit at a different pitch. Thus repetition is mediated by its use in the construction of a longer, more hierarchically organised phrase.
15. P. Tagg, 'Analysing popular music', *Popular Music*, vol. 2, 1982, p. 45; see also P. Tagg, *Kojak — 50 Seconds of TV Music*, Skrifter fran Musiitvetenskapliga Institutionen, University of Gothenburg, 1979, pp. 71–2.
16. See Tagg, *Kojak*, pp. 184–5.
17. J. Maróthy, *Music and the Bourgeois, Music and the Proletarian*, Budapest, Kaido, 1974, pp. 17–22.
18. See P. Oliver, 'Blues and the binary principle' in P. Tagg and D. Horn (eds), *Popular Music Perspectives*, Gothenburg and Exeter, 1982; and P. Oliver, 'Binarism, blues and black culture', *Popular Music*, vol. 2, 1982, pp. 179–200.

Richard Middleton

19. J. Maróthy, *Music and the Bourgeois*, pp. 11–127 *passim*.

20. Without even considering the *self-conscious* use of repetition by such bands as Velvet Underground and certain recent 'minimalist' groups. The practice of repetition for 'aesthetic' reasons (for instance, to represent 'monotony') raises a whole extra level of problems, not considered here.

21. P. Fuller, *Art and Psychoanalysis*, Writers and Readers, London, 1980.

22. Jameson, 'Reification and utopia', pp. 136–8.

23. Barthes, *Image-Music-Text*, p. 10.

24. S. Heath in ibid., p. 9.

25. R. Barthes, *The Pleasure of the Text*, trans. Richard Miller, Jenakhan Cape New York, 1975.

26. Ibid., p. 4.

27. See ibid., pp. 40–1; Jameson, 'Reification and utopia', pp. 135–6.

28. See D. Avron, 'Vers une métapsychologie de la musique', *Musique en Jeu*, vol. 9, p. 104.

29. J. Lacan, *The Four Fundamental Concepts of Psycho-Analysis*, trans. Alan Sheridan, Penguin Books, Harmondsworth, 1979.

30. To be fair, Barthes offers the possibility that form — in its most extreme manifestation, 'extreme repetition' — could be a source of *jouissance*; but he does not pursue this (Barthes, *Pleasure of the Text*, pp. 41–2).

31. G. Rosolato, 'Répétitions', *Musique en Jeu*, vol. 9, pp. 33–44.

32. Freud's *Trieb*, usually mistranslated as 'instinct'.

33. Rosolato, 'Répétitions', p. 41.

34. S. Freud, *Beyond the Pleasure Principle*, Standard Edition of *The Complete Psychological Works of Sigmund Freud*, trans. J. Strachey, vol. 18, The Hogaski Press, London, 1955, p. 37.

35. P. Ricoeur, *Freud and Philosophy*, trans. Denis Savage, Yale University Press, London, 1970, pp. 286–322.

36. Freud, *Pleasure Principle*, pp. 23, 36.

37. Ricoeur, *Freud and Philosophy*, p. 320.

38. Quoted in ibid., p. 321.

39. Ibid., pp. 292–3.

40. See ibid., p. 319.

41. Lacan, *Psycho-Analysis*, pp. 62–3.

42. Rosolato, 'Répétitions', p. 43.

43. See S. Heath, 'Notes on suture', *Screen*, vol. 18, no. 4, pp. 48–76.

9

Colin Mercer

That's Entertainment: The resilience of popular forms

The original intention of this contribution was some commentary on what has come to be known as the 'realism debate'. It was intended to take up and develop some of the themes concerning the relationship between the categories of realism and the 'popular' which James Donald and I had sketched out, within pedagogical constraints, in an Open University course unit called *Reading and Realism*.[1] Aside from a certain weariness which mitigated against talking about realism again at all, the project of bringing together questions of realism and of the popular began to establish its own internal resistances. It couldn't be done. The terms in which the realism debate had been consolidated and developed were simply incommensurable with the ways in which the question of the popular has more recently been formulated. Another prospective title at that stage was 'Recasting Realism' which, assimilating certain elements of the debate, would attempt to displace the rather insistently *politicised* terms in which it had been set up. (A politics, that is, while claiming to be everywhere, turns out to be so general and blunt as to be nowhere). It then occurred to me that perhaps the 'problem' was being sought in the wrong place. Certainly, there are issues of immense importance at stake in the realism debate but perhaps they are not so much to do with the nature of realism *per se* — whether as an aesthetic school, or set of formal techniques, or as a claim to political veracity — but with the terms of its *persistence* in whatever form.

This brings us to the final stage in this preliminary process of 'naming' and the current title.[2] Perhaps, the argument continues, the persistence of realism as an *issue* — there are no valid *formal* comparisons to be made between Balzac, George Eliot, de Sica and *Coronation Street* — has *nothing* to do with aesthetic theory, not even a Marxist one if such were necessary or possible. Perhaps it is much more usefully approached *via*, or even discarded in favour of, a concentration on the ways in which certain techniques of representation are deployed in a much wider field: that of *entertainment*. This is a category or rather a definite set of 'moral technologies'[3] and imperatives which can embrace and say much about the *resilience* of both Balzac and *Coronation Street*. It can say much more about this resilience because, unlike realism which constantly returns us to foundational principles of epistemology, or truth, or ideological *effect*, the focus is shifted, broadly speaking, to what is sometimes vaguely called the conditions of their production and consumption. We can be more specific though and say that to consider the moral technologies and imperatives within the category of entertainment is to consolidate our attention around such issues as the form and material in which a given 'text' appears: as a 'novel' in one, two, or three 'decks'; in magazine form next to articles on domestic hygiene or criminal pathology; as what the Germans called a *Gartenlaube* (an arbour) which was a 'family literary journal'; as 'railway fiction' designed to be read quickly and discarded; as 'soap opera' — itself originally a 'magazine' form on television between advertisements; or as a form of tele-visual documentary. Across these diverse technologies of representation we can establish no unifying principle of realism (though they have all been claimed as such) but we *can* establish certain convergences within the category of technologies of entertainment. Basically, the argument I shall be developing here is that the issue is not concerned with 'realism' or 'texts' at all but with the conditions of the effectivity, and, correspondingly, resilience of, popular forms. Put another way, the question might emerge as what are the conditions of their legibility, their generation into, roughly *consensual* forms? It is possible that at this stage you will be thinking that if you abandon a category like realism then there's a good chance that all those other meaty aesthetic categories — anti-realism, symbolism, avant-gardism, neo-realism, modernism and so on — will disappear with it. They will still remain as names of course, but there's a good chance that much of their conceptual validity will begin to evaporate. Perhaps, but amen.

From the real to the popular

And amen initially and paradoxically in the name of Brecht who is so often wheeled on in the name of a *certain* 'open-ended' realism, but who reminds us, firstly, that there is no representational foundation to realism, or rather no essence against which its adequacy might be calculated: 'Nothing prevents the realist Cervantes from seeing knights tilting at windmills or the realist Swift from seeing horses founding states.'[4] And secondly — and this might be harder to take — that the question of realism, in spite of certain recent summaries,[5] is not about the formal 'conventions' of particular 'texts' because it is, as Brecht put it, 'sovereign over all conventions'.[6] In effect, what Brecht did when he skilfully turned Lukács's accusations of 'formalism' back on the the accuser's own obsession with the 'forms' of the nineteenth-century novel, was not to meet him on his own ground and win the game of dialectics but to displace completely the terms of the debate on to quite a different ground: that of *popular entertainment*. If, for Lukács, the 'task of art is the reconstitution of the concrete . . . in a direct, perceptual self-evidence'[7] or dependent on the 'correct reflection of the totality'[8] then for Brecht these are at least secondary issues, or perhaps not issues at all. And this is because the 'sovereignty' of realism as a *political* choice — which is why it is important for Brecht — effectively recognises that there is a different, perhaps much more 'superficial', set of concerns which are related to strategies of entertainment and to corresponding ways of engaging with the popular, of addressing that complex and variously formed entity known, since the end of the eighteenth century, as 'the people'. No matter how overladen — as Brecht acknowledges — with ideological assumptions and prejudices, this entity and the 'technologies' which form it, must be engaged with.

It is worth stating, of course, that Brecht could only go so far in this matter. Contemporary 'Brechtians' seem reluctant to admit these limitations but it is worth stating them here: he worked in the *theatre* (and, to a certain extent in radio and film) in a Germany where 'the people' had massively become the *Volk* of Nazism and, as a matter of political choice and calculation, he referred to himself as a realist. None of this, including his win over Lukács, allows him to be constructed as a model for cultural theory and practice. This is not a theoretical flaw, not a contradiction: simply a recognition of the fact that his appeals to realism were — like the best, though not always recognised as such — a matter of choice and strategy formulated in relation to particular aims. It is the choice of a strategy for working within the apparatuses of theatre, film and radio. And, before it is objected that in spite of these naunces Brecht's *general* aim was a fissuring of bourgeois ideology, let it be noted, firstly, that his strategies across different media are significantly different and, secondly, that anybody who believes in a general bourgeois ideology independent of the technologies of its implementation, will spend a long time looking for it. We have only to consider the fate of 'Brechtian' theatre in both its agit-prop and West End/television/filmic forms today to confirm this point. Pierre Bourdieu is certainly right to argue that Brechtian 'distanciators' today can only confirm the old authority of the intellectual in the cultural field.[9] And this is because such strategies are formulated in the terms of the 'realism debate' and not in terms of entertainment and its technologies.

Brecht was keenly aware of this and what we should take from his work is not a 'theory of cultural action' but a piecemeal strategy of detailed investigation and reformulation. The fact that he was a Marxist and a Communist does not militate against such procedures. The displacement of the concern with 'conventions' towards the apparently more 'humanist' area of 'general human interest' in fact takes the paradoxical form of an immense *technical* (perhaps technological in view of what I have said above) investment in the elaboration of diverse and particular 'dramatic' strategies to meet and engage with the equally diverse and particular strategies which had formed the resilient categories of 'the people', 'popular', 'pleasure' and 'entertainment': we can look long and hard at a any of these strategies and still not find any foundational principle of realism either in the 'form' or 'content' of given productions. In Brecht what we find much more insistently are particular techniques of writing, of visual and aural representation (or performance), of the technical disposition of people, objects, lights, sounds in the self-consciously recognised space of the theatre. This went as far, we know, as the organisation of these elements in the auditorium and the audience itself: smoke, noise, the clinking of wine and beer bottles, the screeching of chairs. These were not components of a genial familiarity but of a technically elaborate set of 'counter-technologies'. We also know that Brecht's acting techniques were all about 'surface' features as against the 'depth' of Stanislavskian methods: Charlie Chaplin against Marlon Brando perhaps. In his writings he constantly reminds us of these 'surface' movements (of entertainment) counterposed to the 'psychological depth' (of realism?): the *gestus* is the discrete and particular technology of the body and its capacities — movements, intonation of the voice, special techniques of moving in relation to other actors, turning, confronting, glancing and so on. All of this pitched against the 'glowing soul' of traditional cultural forms centred on a particular psychology.

Entertainment

But that 'glowing soul', that 'psychology', were essential components of the repertoire of popular entertainment. They too were the outcome of particular procedures and techniques of representation — character, monologue, gestures, speech, silence, exchanges of looks which were, in turn, only the surface technology of entertainment. The 'realism' of Brecht's strategies is another way of saying 'look, these are "superficial" and surface features too'. It is only conjuncturally and politically formulated *claims* to realism which give them the appearance of depth. If we are to allocate to Brecht a special place it is not in terms of a realism but rather in the way in which he was able to disinter previous 'depths' and to reveal them for what they were: another series of techniques and technologies with a longer history.

A substantial part of the history of entertainment was bound up with particular claims to address formative political entities such as 'the people'. The press, as has been well documented, was particularly concerned with addressing people within a particular and circumscribed community. As one commentator notes rather casually,'that which is taken to be entertainment . . . has as long a history as the press itself'.[10] He goes on to cite a German author of 1690 who noted that '[t]he purpose of the new newspapers is to supply its readers with information about current affairs and events together with some useful advice and entertainment'.[11] While noting, perhaps, some ambivalence concerning precisely what 'entertainment' actually means there, we can register a possible convergence of concerns, signalled in different ways, by Richard Sennett and Jürgen Habermas[12] about the profound significance of the press for the elaboration of particular conceptions of 'the people', 'public opinion' and the 'public spheres'. All of these concerns became central to the emergence of specific sets of techniques of governmentality: a 'policing' of the people. More recently Benedict Anderson has contributed a further dimension to this by arguing that these 'spheres' were also *nationally* delimited in ways which have strong implications for the nature of contemporary nationalism. He argues, for example, that the newspaper (along with the novel) 'provided the technical means for "re-presenting" the *kind* of imagined community that is the nation.'[13] Anderson describes the reading of a newspaper as 'mass ceremony' of 'almost precisely simultaneous consumption' which is

> performed in silent privacy, in the lair of the skull. Yet each communicant is well aware that the ceremony he performs is being replicated simultaneously by thousands (or millions) of others of whose existence he is confident, yet of whose identity he has not the slightest notion. Furthermore, this ceremony is incessantly repeated at daily or half-daily intervals throughout the calendar. What more vivid figure for the secular, historically-clocked, imagined community can be envisioned? At the same time, the newspaper reader, observing exact replicas of his own paper being consumed by his subway, barbershop, or residential neighbours, is constantly reassured that the imagined world is visibly rooted in everyday life . . . creating that remarkable confidence of community in anonymity which is the hallmark of modern nations.[14]

Given this elaboration of depth, of the ascription of individual and national capacities, it is not surprising that the idea of entertainment as a technique of 're-presentation' in the technology of news production should assume distinctive features in relation to other national imperatives. This is true, as Heinz-Dietrich Fischer notes of early literary genres, and especially the popular novel with its origins in the eighteenth century and which 'correspond with at least part of the modern concept of entertainment'.[15] In the words of another author, these were 'the most widely read books of the day, showing great *variety* and satisfying *qualitatively different needs'*.[16] The nature of that 'variety' was to be adequately summarised under the heading of '*chivalry, crime and suspense'*.[17] and the nature of the 'qualitatively different needs' is negatively suggested by the German term *Konfektionsliteratur* or literature which is 'made to measure'.[18] Made to measure for whom and on what terms is the question we would need to pose of this proposition. In relation to the *Gartenlaube* or the 'arbour' genre mentioned above, Habermas provides part of the answer when he writes that this genre

> already represents the idyllic mystic genre through which the flourishing cultural tradition maintained by the grand bourgeois family of past generations through their patronage of literature was passed on to the petit bourgeois

town family but which the latter could only imitate. The art almanacs and poet's journals, whose tradition in Germany dates back to 1770 . . . were replaced around 1850 by a variety of family literature journals, such as . . . *Gartenlaube*, published by sound financial enterprises which were in a position to foster (large-scale) reading habits of almost ideological fervour. Such literature, however, still required the family as a literary sounding board.[19]

It might be possible, and more fruitful, to argue, therefore, that these genres and, indeed, the 'magazine' publication of the 'realistic' Dickens and Eliot in nineteenth-century Britain, were much more to do with what has now been called the 'policing of families' and with discrete technologies which elaborated certain 'occasions of reading' than with the establishment of a canonical literary realist tradition. Habermas argues, as a first stage, that at this point 'culture attempts to broaden its base through adapting itself to the relaxation and entertainment needs of consumers'.[20] But, to return to some of the arguments I outlined above in the introductory section, perhaps it is necessary to see this 'culture' in a less uniform and self-conscious way. In order to relate, say, the question of realism in Dickens to the popular it is important that the transaction be established via certain technologies of entertainment. Ian Hunter, for example, argues that, in the context of other discrete strategies of 'popular family entertainment',

> Dickens' 'descriptions' . . . have the primary function of deploying new norms of public behaviour and morality . . . They do not attempt to give information about social life but help to constitute the new 'surface' of public morality on which a whole range of formerly tolerated activities (public indecency, drunkenness, profligacy, child-labour, dereliction of family duties, etc.) would show up as unacceptable.[21]

Developing this argument against 'realist' concerns with foundational principles of veracity and against also the more contemporary (structuralist) concern with the 'language' of realism, Hunter argues that both of these foci are wide of the mark because the point of resilience of these forms lies not in questions of adequacy but rather insofar as they are 'deployed within the great correctional apparatuses associated with the regulation of the health and well-being of populations, the reform of family life, the disciplinary investment of children and the policing of the metropolis'.[22]

'Entertaining and educating in an entertaining manner' was the motto of the *Gartenlaube*.[23] This was also the substance of the *feuilleton* which emerged in newspaper and magazine form at around about the same time (the early nineteenth century) and was later to give its name to a particular sort of novel most easily designated as 'light reading'. As Fischer notes, the subject matter of the *feuilleton* would be 'theatre, arts, literature; experiences of town life and all kinds of news coming from behind the scenes; the immediate environment and day-to-day life . . . not always important but nonetheless worthwhile, for some readers even significant; all attractively written'.[24] The word *'feuilleton'* eventually came to be applied to all aspects of journalism concerned with culture, entertainment, domestic life and household hints. The word 'entertainment' also comes at this time to assume the sense of, according to the *Oxford English Dictionary*, 'occupation of time, amusement' and that of a 'public performance' castigated, for example, by Samuel Johnson in 1775, as being a 'lower form of comedy'. But perhaps the good Doctor should have known better for it was he who was to write, a couple of years later that

> it must be remembered, that life consists not of a series of illustrious actions, or elegant enjoyments [but] . . . in the performance of daily duties, . . . in the procurement of petty pleasures . . . The true state of every nation is the state of common life. . . . The great mass of nations is neither rich nor gay: they whose aggregate constitutes the people, are found in the streets, the villages, in the shops and farms . . .[25]

The 'national character' of this people, Johnson insists, can only be obscured or obliterated in the 'schools of learning' and 'palaces of greatness'. This recognition of 'the people' and their strategic significance for national character and national life returns us to the issue raised above by Benedict Anderson concerning the nature of this newly addressed and elaborated 'community in anonymity' to which the technologies of entertainment were directed. Dr Johnson's worry that 'diminutive observations' might 'take away something from the dignity of writing' is simply another way of saying that the old classical advice of 'educate, animate, amuse' would need now to operate with a new range of techniques and technologies in the formation of a distinctive new 'community'. I will be developing this theme in more detail below. For the present there may be some problems arising over the conjunction of Samuel Johnson and popular culture!

This can be moderated by the argument that what have now come to be recognised as popular cultural forms even in a basically descriptive sense of 'well liked' did not spring from the head of Minerva — or Dr Johnson, or Lord Northcliffe — at some stage in the latter part of the eighteenth century or the nineteenth. They emerged rather as resultant forms of a series of confrontations, transactions and negotiations marked by different power relations and variable economic and political imperatives. Equally, therefore, if they did not spring from the head of Minerva, neither did they emerge from the bosom of the people. Again, equally, if construed in this way, these diverse forms — *feuilletons, Gartenlaube*, magazines, the newspaper, serialized novels, 'household words', little books of hints and self-help, all 'entertainingly written' — cannot be taken to be, even in their 'realist' forms, expressive of a totality which might be a society, a class, a community or history. On the contrary, they must be understood not as evidence of something to be located elsewhere, something profound or deep and underlying them, but as the composite of surface technologies which elaborate and inscribe the relations between class, community, nation and history. Not that there is nothing happening elsewhere — in the economy, in the courts, in the streets — but that these forms cannot be read off against that 'elsewhere'. And for this reason: that, in order to understand entertainment as a set of effective technologies concerned with the 'occupation of time' of the population, and to displace the false dichotomies of the concern with realism, an 'occasion of reading' must be taken to be as real as any other social phenomenon. Occasions of viewing and listening must be construed in the same way: as invested with these technologies of deportment, response and inflection which Brecht was so concerned with.

'And one of the places that bind potentially destructive antagonisms in a neutralising mutuality is texts — occasions of reading.'[26] It is much more fruitful to understand 'texts' in this way, as *occasions* located in historical time and space, determined by conditions of circulation, distribution and legibility than to treat them as either expressive of a totality or as the *simulacrum* of a structure. Indeed, a form like the *Gartenlaube* inscribes its own occasion and place: in the arbour in the garden if you had one. But if you did not then you could imagine that this was the place where it should be most appropriately read. 'Railway literature' in nineteenth-century Britain furnishes other such occasions, perhaps more demotic in its impetus than the *Gartenlaube*. As Tony Davies notes, there were two distinct 'social destinations' for cheap and popular fiction in Victorian Britain: 'the family home and the railway'. For the former destination he registers such forms as the 'Parlour Novelist' (1847), the 'Parlour Library' (1849) and magazines such as *'The Home Circle'* (1849), *Household Words* (1850), and *The Family Paper* (1856).[27] It was the firm of W.H. Smith and Son with their railway bookstalls which quickly monopolised the latter market with their 'Run and Read Library [which] consisted of 'Tales uniting Taste, Humour and Sound Principles, written by competent Christian writers with a view to elevating the character of our popular fiction.'[28] But as Davies notes, this technology of literature and its preferred occasions of reading quickly became also the occasion for 'potentially destructive antagonisms' insofar as the form known as the 'railway novel . . . became a metonym for the unregenerate tastes of the "unknown public" '.[29] There was a profound ambivalence present within the formulation of appropriate technologies of this 'public sphere' of entertainment which had not been so much of a problem in the 'private sphere' of the domestic parlour. As Davies notes, the railway remained 'a deeply ambiguous symbol, incarnating the modernising optimism of bourgeois order, profit and legality, but ruthlessly destructive too of older pieties'.[30] The railway was to become both a way of coordinating the metropolis but also a sign of degeneration amongst the populace. Davies cited Ruskin's conviction of 'the certainty of the deterioration of moral character in the inhabitants of every district penetrated by a railway'.[31]

At the point of this contradiction, and in this new moral topography of the city there emerges a work like G.M.W. Reynolds's *Mysteries of London*, in four volumes and another eight volumes of *Mysteries of the Court of London*. Davies notes that Reynolds's 'sensational tales of love, crime, poverty and riches . . . outsold Dickens in his heyday'.[32] The contradiction embedded here is nicely summarised — again by Ruskin — in a response to Reynolds's work where he laments:

> it is impossible to distinguish in these tales of the prison house how far their vice and gloom are thrown into their manufacture only to meet a vile demand, and how far they are an integral condition of thought in the minds of men trained from their youth up in the knowledge of Londonian and Parisian misery.[33]

The problem was of course — and here we must register some of the ambivalences of technologies of entertainment, some of their negotiated and uneven characteristics — that Reynolds was a well-known radical political activist, founder of *Reynolds News*, a radical weekly which lasted well into the twentieth century. As Davies notes, it is possible for the technologies of entertainment and the preferred moral topography of the city to be inflected otherwise:

> it may be that Ruskin's fear and contempt were prompted less by the technical virtuosity, brilliant vulgarity and sheer energy of Reynolds' novels and serials than by their republicanism, their persistently enunciated solidarity with popular emancipation and democratic causes, and by the deplorable fact noted by Margaret Dalziel, that 'his lovers, the women as well as the men, *enjoy* themselves'.[34]

The fact that Reynolds has been ignored in favour of the more 'classic' status of Dickens is due not to the 'adequacy' of their representations of metropolitan life but rather to a systematic exclusion of the possibility of other technologies of entertainment than those provided by the criteria of 'aesthetico-moral criticism' and its attempts to 'provide a single general criterion for evaluating writing, based on the allegedly unique appropriateness of literary language to experience.'[35]

The 'co-creation of contemplators'

The positing of a range of technologies of entertainment is not sufficient of itself of course. But it does have the advantage of moving away from a number of problematic positions which may have been formulated in the field of 'cultural politics' in the post-1968 era. A number of these problematic positions can be identified. The first of these — not peculiar to this period but resurrected by it in different ways — is that popular forms constitute something of a 'transmission belt' for the dominant ideology. The *empirical* example of Reynolds, cited above, might be taken as a counter-position. But there is also an important theoretical point to be registered here: that there is no such thing as a 'dominant ideology' to be transmitted. The 'ideology effect' of such forms, if we want to put it in that way, lies not in a construed uniform dominance but in the techniques and procedures of the transmission itself. The second problematic position arises directly from the first and lies in the search for 'progressive texts'. These are sometimes accorded this status because they are 'realist' and sometimes because they are 'anti-realist', but both misconstrue the nature of a text, perhaps because of the nature of the term itself. The 'text' taken in that singular way is understood as somehow *indicative* or, in more complex ways, as a *vector* which is sufficient in itself to designate whether it is 'pointing' in a progressive direction or a 'reactionary' one. The host of technologies involved in the elaboration of 'occasions of reading' — the range of domestic, public, topographical determinants upon such occasions — are occluded in this narrowly conceived political 'search'.

The third position, more sophisticated than the first two, is that of the 'classic realist text' in which the realist novel is seen to organise as an exemplary form not one, but a 'hierarchy of discourses' in order to play them off against each other and, more importantly, to establish the 'referee' category of the dominant discourse of reasoned truth or metalanguage. This approach is closer to the method I have been advancing on its concentration of what might be called 'literary technologies' for dealing with differences of voice, character, etc. But there are two major problems with this. Firstly, it too allows no scope for the investigation of 'occasions of reading', conditions of legibility, and the ways in which this 'hierarchy' of discourses might intersect with others — on the family, forms of appropriate reading, etc. — which are not at all textual. Secondly, when combined with the search for a 'progressive' text as it frequently is, the idea of the 'classic realist text' is disastrously elevated to the status of an *empirical* and historical category: from, say, Walter Scott to George Eliot to *Days of Hope* and Kingsley Amis. As a counter-position to this it might still be useful to speak of 'classic realist tactics' operating within a definable historical moment but like all tactics, only understandable in relation to the *occasions* — of reading, viewing, listening, *entertainment* — of which they form a part. And in that context the question of realism loses its status anyway.

None of these positions effectively addresses the central issue of conditions of legibility. This does not mean just literary, visual capacities, recognition of generic forms and so on but also the institutional modes of their representation, the 'machinery' of techniques, the question of cultural, political and economic dispositions, the pre-established or formative powers of 'non-textual' categories such as entertainment, amusement, education, improvement. To these factors we might add also the power of notions such as a 'reading public' the 'common reader' and, more insistently, of categories such as 'rational recreations' and 'really useful knowledges' which constituted a powerful and politically ambiguous impetus to occasions of reading in the nineteenth century.

Put in a simpler form, this is a question of the conditions for what the Soviet linguist V.N. Voloshinov called the 'co-creation of contemplators'. While registering some reservations about the terminology used here it is possible to sketch out a couple of important theoretical points. Voloshinov argues, for example that the 'meaning' of a given utterance can only be understood if we understand the 'shared spatial and ideational purview' of the verbal scenario. As a limit case he offers the example of two men sitting in a room and a conversation comprising a single word — 'well'. The 'purely verbal part' of the utterance gives us very little to go on here. A syntactic, morphological or semantic analysis won't do. We need to know more about the 'extraverbal context' of the utterance. For Voloshinov, this is comprised of three components. The first of these is the *common spatial purview* of the participants, the interlocutors: in this example the fact that they are both sitting in a room with a shared view of the window. The second is the *common knowledge and understanding of the situation*. The third component is their *common evaluation of the situation*. The cause of the utterance was that they had both looked up at the window and noticed that it had begun to snow. Furthermore, it had begun to snow in May! Thus,

> [O]n this 'jointly seen' (snowflakes outside the window), 'jointly known' (the time of the year — May), and 'unanimously evaluated' (winter wearied of, spring looked forward to) — on all this the utterance *directly depends*, all this is seized in its actual living import — is its very sustenance.[36]

And all of this, Voloshinov stresses 'remains without verbal specification'. This may seem fairly limited but it does provide the author with the opportunity for an important theoretical statement: 'the discourse does not at all reflect the extraverbal situation in the way a mirror reflects an object . . . the discourse *resolves the situation* bringing it to a *evaluative conclusion*, as it were'. There is no 'inside and outside' here, no problem of signifier and referent: it is a question of 'that unity and commonness of being surrounding the speakers'. The focal point of the analysis of the utterance is the series of transactions between the 'actualisation' of the utterance and the *assumed* part of it — the pregiven, the preconstructed or the enthymemic — the common purview. And this purview itself is constructed — implemented — via a silent contract between three participants: 'the *speaker* (author), the *listener* (reader), and the *topic* (the who or what) of speech (the hero)'. In this sense we would be looking for something not as the context or background to a given cultural form, not something outside of it or adjacent to it, not something in 'history' which is represented in a given text in more or less mediated ways and not something which is 'coded' in the text, but the nature of the pact, the contract, the complicity which that text establishes within a whole set of techniques and procedures at a given historical moment.

There are three main points here which seem germane to the analysis of cultural forms as entertainment. The first is the rather crudely sketched idea of a 'spatial and ideational purview' which corresponds, roughly speaking, to the idea of a temporally and spatially constrained 'occasion of reading' which I have been using above. There is no 'meaning' to the limit-text of 'well' which can be provided by a purely linguistic analysis. It depends, once more, on both discrete gestures — eye and head movements — and on something which can only be transacted by virtue of *those* movements on *this* occasion — the fact that it is snowing in May. Unfair perhaps; a literary text can't perform such movements but the response to that is: then why only look at the text for evidence of such movements?

The second point is that discourse in general is not reflective but 'evaluative' in its functions. This, though simply formulated, has considerable theoretical implications. It returns us again to the 'surface' of a range of competing and congruent techniques: of persuasion, of the mapping of social and moral imperatives, rather than to the 'depths' of what 'really happened' in the 'extraverbal scenario'. It reminds us, in other words, that there are a series of evaluative criteria at play in cultural forms — entertainment, instruction, moral investment — which it would be quite inappropriate to analyse in terms of the single evaluative criterion of realism or veracity.

The final point to be raised here is that of, broadly speaking, the 'commonness of being' or, more adequately, the *contractual* nature of discursive forms insofar as they establish relationships of complicity, of dependence, of subordination between the contracted parties of, in Voloshinov's example, author, listener and topic. This contract is established on the basis of the 'assumed' or enthymemic components of a discourse: it is the mechanism by which contemplators are 'co-created' and, as Voloshinov argues later in his essay, this 'assumed' may be the 'occasions' of the family, the clan, the class, the nation or the whole epoch. But before stepping over the line into what might become a behaviourist theory of linguistics it is worth noting that what Voloshinov is speaking about here is not linguistics at all but *rhetoric* construed in its original sense and not its contemporary pejorative one.

Entertainment as a rhetoric

'Rhetoric' according to one seventeenth-century commentator, 'is concerned with particulars and not universals'. In view of what I have argued above concerning the replacement of the 'realism debate' and its 'universals' by the 'particulars' of entertainment technologies, this is a useful emphasis. But there are other ways in which the concept might be usefully redeployed in cultural analysis. The first of these is, roughly, its empirical range and its analytical concern with the 'typically *social* character of . . . forms of sophism: they are linked to man's relations to other men within the nation, the social group or the institution'.[37] Which is another way of saying that they don't 'tell you' about these relations; they actively *constitute* them. This is supported by the second, more *theoretical*, direction of rhetorical analysis nicely summarised here by Terry Eagleton:

> Rhetoric in its major phase was neither a 'humanism', concerned in some intuitive way with people's experience of language, nor a 'formalism' pre-occupied simply with analyzing linguistic devices. It looked at such devices in terms of concrete performance — they were means of pleading, persuading, inciting and so on — and at people's responses to discourse in terms of lin-guistic structures and the material situation in which they functioned.[38]

Following the sense of this formulation it would seem plausible to argue that an adoption of some of the procedures of rhetorical analysis in its full sense of recognising persuasion, incitement, etc., would provide a way out of the disabling dichotomy, not unknown to humanism, of the resort to experiential verification and the formalism of the linguistic — or linguis-tically informed — analysis of the devices of realism.

Franco Moretti is another contemporary critic who underscores the importance of avoiding this dichotomy through the deployment of rhe-torical analysis when he argues, for example, that rhetorical figures show themselves to be 'unrivalled mechanisms for welding into an indivisible whole description and evaluation, "judgements of fact" and "judgements of value" '.[39] For Moretti it is the persuasive and consensual procedures of literary technique and the ways in which its ' "educational", "realistic", function consists precisely in training us . . . for an unending task of mediation and conciliation' which urgently needs to be analysed as a sub-stitute for the more 'earnest' attempts to 'get behind' the historical tissue of such forms.[40]

Taking these emphases on persuasion, incitement, consent, evaluation and conciliation it would seem that rhetoric is a more appropriate category for addressing both the complex issues of the *popular* and of *entertainment*. In the case of the first category it is more appropriate because rhetorical forms are not just addressed to anyone but to a particular *people*, or, more cor-rectly to the relations between the 'persons' which constitute a people as a specific and delimited political entity. In this sense the novel, and the 'novelistic mode' of representation, need to be accorded a primary rhe-torical significance not because of its realism or its embodiment of a humane ideal of character and criticism but because it is intimately con-nected in its formation with ways of addressing a delimited people. The novel, as Anderson argues, offers an appropriate mechanism for the 'kind of imagining' of a community because of its privileged relationship to the formation of national secular and vernacular languages. The novel, since the eighteenth century, is explicitly concerned with the 'conciliation' of competing voices and with the coordination of a 'common language' and 'public opinion'. Mikhail Bakhtin argues, for example, that the novel is a pre-eminently 'persuasive' technique of writing insofar as it consistently engages in a *dialogue* with 'the words of another'. The 'plurilinguism' of the novel, as he calls it, is, in turn, 'indissolubly linked to the problem of the differentiation and stratification of every national language.'[41] The nature of the novel, furthermore, 'presupposes a strongly differentiated social group in a relation of tension and active reciprocity with other social groups'.[42] It is analogous, for Bakhtin, to the overheard speech in the public place and the constant interplay of expressions like 'he says . . . we say . . . he said . . . you say . . . I said' and the composite affirmations 'everybody says' or 'I was told'.

To argue then that the novel, in its eighteenth and nineteenth century forms, was popular is not to say that it was 'well liked' but rather that it engaged and technically elaborated the distinctive procedures by which people are held together within a delimited space. In this sense both its 'internal' technologies for the coordination of the different strata of language — the picaresque, the epistolary forms — and its 'external' technologies — new techniques of reading, 'silent scanning', 'family readings' and so on, constitute a complex of persuasive rhetorical forms within the national sphere. We would need to make various distinctions between the eighteenth-century novel's concern with, as Bakhtin puts it, 'traversing the native land' and the nineteenth-century novelistic concern with more localised 'communities' — the family, the household, the metropolis, the rural community. But the essential point remains that what is frequently called the 'novelistic mode' has little to do with a postulated realism and a great deal to do with the popular and rhetorical imperatives of entertainment both in its older, contractual sense of 'support' and in its more modern sense as occupation of time, amusement and public *performance*. (The French word for 'performance' is, funnily enough, *représentation*.)

Entertaining the nation

[I]f the body of objects we study — the corpus formed by works of literature — belongs to, gains coherence from, and in a sense emanates out of the concepts of nation, nationality, and even of race, there is very little in contemporary critical discourse making these actualities possible as subjects of discussion.[43]

Edward Said's justifiable impatience there needs to be extended beyond the corpus of literature to, for example, national film cultures, television programming and to the sort of cultural phenomena analysed by Colin MacArthur elsewhere in this collection. But the point is well taken. Said's quite basic insistence that, at least since the nineteenth century, the idea of culture has inexorably come to include the meanings of '*belonging to* or *in a* place, being *at home in a place*' and that as such it 'also designates a boundary by which the concept of what is extrinsic or intrinsic to the culture comes into play',[44] is an important one across the range of cultural forms and strategies. Many of the features of this internal and external differentiation are inextricably and simultaneously formed alongside those technologies for supporting, addressing and entertaining the people. This is certainly evident in a different range of technologies of entertainment which emerges in the early days of the BBC.

From its earliest days the explicit mode of address of the BBC has been encapsulated in its advice to producers, technicians and speakers, that you are not speaking to millions of people but rather to one person (or family) multiplied by millions.[45] This assumes contemporary and potent populist forms in the shape of the now defunct *Nationwide* or more recently, Breakfast Television, where the addressee is dominantly the 'man in the street' or the 'ordinary family'. Like the eighteenth-century novel it elaborates and works upon a construed public opinion, a network of 'I say-you say-everybody says-we say' and invests the individual or the family with a delimited range of capacities. And like the nineteenth-century *feuilleton, Gartenlaube* and 'railway fiction' it establishes its own occasions for viewing and a specific moral and political topography of the nation based centrally on the theme of 'unity in diversity'. Also like the *feuilleton*, programmes of this nature are about 'all kinds of news coming from behind the scenes; the immediate environment and everyday life . . . all attractively written'.

In this the BBC has been remarkably continuous from the earliest days. In spite of Lord Reith's loathing for the idea of 'mass culture' and the pejorative associations of entertainment he was none the less keen to argue that the investment and support of individual capacities and the character of the community was the prime function of radio in that if it was 'valuable as an index to the community's outlook and personality . . . it was of first importance that the service should be trusted; it must not abuse the confidential footing it had obtained on everyman's hearthrug'.[46] Certainly without knowing it Reith was stating the first principle of what was to become known as the *socius function* of entertainment: 'analogous to the function that a companion or a conversation partner during leisure might fulfil'. But, like Voloshinov's example of the 'well' conversation this would also need a 'spatial and ideational purview'. The first (spatial) component of this was provided by Reith's colleague, C.A. Lewis, who argued that

> Broadcasting means the rediscovery of the home. In these days when house and hearth have been largely given up in favour of a multitude of other interests and activities outside . . . this new persuasion may to some extent reinstate the parental roof in its old accustomed place . . .[47]

And it was Reith himself in his valedictory speech who provided the second (ideational) component when he said, in characteristic tones:

191

> We believe that a new national asset has been created . . . the asset referred
> to is of the moral and not the material order — that which, down the years,
> brings the compound interest of happier homes, broader culture and truer
> citizenship.[48]

The idea of 'citizenship' was crucial to Reith and his associates: what better
category for investing the individual with discriminating and reflexive
capacities (hence the resistance to radio 'on tap' and the punctuation of
programmes with silences for reflexion) and at the same time with the sense
of duty and belonging to the national community. And what better category for supporting that *socius function* through specific techniques:

> The problem was to fit entertainment as occasion into an intimate routine
> . . . The solution lay in the development of a particular sort of *voice* —
> intimate and authoritative — and a particular sort of *personality* — relaxing
> and knowable. The radio star was public figure as private friend.[49]

There was no contradiction here between the 'serious' qualities of citizenship (the public service ideal) and the 'frivolous' features of being
amused (the 'light entertainment' ideal): they fuse through a series of techniques to form a particularly enduring relationship between the categories
of individual, citizen, family and nation. Contrary to George Orwell's
complaint in 1937 that 'palliatives' such as the radio were 'mitigating the
surface of life',[50] it might well be argued that these forms were actually
elaborating that surface.

Conclusion: From representation to performance

As I noted above, the French word for performance is *représentation*. Perhaps
it would have been easier if the English word for representation had been
'performance'. This is because the general drift of my argument has been
that questions of representation, rather than being taken on their own
terms of adequacy or realism, need persistently to be transacted through
the quite different theoretical grid of their performative 'occasions' within
the field of entertainment. This field of technologies is, as I have argued,
not reducible either to 'linguistic' questions or formal devices. They need
to be understood in relation to the particular occasions in which they
operate as contractual and rhetorical forms which invest individuals,
peoples, communities, nations in resilient and complex relationships.
'Rhetorical discourse' as Giulio Preti puts it, 'is a discourse addressed to a
particular . . . audience . . . In other words, rhetorical argument starts from
presuppositions as well as from feelings, emotions, evaluations — in a word
'opinions' (*doxai*) — which it supposes to be present and at work in its
audience'.[51]

Representation as performance and as entertainment must be understood in terms of this particularity. Even explicit and practising realisms acknowledge this point. When John Grierson complained in the 1930s that 'our culture is diversed from the actual' and that 'our gentlemen explore the native customs of Tanganyka and Timbuctoo, but do not travel dangerously into the jungles of Middlesborough and the Clyde'[52] or when Robert Flaherty says that '[A] story must come out of the life of a people, not from the actions of individuals'[53], they were not — or not only — making claims to veracity but also, and more importantly for contemporary forms, investing a series of techniques, strategies, and occasions for, once more, the national community, in the form of documentary. *This* is the form of resilience, not its realism. Grierson was explicit about this *particular* and *performative* function: 'the major problem remains . . . what final honours and final dishonours we shall reveal in this English life of ours: what heroism we shall set against what villainy?'.[54]

Clearly the terms of that question are still very much up for grabs. But it cannot be answered in terms of a 'politics of interruption' which, while keen on revealing contradictions between 'representations' and the 'real', has very little to say about the dense fabric of technologies of entertainment, of performance; in short, of some of the reasons for 'the popular' which, as Brecht reminds us, we 'so emphatically need'.

Notes

1. James Donald and Colin Mercer, *Reading and Realism*, Open University Press, 1981.
2. Suggested by James Donald whom I would like to thank for much assistance in the writing of this article.
3. The term is adopted, perhaps without sufficient justification, from Ian Hunter, 'After Representation', *Economy and Society*, November–December 1984. Many of the arguments presented in this article are directly indebted to Ian Hunter's work.
4. Galvano Della Volpe, *Critique of Taste*, New Left Books, London, 1978, p. 239.
5. See, for example, Terry Lovell, *Pictures of Reality*, British Film Institute, London, 1980.
6. Bertolt Brecht, 'Against Georg Lukács' in E. Bloch *et al.*, *Aesthetics and Politics*, New Left Books, London, 1978, p. 82.
7. Georg Lukács, 'Art and Objective Truth' in Lukács, *Writer and Critic*, Merlin Press, London, 1970, p. 47.
8. Ibid., p. 43.
9. Pierre Bourdieu, 'The Aristocracy of Culture', *Media, Culture and Society*, vol. 2, no. 2, 1980, pp. 237–8. See also C. Mercer, 'A Poverty of Desire: Pleasure and Popular Politics' in *Formations of Pleasure*, Routledge and Kegan Paul, London, 1983, pp. 85ff.
10. Heinz-Dietrich Fischer; 'Entertainment — An Underestimated Central Function of Communication' in Fischer and Melnik (eds), *Entertainment: A Cross-Cultural Examination*, Hastings House, New York, 1979.
11. Ibid.

12. See Richard Sennett, *The Fall of Public Man*, Alred A. Knopf, New York, 1977; Jürgen Habermas, *Strukturwandel der Öffentlichkeit*, Neuwied, 1962.
13. Benedict Anderson, *Imagined Communities: Reflections on the Origin and Spread of Nationalism*, New Left Books, London, 1983, p. 30.
14. Ibid., pp. 39–40.
15. Fischer, 'Entertainment', p. 3.
16. Ibid., pp. 3–4 (emphasis added).
17. Ibid., p. 4.
18. Ibid.
19. Cited in ibid., p. 5.
20. Cited in ibid.
21. Ian Hunter, 'After Representation' p. 407.
22. Ibid., p. 408.
23. Cf. Fischer, 'Entertainment', p. 4.
24. Ibid.
25. Samuel Johnson, *A Journey to the Western Isles of Scotland.*, ed. Mary Lascelles, Yale University Press, London, 1971, p. 22.
26. Tony Davies, 'Transports of Pleasure: Fiction and its Audiences in the Later Nineteenth Century' in *Formations of Pleasure*, p. 46.
27. Ibid., p. 49.
28. Ibid.
29. Ibid.
30. Ibid., p. 51.
31. Ibid.
32. Ibid., p. 53.
33. Cited in ibid., p. 52.
34. Ibid., p. 53.
35. Hunter, 'After Representation' p. 409.
36. V.N. Voloshinov, 'Discourse in Life and Discourse in Art', in *Freudianism: A Marxist Critique*, Academic Press, London, pp. 98ff.
37. Franco Moretti, *Signs Taken for Wonders*, Verso, New Left Books London, 1983, p. 3.
38. Terry Eagleton, *Literary Theory*, Blackwell, London, 1983, p. 206.
39. Moretti, *Signs*, p. 4.
40. Ibid., p. 13.
41. Mikhail Bakhtine, *L'Esthétique et théorie du roman*, Gallimard/NRF, Paris, 1978, p. 183.
42. Ibid., p. 184.
43. Edward Said, *The World, The Text, and The Critic*, Faber, London, 1984, p. 169.
44. Ibid., pp. 8–9.
45. The idea was still current at a BBC course on presentation for Open University academics in 1982 which I attended.
46. Cited in Simon Frith, 'The Pleasures of the Hearth' The Making of BBC light entertainment' in *Formations of Pleasure*, p. 110.
47. Ibid.
48. Ibid., p. 108.
49. Ibid., p. 115.
50. Ibid., p. 119.
51. Cited in Moretti, *Signs*, p. 3.

52. Cited in Christopher Williams, *Realism and the Cinema*, Routledge and Kegan Paul/British Film Institute, London, 1980 p. 105.
53. Ibid., p. 101.
54. Ibid., p. 105.

10

Janet Woollacott

Fictions and ideologies. The case of situation comedy

Escapist fiction, that which purportedly allows its viewers or readers to 'escape' from the problems of the real world, was the category within which situation comedies found their home in terms of television criticism. Whereas some popular genres show obvious connections with the more general ideological formations in play at the time of their popularity (the spy thriller during the 1960s, for example, or the television crime series during the seventies), situation comedies could be held to have a more general grip on their audience. Over a longer period of time, at least for the last three decades, they have been a consistent part of the flow of the evening's television entertainment, a necessary and vital ingredient in the television controller's strategy for keeping the audience 'tuned in'. Moreover, the popularity of situation comedies has remained, throughout major shifts in more general ideological configurations in the period, and through the rise and decline of other popular genres such as the crime series. It is the aim of this article to outline some of the general characteristics of situation comedies, their narrative and comic strategies, use of character and performance; to consider some of the 'pleasures' of situation comedies and to suggest some of the issues raised by the role of situation comedies in considering the relations between fictions and other ideologies.

Despite the very wide range of targets for joking and humour in situation comedies, the programmes do conform to relatively strict conventions. Clearly some aspects of their formal organisation are related to institutional constraints; the weekly half-hour slot, the limited number of characters and the cheap sets. In this respect and others they can be considered as a television genre. Ryall suggests in relation to film genres that 'genres may be defined as patterns/forms/styles/structures which transcend individual films and which supervise both their construction by the film-maker and their reading by an audience'.[1] In the mutual expectations of television producers and audiences, genre conventions are constantly varied but rarely totally exceeded or broken. Generally situation comedies are pre-eminently texts which are linked to a comfortable practise of reading. As Stephen Neale remarks of all popular genres, 'the existence of genres means that the spectator, precisely, will always know that everything will be made right in the end, that everything will cohere, that any threat or danger in the narrative process itself will always be contained'.[2]

The narrative organisation of situation comedies, involves making everything right in the end in a particular way. *Steptoe and Son*, for example, was an early and popular situation comedy, frequently referred to as one of the first British situation comedies. The first version of *Steptoe and Son* was a Comedy Playhouse production transmitted in January 1962 and called 'The Offer'. The titles show Harold Steptoe returning with his horse and rag and bone cart to the yard where he and his father live. *Steptoe and Son* is inscribed on the gates of the yard. 'The Offer' establishes the claustrophobic world of the Steptoes, moving between their house, furnished and cluttered with objects selected from the yard and the yard itself. The relationship between father and son is equally claustrophobic, quickly established as one of constant mutual complaining and bickering.

Albert	That's another thing, you don't look after that horse. How can you expect to get round quick if your horse ain't in good nick.
Harold	Look, dad, you look after the yard and I'll look after the horse and cart, all right?
Albert	He don't get enough to eat. He's entitled to eat, that horse, same as you and me.
Harold	For gawd's sake, dad, don't keep on about the horse.
Albert	He's a dumb animal, he can't tell us when he's hungry.
Harold	Well, this one can. Greedy, hungry gutted great clodhopper.

The culmination of the arguments between Albert and Harold, as they unload the cart is Harold's threat to leave and live and work elsewhere.

Harold	Yeah, well, that's it ain't it . . . you don't want to say anything do you . . . otherwise I'll jack this lot in and be off. I'm sick to death of you, the yard, the cart and the horse.
Albert	Dah, what do you know, what could you do?
Harold	Look mate, don't you worry about me. I can look after myself. I'll be all right, I've had an offer.
Albert	Get out of it.
Harold	Oh yes I have. And it don't include you or that rotten horse. See? OK? All right? Well, watch it then.

The offer disturbs Albert and he attempts to persuade Harold to stay, pointing out that he belongs here, that he will inherit the business and that Albert himself is old and likely to die soon. They continue to unload the cart with Harold complaining that Albert keeps all the best items for himself. Albert nevertheless manages to snaffle a plate for the wall and to conceal a barometer from Harold. The two move into the house where Harold proceeds with the help of Albert to fill his 'cocktail cabinet' with drops from the bottoms of empty bottles he has collected. The final argument emerges from Harold's discovery that Albert has been drinking his gin.

Harold   I am looking at you. I put a mark on this label, see. That's where the mark is, and that's where the gin is. Two inches beneath it.

Albert   It must have evaporated.

Harold   Yeah, and I know where to. You been at it, haven't you. I been out on the cart and you've been at the gin. Oh well, that's put the old tin hat on that, then, I'm off. I'm taking that offer.

Harold collects various items, including the barometer, and loads them on the cart. Albert refuses to let him use the horse and Harold finds that he cannot move the cart.

(*He strains and strains and gradually gets weaker. He relaxes and has another go. He is panting with effort.*)

Harold   (almost crying) Move, you rotten, stinking cart . . . move . . . I got to go . . . I got to get away. Move . . . move.

Albert persuades Harold to return inside, coaxing him with promises of sausages and tea.

Harold   I'm going, I'm not staying here . . . I'm taking that offer.

Albert   'Course you are. He'll keep the offer open for you. You can go another day. Or you could stay here with your old dad and wait till a better offer comes along . . .

They both go into the room but Albert comes out again and retrieves the barometer which Harold was going to take with him.

This basic format was repeated in most episodes of *Steptoe and Son* with Harold attempting to 'get a bird', or to go on a skiing holiday, but always being foiled and forced to remain in the family home. Harold's failure to leave and to 'better himself' is always linked to his father's domineering and manipulating presence.

In Eaton's attempt to outline a typology of situation comedy, he suggests that the two basic 'situations' of situation comedy are those of home and work. *Steptoe and Son*, of course, combines the two. Within these parameters, he argues that the narrative form of situation comedies is organised around an 'inside/outside' dichotomy. Moreover, the dichotomy 'affects every aspect of production down to its finest budgetary details'.[3] In plot terms, this means that events or characters from the outside can be allowed to enter the situation but only in such a way that the outsiders don't affect the situation which can be maintained for future weekly episodes. 'The Offer' clearly follows this pattern as does *Steptoe and Son* generally with Harold constantly threatening to leave his father in response to some 'outside' event or character, but always failing to do so, in order to return the 'situation' to its normal 'inside' nature. In Eaton's typology, the inscription of the viewer within situation comedies is made manifest rather than being rendered invisible as in so many forms of novelistic fiction. However, this particular form of inscription is not typical of *Steptoe and Son*, nor of many other situation comedies. Moreover, as Eaton acknowledges, he pays little attention to the pleasures of situation comedy, suggesting only that an analysis of such pleasures would not be incompatible with his typology. One of the problems of Eaton's analysis is the extent to which it relies on simply listing the typical characteristics of situation comedies. For example, the circumstances which Eaton perceptively categorises as 'typical', the small number of characters 'stuck with one another' at work or at home, or in some other boundaried setting, may occur in other genres. The situation of *Blake's Seven*, for example, in which the characters are confined to their spaceship, with fleeting teleported trips to other worlds, is not markedly dissimilar to that described by Eaton as a feature of situation comedies, and for rather similar institutional reasons. Even jokes or comic situations are not limited to situation comedies. Soap operas usually have their comic characters and situations. Regan's wit, in a crime series like *The Sweeney* is one much quoted reason for his popularity, while part of the format of a James Bond film is to follow an exciting 'action' sequence with a one-line joke from the hero. Indeed, the generic specificity of situation comedy is not really a question of certain exclusive elements ('situation', jokes, etc.) but of particular combination of elements. In Neale's terms, it's a matter of 'the exclusive and particular weight given in any one genre to elements which in fact it shares with other genres'.[4]

Narrative and situation comedy

Most forms of popular fiction involve a narrative which is initiated through the signification of a disruption, a disturbance, which the narrative proceeds to resolve. The narrative offers to the readers or the viewers a transformation of the initial equilibrium through a disruption and then a reordering of its components. Hence, it could be argued that one of the pleasures of reading a Bond novel rests on the simultaneous existence within the Bond novels of a disturbance both in a discourse of sexuality and in a discourse of imperialism and a progression towards the resolution of those disturbances through the activities of the hero. It is possible to suggest that all genres play with a disturbance, process and closure within the narrative, although in different ways. In so doing, genres construct particular temporal sequences. In the detective story, for example, the enigma with which the narrative begins structures suspense not simply by organising the narrative as a puzzle, but also by setting up a particular temporal sequence. The enigma or disturbance involves separate times; the time of the story behind the crime and the time of its reconstruction in the narrative. Closure is effected through the bringing together of the two times. Thus detective films construct a memory from instances of the story

199

of the crime, from the story of its investigation and from the process of the text itself so that the 'memory constructed within the film duplicates the memory constructed by the film'. The temporal tension produced is the main characteristic of the suspense of a detective story.

The suspense of the thriller form is achieved slightly differently, but one common structure is that of the playing of the protagonist against a grouping of apparently disparate threats. In the Bond novels, the symbolic phallic threat takes a number of forms, that of Bond's substitute father M, that of the villains and that of the heroine. In a crime series programme such as *The Sweeney*, Jack Regan is threatened by criminals and by bureaucratic elements in the law and on occasion by problems with his family or private life. This doubling and occasionally trebling of threats to the hero not only increases the danger to him, but also sets up a temporal sequence involving both the number and complexity of the tasks which have to be performed for an effective and coherent closure to the narrative, for the story to 'end satisfactorily'. Suspense resides in the tension between the viewer's desire for the narrative to progress, although this involves a degree of risk for the hero, and the viewer's desire for the narrative to end, although this requires the full working out of the complex interconnections of the threats to the hero or heroine.[6]

Situation comedies also order the narrative and effect a particular closure, setting up a temporal sequence and positioning the subject, not in suspense but amusement and laughter. Eaton's argument suggests one aspect of the narrative of situation comedies, the lack of 'progression' involved in many situation comedies. In a sense, this lack of progression can only be identified in comparison with other genres, in which the progressive aspect of the narrative, that is the impetus towards the resolution of the initial disturbance, is more strongly weighted. In the opening episode of *Steptoe and Son*, the disturbance from the 'outside', the 'offer' does not lead to an obvious resolution in which either Harold takes the offer and leaves or rejects the offer and stays, but to Harold's inability to take the offer and his remaining without acceptance. In situation comedies, the viewer's pleasure does not lie in the suspense of puzzle solving nor in the suspense surrounding the hero's ability to cope through action with various tasks and threats. Rather the tension of the narrative to which the viewer responds revolves around the economy or wit with which two or more discourses are brought together in the narrative. The pleasure of situation comedy is linked to the release of that tension through laughter.

Eaton's account of the 'inside/outside' dichotomy in situation comedies indicates the narrative structuring of many situation comedies around an intersection of two discourses. The resolution of the disturbance, the contradictions and resistances of the bringing together of the two discourses has to be accomplished with economy and wit, with conscious and overt fictional manipulation. The 'circularity' of many situation comedy plots is precisely an indication of that formally articulated wit. In Tony Hancock's

'The Blood Donor', you may remember the narrative follows this type of economic circularity. The episode begins with Hancock's entry into the Blood Donor Department of a hospital.

Nurse Good afternoon, sir.

Tony Good afternoon, miss. I have come in answer to your advert on the wall next to the Eagle Laundry in Pelham Road.

Nurse An advert? Pelham Road?

Tony Yes. Your poster. You must have seen it. There's a nurse pointing at you, a Red Cross lady, actually, I believe, with a moustache and a beard — pencilled in, of course. You must know, it's one of yours, it's next to 'Chamberlain must go', just above the cricket stumps. It says, 'Your blood can save a life'.

Nurse Oh I see. You wish to become a blood donor.

Tony I certainly do. I've been thinking about this for a long time. No man is an island, young lady. To do one unselfish act with no thought of profit or gain is the duty of every human being. Something for the benefit of the country as a whole. What should it be, I thought. Become a blood donor or join the young Conservatives. But as I'm not looking for a wife and I can't play table tennis, here I am. A body full of good British blood and raring to go.[7]

The two discourses are present from the beginning. On the one hand there is Hancock's discourse, in which the hero constantly and ineffectively seeks higher status, from his name ('Anthony Aloysius St John Hancock' rather than Tony Hancock), his conviction that he has aristocratic connections ('It's blood you're thinking about isn't it? British. British. Undiluted for twelve generations. One hundred percent Anglo-Saxon with perhaps just a dash of Viking but nothing else has crept in. No, anybody who gets any of this will have nothing to complain about. There's aristocracy in there you know.') to his desire to be given a badge for giving blood ('I just think we ought to get a badge as well. I mean nothing grand, a little enamelled thing, a motto that's all, nothing pretentious, something like, "He gave for others so that others might live" ').[8] On the other hand, there is the discourse of the hospital and the other blood donors, the resisting world against which Hancock's delusions normally clash. The intersection of the two discourses is finally marked in the text of 'The Blood Donor', by Hancock's return to the hospital to be given the pint of blood he had donated earlier. He has cut himself with a kitchen knife.

The doctor goes over to Tony.

Doctor Well, you're going to be alright, old man. We're going to give you a transfusion.

Tony I'm a very rare blood type, you know.

Doctor Yes, yes, we know. We've got just one pint of your group in stock — you're to have that.

Doctor MacTaggart comes in.

MacTaggart	Who wants the pint of AB negative?
Doctor	Over here.
MacTaggart	(spots Tony) Oh no, it's not for him.
Doctor	Why?
MacTaggart	He only gave it yesterday. (*To Tony*) Waste of time wasn't it?
Tony	Well, I would have been in a right state if I hadn't. There's nothing else here for me. At least I know it's going to the right sort of person. These blood banks. They're like ordinary banks really. Put it in when you're flush, draw it out when you need it. Come on, bang it in, I'm getting dizzy. I'll let you have it back later on. (*To nurse*) What's on the menu tonight? You got any mince? I like mince, particularly hospital mince . . .[9]

The pleasure and coherence of this ending is partly one of Hancock's triumph over the hospital and blood donorship. Hancock overcomes the resistance of the hospital and subordinates it to his personal demands, thus reordering the discourses in another relationship to that of the beginning, from one of altruism to one of self-interest. But our amusement is also linked to the way in which Hancock's mixture of self-interest and would-be altruism comes full circle.

The narratives of most popular situation comedies within each episode tend to follow this pattern, although over a whole series the narrative sometimes develops beyond a constant return to square one. *Whatever Happened to the Likely Lads?* sees Terry's return from the army, the re-establishment of his friendship with Bob and the events leading up to Bob's wedding to Thelma and his removal to the Elm Lodge housing estate. The three series of *Agony* see the breakup of agony aunt, Jane Luca's marriage to Laurence, her living alone, her affair with Vincent Fish and with Laurence, her pregnancy, return to Laurence and the birth of her child.[10] At the same time, although events happen, the discursive relationships often remain the same. In *Whatever Happened to the Likely Lads?* the clash between Bob and Terry's long-established friendship and common interests and Bob's new relationship with Thelma, remains at the centre of the narrative of each episode. Similarly, in *Agony*, the contradiction between Jane's public image of helping others and her private difficulties in helping herself, her husband and friends, continues to provide the mainspring for the comic strategies of each episode.

In one sense, it is quite clear that while watching situation comedies we already know the likely outcome, just as we know the likely outcome of a detective story or a thriller. This does not, however, eradicate a sense of narrative tension. The tension and suspense of situation comedy is produced through a particular organisation of narrative time. A simple internal example of this is the use in situation comedies of the 'anticipation of the inevitable'. The joke is telegraphed in advance and the pleasurable effects are achieved through the viewer's foreknowledge of it. The comedy stems from the timing and economy with which a scene or a series of scenes are treated. For example, the opening episode of *Whatever Happened to the Likely Lads?* uses four scenes to build up suspense around the reunion of the heroes, Bob and Terry. The four scenes work to tie together a series of jokes, which move cumulatively to the joke of their meeting. The titles of the series and the credits which show stills from the previous series, *The Likely Lads*, establish the past friendship of Bob and Terry and the differences between them now. The title song, plaintively asking 'What happened to the people we used to be?', is sung over the film and freeze frame of Bob shown in a smart suit next to his car and suburban house, while Terry is shown in a casual jacket, against a background of slum clearance, missing a bus (or 'the' bus).

As viewers we know simply from the titles that we are to be reintroduced to Bob and Terry and, regardless of whether or not we are familiar with the previous series of *The Likely Lads*, we also know that they were friends in the past. The scenes which follow establish Bob and Terry's differences and lead inexorably to their meeting. The first scene sees Bob and Thelma looking at slides of the building of their new house, the damp course, the main drainage, etc. The first slide, accompanied by Thelma's sighs, is intercut with a shot of their clasped hands. This happy scene is interrupted by Bob accidentally inserting a slide of Terry Collier, obviously drunk and on a works outing. Thelma reacts with horror, turning accusingly to Bob:

Thelma	You did that on purpose.
Bob	Of course, I didn't, darling. I just picked one at random.
Thelma	Some jokes I can understand. Like electrocuting people or putting a piranha in their bath but suddenly just like that producing him — that's not funny.

Bob reassures Thelma that it was an accident, that he hasn't seen Terry for four years and that she's only really worried about his forthcoming trip to London. When Thelma leaves to get him some tea, however, he turns back to the screen, the anxious expression fading as he smiles reminiscently at Terry's image.

The second scene shows Terry also on his way to London sharing a train compartment with a mother, child and baby. It's established that Terry is home after five years in the army and still chasing women. The blonde attractive young mother suggests that he comes home with her and puts his feet up for the day. Terry's face instantly freezes at the implied sexual promise only to drop disappointed at the mention of the lady's husband, who is a marine. Grasping for excuses, he gets out of the visit. 'Oh, well, it's very nice of you but . . . the thing is I'm only here for the day, so I should see relatives. Yes that's it. Must spend the day with the family.' The film cuts from Terry's face cosily talking about seeing the family to a striptease. The camera cuts from the girl's gyrations to Terry sitting smoking in the audience, back to the girl's act and back to Terry's absorbed face, as unnoticed by him the ash from his cigarette drops down his front. Terry checks his watch and then with an expression of irritation starts to move but stops still watching the act; he stops in front of another intent member of the audience, who impatiently pushes him to move along. It's Bob but neither Bob nor Terry notice one another.

The fourth scene opens with Terry tossing copies of Mayfair on to various seats in a train compartment. As he sits down, Bob enters carrying a large parcel and therefore not seen by Terry. At that precise moment the lights go out.

Bob	Sod it . . . sorry, was that your foot?
Terry	I've got another.
Bob	What's the matter?
Terry	Power failure. Typical.
Bob	Would you believe it. The jet age. High speed gas and all that. 'Inter-city makes the going great'—.
Terry	Typical of this country.
Bob	That'll mean no heat as well. Any heat on your side?

Bob attempts to check and there's a scuffle.

Bob	Oh . . . sorry again.
Terry	It was my knee that time.
Bob	Sorry, mate.
Terry	How far are you going?
Bob	Newcastle.
Terry	Well sit still will you. Or I'll be black and blue by the time we get there.
Bob	You live up that way?
Terry	Near there. Haven't been back for ages. Just come out of the army.
Bob	Oh aye, Enjoy it?
Terry	Got a lot out of it, got a lot out of it.
Bob	I nearly went in once.
Terry	Could've done a lot worse.
Bob	Actually, there's a funny story attached to it, really you see, I had this mate, my best mate, you know, really close. Anyhow, a few years back, I decided to go into the Services. You know — get away for a bit, see something of the world. So I signed on. Well when I went away, this mate of mine couldn't take it. Went to pieces. Couldn't function without me. I suppose it was like losing your right arm. So he signs on too. Just to be with me. Only you'll never guess . . .

In the latter part of this speech the camera cuts from Bob talking to the shadowy outline of Terry's head, clearly stiffening and aware who his companion in the railway carriage is. But Bob continues.

Bob   . . . He gets in and I get discharged — flat feet. So I'm free again and he's lumbered for three years! You should have seen the look on his face. I still laugh when I think of it. I mean it's a sad story in some ways because he's never spoken to me since. But when you're telling the story, like when you tell someone else, you do see the funny side. I mean you've got to laugh.

As Bob laughs, the camera cuts again to Terry's silent presence and there's a pause before Terry explodes.

Terry   You bastard.

The lights come on dramatically. We see Bob and Terry face to face before the camera cuts to Bob's face, aghast and taken back.

Jokes and the comic strategies of situation comedies

It is often assumed that 'jokes' are what distinguish situation comedies from other narratives. It is worth looking more closely, therefore, at the formal characteristics of jokes and their relationship to the comic and narrative strategies of situation comedies. In Freud's work on jokes and joke-telling, he identifies the main characteristic as that of a verbal play in which two meaning systems intersect and a phrase or action is replaced by something linked to it in a conceptual connection. Freud also suggests that the pleasure of the joke resides in the way in which the listener or third person is 'given' a release from internal anxieties and inhibitions through the mechanism of the joke.

> If we can see that the hearer of a joke laughs but that its creator cannot laugh, this may amount to telling us that in the hearer a cathectic expenditure has been lifted and discharged, while in the construction of the joke there have been obstacles either to the lifting or to the possibility of discharge. The psychical process in the hearer, the joke's third person, can scarcely be more aptly described than by stressing the fact that he has bought the pleasure of the joke with very small expenditure on his own part. He might be said to have been presented with it. The words of the joke he hears necessarily bring about in him the idea of the train of thought to the construction of which great internal inhibitions were opposed in him too. He would have had to make an effort of his own in order to bring it about spontaneously as the first person, he would have had to use at least as much psychical expenditure on doing so, as would correspond to the strength of the inhibition, suppression or repression of the idea. He has saved this psychical expenditure . . . we should say that his pleasure corresponds to this economy.[11]

The 'jokes' in the situation comedies which we have discussed so far are not predominantly verbal nor are the pleasures of watching situation comedies solely those of jokes. Situation comedies constitute one form of realist fiction. If you think back to the opening scenes of 'Strangers on a Train', jokes are part of the text. When Thelma responds angrily to Terry's unexpected appearance among the slides, Bob reassures her. 'I just picked one out. Like a lucky dip — or an unlucky dip. It could have been anything. It could have been my first bicycle or your sister's wedding — or us caravanning in East Lincs', and jokes, 'It just happened to be the Creature from the Black Lagoon'. The joke is visually reinforced by the camera cut to the slide of Terry's drunken face. Yet the pleasures of watching 'Strangers on a Train' are the pleasures of watching a realist text. The illusion, generally, is not that we are listening to the telling of a joke, but that we are finding a situation or characters comic.

When Galton and Simpson first started writing *Hancock's Half Hour*, they stressed that they were increasingly interested in writing not jokes, but a fictional form in which situations and character provided the humour.[12] Indeed, it is possible to see, it you think back to Hancock and to *Steptoe and Son*, how central to the jokes are the characters in comparison with jokes which could be bought and used by any stand-up comic.

The institutional form of situation comedies, the half-hour slot in the evening's viewing and the textual characteristics with which we have been concerned so far, add to the likelihood that we will find situation comedies amusing or comic. Freud suggests that the most favourable condition for the production of comic pleasure is a generally cheerful mood in which one is inclined to laugh but he also argues that

> a similarly favourable effect is produced by an expectation of the comic, by being attuned to comic pleasure. For this reason, if an intention to make something comic is communicated to one by someone else, differences of such a low degree are sufficient that they would probably be overlooked if they occurred in one's own experience unintentionally. Anyone who starts out to read a comic book or goes to the theatre to see a farce owes to this intention his ability to laugh at things which would scarcely have provided him with a case of the comic in his ordinary life.[13]

Finally, Freud also warns us — not that, by now, you would need warning — that the comic is inimical to intellectual or analytic work just as the analysis of jokes inevitably renders them unfunny.

Ideology and situation comedy

One of the recurring interests in the study of comedy is the issue of its 'subversive' nature. In the British Film Institute's Dossier on situation comedy, the question of whether situation comedy is ideologically incorporative or ideologically subversive is broached time and again and with conclusions varying from seeing situation comedy as essentially conservative despite its reputation for subversion to seeing it as a fictional form which is capable of both inflections.[14] The centrality of the issue of whether comedy subverts or not can only be understood in relation to the theoretical traditions through which popular fiction is normally studied. The mantle of Leavis in English literature carries with it a condemnation of popular fiction. Much Marxist criticism echoes this. High culture, works of 'great art', have always been seen within Marxism as representing something of a problem, something above and beyond ideology, but, on the whole, no such reservations have been held about popular cultural forms. Lowenthal, for example, suggests in his introduction to a discussion of popular culture and literature that it is necessary to distinguish between 'art on the one hand' and a 'market oriented commodity on the other'.[15] The discussion of popular fiction as 'mere ideology', an indicator of something else, be it the socio-psychological characteristics of the multitude or a distorted view of 'real' conditions of existence influenced and moulded by ruling-class interests, has led to a number of problems of 'reductionism' in Marxist and other accounts of popular fiction.

Probably the most typical aspect of accounts of popular fiction is the attempt to read 'through' fiction to a reality constructed by Marxist theory, and in so doing to reveal the 'distortion' involved in any particular popular text. Sometimes the analytic task is seen to be solely concerned with the unmasking of 'distortion' in the text and a deploring of its assumed influence. In an account of children's fiction, for example, we get this castigation of the work of Enid Blyton:

> Naturally, the stress on the middle-class English (perhaps I should say upper-middle-class English judging by the number of servants of all kinds, even governesses) implies its opposite which is that other people will be held in contempt, despised or hated to the degree that they deviate from this assumed norm. Thus the English working classes, when they appear at all, are figures of fun, if submissive to their natural masters, and only disliked and portrayed as rather stupid if they are rebellious.[16]

Dixon's reading of *Five Fall into Adventure*, one of Blyton's series of 22 Famous Five adventures, is almost completely concerned to reveal the 'bias' of the text.

Apart from the combination of moral indignation and aesthetic evaluation which marks Dixon's analysis, the problem is that the focus on 'class bias' diverts attention from the formal organisation of the book and from the way in which the Famous Five narratives work upon their readers. The process of identification which operates in the Famous Five stories is treated only casually and accidentally. Dixon has no way of accounting for the popularity of the Blyton books except, perhaps, through girls' identification with characters such as George, the tomboy. He blames the popularity of the books on a combination of children's need for security and reassurance and effective marketing. Yet the narrative organisation of the

Famous Five books repays attention. In all the books, the children 'have an adventure' outside the parameters of adult control. Moreover, in so doing the Five accomplish something, catch a criminal, correct injustice or solve a puzzle, which adults are shown to have been incapable of accomplishing. Often the narratives play with parental or pseudo-parental disapproval of the activities of the Five which the development of the narrative shows to have been mistaken. In a sense, the Famous Five books are simple forms of a detective story cum thriller, which are addressed, however, directly to children, and in which children figure as the heroes and heroines. The class and sexual coding which is undoubtedly present in Blyton's books only works through this narrative.

Dixon's work shares some characteristics of a fairly crude Marxism of this sort of order. Given that the production of fiction is, in the broadcast sense, a reflection of fundamental conflicts in the social order then the business of Marxists is to identify the conflicting forces and then to distinguish progressive or reactionary forms of fiction. At the same time, Dixon's work undoubtedly also draws upon a long tradition in literary criticism, that of mimesis, in which fiction is judged by its ability accurately to reflect social reality. Comedy has been just as liable as other fictional forms to the notion of 'distorted reflection' and the identification of progressive or reactionary texts. Dorfman and Mattelart's fascinating and vitriolic attack on the Walt Disney comics in circulation in Chile takes up both these classically Marxist challenges. The ideology of Donald Duck, they argue, reflects particular class interests. Dorfman and Mattelart assume that the Disney comics can impose false consciousness on their readers: 'It is the manner in which the U.S. dreams and redeems itself, and then imposes that dream upon others, which poses the danger of the dependent countries. It forces us Latin Americans to see ourselves as they see us.[17]' Their reading of the Disney comics suggests that the transformations which the real world undergoes in the Disney comics are a tool in the exploitation of the Third World by American capitalism. The analysis of the jokes in the Disney comics focuses on the use of colonial stereotypes. Hence the following tale is used to illustrate 'Disney's colonial attitudes' to African independence movements. Donald has parachuted into a country in the African jungle. A pig pursuing him lands and discloses the whereabouts of some enemy ducks. To effect his escape, the pig decides to scatter a few coins as a decoy. The natives are happy to stop, crouch and cravenly gather up the money. Elsewhere, when the Beagle Boys dress up as Polynesian natives to deceive Donald, they mimic the same kind of behaviour. As they prostrate themselves and offer to be Donald's servants, Donald observes that they are natives too, but a little more civilised.

It is not necessary to claim that the Disney comics are ideologically innocent to suggest that the jokes and the comics here require rather more detailed attention than they tend to be given by Dorfman and Mattelart. The joke about the bowing and scraping natives, for example, would seem to work on the basis of the foolishness of Donald Duck rather than inherent slavishness on the part of the natives. Clearly Dorfman and Mattelart are more concerned to make a political intervention in this area than they are to investigate why the Disney comics should have any popular appeal. Dorfman and Mattelart's work is not untypical of the neglect in the earlier Marxist tradition of the area of popular consent.

Stereotypes

In the case of situation comedies, one characteristic mode of identifying ideological 'bias' has been that concerned with the use of stereotypes. Stereotypes are forms of characterisation which are simple, memorable, widely recognised and frequently repeated. 'Dumb blondes', for example, are a recognisable type through a range of texts from Judy Holliday in *Born Yesterday*, to Marilyn Monroe in *Some Like It Hot*, to Lucy in the *I Love Lucy* show, to Wendy Craig in situation comedies such as *And Mother Makes Five*. The notion of stereotype assumes, not altogether unjustifiably, that there are important consequences stemming from the repetition of character types.

Stereotyping is not simply a 'neutral' exercise. Forms of stereotyping in the media have been identified as part of the way in which the media define and reinforce the deviant status of particular groups. Pearce sums up news coverage of homosexuality as 'How to be immoral, and ill, pathetic and dangerous, all at the same time'.[18] In a monograph on *Gays and Films*, Sheldon suggests the difficulties for homosexuals of responding to films with negative stereotypes: 'I remember being depressed for days after seeing *Sister George*, feeling "Sure, such a relationship may exist, but what a miserable one, and what's it doing on film to pervert young minds about lesbians" '.[19] Particular stereotypes are often attacked for their failure adequately to convey the 'real', either in terms of the complexity of any one individual or in terms of the range of real concrete individuals, homosexuals, blacks or women, who make up the membership of any particular stereotyped group. Criticism of the characterisation offered in stereotypes often explicitly demands more 'realism', in the sense of being truer to the real individuals outside the text, but it may also, of course, implicitly endorse some forms of signification at the expense of others. The typical characterisation of the nineteenth-century bourgeois novel, for example, is normally seen to be more adequate than that of a popular, contemporary situation comedy. Stereotypes are also attacked, however, for their failure to offer an ideal, a positive rather than a negative image.

Richard Dyer attempts to theorise the positive and negative aspects of stereotypes, by taking up Klapp's distinction between social types and stereotypes:

stereotypes refer to things outside one's social world, whereas social types refer to things with which one is familiar; stereotypes tend to be conceived of as functionless or disfunctional (or, if functional, serving prejudice and conflict mainly), whereas social types serve the structure of society at many points.[20]

As Dyer makes clear, most social types turn out to be white, middle class, heterosexual and male, and the distinction between social type and stereotype refers to those characters or types who are to be seen within and outside the boundaries of normal acceptability. Stereotypes in this formulation are inevitably negative. Indeed, Dyer suggests that they form part of a wider strategy of social control.

> The establishment of normalcy through social and stereotypes is one aspect of the habit of ruling groups — a habit of such enormous political consequences that we tend to think of it as far more premeditated than it actually is — to attempt to fashion the whole of society according to their own worldview, value system, sensibility and ideology. So right is the worldview for the ruling groups that they make it appear (as it does to them) as 'natural' and 'inevitable' — and for everyone — and insofar as they succeed, they establish their hegemony.[21]

There are one or two problems with this outline of the ideological functions of social types and stereotypes. One problem is simply the extent to which a focus on stereotypes and on their repetition leads to the neglect of differences between characters in situation comedies. Wendy Craig's Ria in the BBC2 series *Butterflies*, for example, undoubtedly plays upon certain aspects of the 'dumb blonde' stereotype, but it also differs substantially from the earlier version. Moreover, any analysis which works on the assumption of relatively unambiguous identification between the viewer or reader and the stereotype, ignores the way in which identification works through textual and inter-textual formations. Identification with a character in a situation comedy follows both from the articulation of a character within a text and from the spectator's position within a particular reading formation. Neale suggests in relation to film that identification with character depends upon identification with the text itself. 'It is this primary identification that provides the basis of the spectator's relationship to the text and its characters and so requires initial attention and analysis.'[22] In one sense, this simply appears as understanding the function of the character in the text. Hence, the appearance of homosexual characters in *Whatever Happened to the Likely Lads?* appears to function simply to reinforce the 'healthy' heterosexuality of Bob and Terry, despite their intimate friendship. In 'Strangers on a Train' after Bob and Terry have re-established their friendship, they quarrel in the train buffet over Bob's marriage to Thelma. As Bob leaves, full of affronted dignity, Terry orders a Scotch and remarks to the barman that he gave the best years of his life for that man (an implicit reference to his stint in the army). The barman, however, who has been listening sympathetically, puts a comforting hand over Terry's and remarks, 'Never mind, sailor, lots of other pebbles on the beach'. The camera focuses on Terry's aghast reaction to this. The typical and dominant response of the viewer is with Bob and Terry and the camera ensures that it remains with Terry in this case rather than with the barman.

Yet to a large extent, the 'reading' relationships or 'viewing' relationships have to be conceived of in terms of an interrelationship between the reading formations of the viewers and the internal characteristics of the situation comedy. Questions about the subversive or incorporative qualities of stereotypes in situation comedy are fraught with problems, but particularly so when dependent simply on a textual analysis of a situation comedy. Medhurst and Tuck, for example, argue that situation comedies such as *Butterflies* or *Solo* lie outside the main pattern of situation comedy, moving towards melodrama because they involve themes untypical of situation comedy, that the woman rather than the male is seen as the victim of marriage and domesticity. To a certain extent this is seen as an explanation of differing views of these two series.

> They are controversial series, liable to cause radical disagreements (not least between the two writers of this essay). Does *Butterflies*, for example, represent any kind of breakthrough in representations of women in comedy, or does it stand as the most insidious example of the method of innoculation? Ria is shown to be unable to cook; do we read this as a positive rejection of the housewifely role or a tired revival of the old jokes about female incompetence? Similarly, in the last episode of the first series of *Solo*, Gemma remarks of her relationship with Danny, 'If only the world hadn't changed and shown me things I really didn't want to see'. This can be taken as a positive acknowledgement of the impact of contemporary feminism, or as a glibly innoculatory gesture towards such an acknowledgement. [23]

But many 'non-controversial' situation comedies allow for different strategies of identification. In *Whatever Happened to the Likely Lads?*, the dominant critical reading undoubtedly involved identification with the 'lads'. Clive James summarises this 'male' view.

> Back from forces, Terry has spent the last couple of months trying to pull the birds. Bob, however, is on the verge of the ultimate step with the dreaded Thelma, and last week felt obliged to get rid of his boyhood encumbrances. Out of the old tea chest came the golden stuff: Dinky toys, Rupert and Picturegoer Annuals, all the frisson inducing junk that Thelma would never let weigh down the shelf units. 'I need those for reference', whined Bob with his arms full of cardboard covered books. There were Buddy Holly 78s — never called singles in those days, as Terry observed with the fantastic pedantry typical of the show. Obviously Bob will have a terrible time with Thelma. [24]

211

But discussions with Open University Summer School students showed a substantial proportion of them, predominantly women, who identified with Thelma as a strong maternal figure, similar to those in soap operas such as *Coronation Street*, against which the activities of Bob and Terry are simply the amusing antics of children. Clearly, this does not show that *Whatever Happened to the Likely Lads?* is a subversive text, but it does indicate that there can be very different readings of a situation comedy depending upon the operations of gendered reading formations and it itself suggests that any judgement about ideological subversion or incorporation can only be made in relation to the analysis of reading formations or viewing formations over time.

Of course, stereotypes are one attempt to bridge the gap between individual readings and more general ideological formations, but they tend to work in terms of a view in which ruling class ideas are handed down to the masses. Dyer, for example, suggests that stereotypes are one way through which ruling class groups project their own worldview. If however, the sphere of popular fiction is viewed as occupying an area of exchange and negotiation between ruling groups and subordinate classes, it could still be said to be the case that stereotypes play a particular role in establishing elements of the ideologies of dominant groups. Homosexuals, blacks and women could all be said to have negative images in contrast with white heterosexual males but it can also be argued that there is considerable negotiation around the use of stereotypes, indicated by the shifts and differences in one stereotype across a range of texts and by the way in which social subjects established in different reading formations negotiate identification with a stereotyped character. Thus, the use of stereotypes in popular fictional forms such as situation comedies may be rather less unambiguously a reflection of dominant group views than Dyer suggests.

Popular fiction and consent

Mick Eaton in a recent article quotes a Tony Allen routine in which the comic is approached by the Anti-Nazi League to perform at one of their benefits. He is questioned over the phone by the organiser over whether his humour is 'anti-black' and replies that it isn't. He is then asked whether his humour is 'anti-women' — he thinks that it isn't. Allen then warns the organiser that his humour has a broader span, 'it's anti-life'. 'That's all right', says the organiser, 'that's not an area of current concern'. Eaton uses the joke to argue that discussions of comedy cannot be separated from the ideological/political positions available in a class society. One way of conceiving the relationships between ideologies and situation comedies is to focus rather less on the 'progressive' or 'non-progressive', 'subversive' or 'non-subversive' polarities of situation comedies and more on the way in which situation comedies perform alongside and in relation to other ideologies.

Traditionally, Marxist theories of ideology were centrally concerned with determination. Indeed, the preoccupation with questions of determination, with the determining relationship between economic base and ideological superstructures, led to the problems of reductionism referred to earlier. Changes in Marxist theories of ideology, initiated largely through the work of Althusser, involved some crucial reformulations in this area. Althusser's 'structuralist' reworking of Marxist theory stressed not the view of ideology as distortion, involving false consciousness, but the notion that ideology constituted the forms and representations through which men and women 'live' in an imaginary relation, their relationship to their real conditions of existence. Althusser's work generally, with its conceptualisation of ideology as determined only 'in the last instance' by the economic base, and in conjunction with developments in semiology, refocused attention on the autonomy and materiality of the ideological and on the notion of articulation, on the relationships between parts within a structure rather than solely on determination. Theories of hegemony make use of the idea of articulation in a particular way to suggest that within a given mode of hegemony, popular consent is won and secured around an articulating principle, which ensures the establishment and reproduction of the interests of ruling groups while at the same time winning popular consent. The success of hegemonic ideological dominance can then be judged by the degree to which the articulating principle secures an ordering of different and potentially oppositional ideological discourses.

The area of popular fiction and popular culture generally works to shift and secure subject positions with the active consent of its readers and viewers. It constitutes a crucial area of negotiation of consent. When forms of popular fiction such as situation comedy rework the subject positions available to viewers they move their viewers on into different ideological frameworks. For example, regardless of whether a series like *Butterflies* truly 'subverts' or really 'incorporates', it does move its viewers on to a different set of ideological coordinates in relation to extramarital sex on the woman's part in terms of past handlings of this theme in situation comedies. In a reading framework of feminist criticism, of course, this move to a new set of ideological coordinates may not appear to be an improvement but it does occur. The popularity of a particular situation comedy or other fictional forms is an indicator of the success of that securing or shifting of subject positions.

In *Policing the Crisis*,[25] the authors outline a number of changes which have taken place in the ideological configurations of post-war Britain. *Policing the Crisis* takes as its starting point the orchestration by the media of mugging as a 'moral panic' and seeks to establish that this represents a movement from a 'consensual' to a more 'coercive' management of the class struggle, which in itself stems from the declining international competitiveness of the British economy following the post-war period, the erosion of which led to attempts to secure 'consent' by more coercive although legitimate means. The immediate post-war period saw the construction of a consensus based on the politics of affluence. Economic decline triggered the disintegration of the 'miracle of spontaneous consent' based on these politics and there was an attempt to put forward a Labourist variant of consent to replace it. The exhaustion of this form of consent, however, combined with the rise of social and political conflict, the deepening of the economic crisis and the resumption of more explicit class struggle, culminated in the 'exceptional' form of class domination through the state in the 1970s, in which the ideological articulating principle was a discourse of 'law and order'.

The media play a central part in this analysis. They are described as a 'key terrain where "consent" is won or lost', as 'a field of ideological struggle'.[26] The key to the media's involvement in the construction of consent lies in the authors' analysis of news as performing a crucial transformative but secondary role in defining social events. The primary definers are those to whom the media turn, their accredited sources in government and other institutions. Although *Policing the Crisis* emphasises the transformative nature of media news reporting, in the selection and structuring of themes and topics, the conception of the media role is one of 'structured subordination' to the primary definers. Further, the creative media role serves to reinforce a consensual viewpoint, by using public idioms and by claiming to voice public opinion. Thus, in the 'crisis' described, the media have endorsed and enforced primary definitions of industrial militancy, troublesome youth cultures, mugging, student protest movements, as part of a 'law and order' problem.

Policing the Crisis confines its account of the media largely to the area of news coverage and only touches upon the area of popular culture tangentially. Yet clearly the idea of the dominant articulating principle of ideological hegemony, a principle which structures ideological discourses and which involves the media in the construction of that articulation, could and should be extended beyond the confines of news coverage. One obvious area for development is in establishing the relationship between the dominant articulating principle and particular popular fictional genres. Given that genres themselves constitute specific articulations of ideological and formal elements, it would seem to follow that shifts in the dominant articulating principle would be registered in the area of popular fiction by the increased popularity of appropriate genre articulations. The police crime series, for example, became popular at a time when there were major shifts in the dominant articulating principle, from the terrain of ideologies of 'affluence' to that of 'law and order'. The television crime series was a form in which both arguments for and reservations about current 'law and order' issues could be put into play in terms of the subject positions produced by the genre.

Similarly the thriller format developed around notions of Britain's internal and external security in programmes such as *The Professionals* and *Sandbaggers*. *The Professionals* stands at one end of a range of programmes which focus directly on themes of 'law and order' and which extend the notion of policing quite radically. Where programmes such as *The Sweeney* suggested the dissatisfactions of a working policeman in the Flying Squad in terms of the barriers placed by bureaucratic police procedures on the arrest of criminals, *The Professionals* begins from the premise that the ordinary police cannot handle certain problems. One of the books derived from the programmes describes the heroes as the 'hard men'. 'They're the hard men. The Professionals. Doing society's dirty work in the ever more bloody war against violence and destruction . . .'[27]

The process of articulation with a hegemonic principle may help explain one of the continuing problems of the study of genre — why particular genres are popular at any one historical moment and why they may increase or decrease in popularity over time. Works of fiction and specific genres are popular precisely because they articulate, work upon and attempt in different ways to resolve contemporary ideological tensions. The case of situation comedies raises two important issues in relation to this, however. In the first place any comparison of situation comedies and television crime series will indicate something of the complexities of the process whereby popular genres both organise ideological themes differently and interpellate their subjects differently. Thus the episode of *Till Death Us Do Part*, 'If we want a proper democracy we've got to start shooting a few people' (transmission October 1972), constructs one version of the 'law and order' discourse with Garnett 'pulling in' a range of problems into the same problem of law and order.

Alf	. . . Enoch's wrong, having a go at the coons.
Mike and Ria	(astonished) Oh!!!
Alf	Yes! He ain't seen the real danger. It's not the coons. We don't want 'em over here stinking the country out with their curries and making a row on their dustbin lids. But they're bloody harmless — not like yer bloody Russian Unions and yer Chinese *Take-Aways* . . . Hot beds of bloody fifth column they are. But we're on to 'em, don't worry. You'll see the next time one of them commy shop stewards goes in the nick he'll rot there. All they organise them bloody strikes for is so they can get on the bleedin' telly. I blame the BBC for encouraging 'em. They'll put anyone on the bloody telly, they will. Rock an' roll vicars . . . and sex maniacs, an' bloody Irish gunmen. Admit they put stockings over their heads first, but still. They only let the Queen go on for one show at Christmas — I don't know what they've got against that woman. She should have her own series, 'cos she's better'n Lulu. (*Rita giggles.*) Blimey, she's the best thing on at Christmas.

215

Garnett's mad logic takes the argument on to cover both prison conditions and the unions and the solution to it all.

Alf And why shouldn't they get bloody slops? Prisons supposed to be a bloody deterrent annit? They ain't supposed to sit about all day scoffing and shagging! (*Else is shocked.*) I mean, blimey, they'll be putting yer Billy Butlin in charge of the prisons soon, and have bloody red-coats for warders! I mean in the old days, they used to put 'em in bloody chains and ship 'em out to the Colonies. But we can't do that now, 'cos your bloody Labour Party gave all the Colonies away. So we have to keep 'em here and feed 'em out of our taxes. And what if five of their ring leaders [of the prison officer's union] defy the law, eh? They can't bung them in prison, 'cos they're already in there.

Else They'll have to fine their union.

Alf Don't be so bloody draft. What are they gonna fine them? Eighty gallons of porridge? A hundredweight of hardtack? And another thing what would yer Russians have done, eh? They wouldn't have put them in prison, would they, eh? And your Chinese, eh? If five of their dockers had defied their laws, eh? They wouldn't have put them in prison, would they? Eh? No. They'd have bloody shot 'em.

Mike And I suppose you'd like to see 'em shoot our dockers, eh?

Alf We wouldn't! That's the trouble with this country. That's our weakness! If we want a proper democracy here, we've got to start shooting a few people . . . like yer Russians do.[28]

Till Death Us Do Part quite clearly registers a political concern with the ideological themes which were the focal point of other popular genres, notably the television crime series. At the same time, it could be argued that *Till Death Us Do Part* handles those themes rather differently. Garnett's suggestion that 'we've got to start shooting a few people' may sound more than reminiscent of the solution that is found in most episodes of *The Professionals*, but it is also a conclusion that we are supposed to laugh at rather than applaud. Moreover while *Till Death Us Do Part* was relatively unusual amongst the popular situation comedies of its period in its direct concern with political issues, it was also organised like many other situation comedies to pull the right-wing views of the inimitable Alf Garnett into a family narrative, playing off his position outside a liberal consensus against his position within the family. Later situation comedies such as *Shelley*, *Citizen Smith* or *Agony* dealt with characters and problems relevant to 'law and order' issues (unemployment in *Shelley*, political radicalism in *Citizen Smith* and sexual permissiveness in *Agony*) in a manner which also tended to pull 'deviance' into a familiar sitcom world of 'universal' problems of family, sexuality and class. The crime series, however, tended to place those same problems and characters as threatening to and outside the parameters of the family, class and 'normal' sexuality. In important ways then situation comedies and the crime series in the 1970s work against one another rendering their themes and subjectivities in opposed directions and in so doing indicating something of the complexity of the relationship between a hegemonic principle and the fictional field.

In the second place, popular and controversial situation comedies such as *Till Death Us Do Part* raise certain questions about the relationship between specific fictional forms and more general ideological formations. It is clearly the case that some fictions are not simply popular but also play a particular part in relation to the ordering of other ideologies. Such fictions have a place in the public arena above and beyond their immediate textual base. The public outcry which surrounded *Till Death Us Do Part* and the way in which Alf Garnett became a figure in the popular imagination even for people who didn't watch television indicates this process at work. At specific historical moments, some fictions, rather than working alongside and in relation to other ideologies, come to provide a nexus through which ideologies may be actively reorganised, shifting the subjectivities at their core, while other fictions work precisely to stabilise existing subjectivities. It is in this area that it is possible to establish in historical rather than formal terms the subversive or incorporative qualities of situation comedies. Without work of this order, the discussion of situation comedies in terms of their potentially subversive effects is simply an exercise in criticism, an attempt to organise situation comedies to mean some things and not others, to establish the protocols of viewing: a perfectly legitimate but rather different exercise.

Notes

1. T. Ryall, 'Teaching through Genre', *Screen Education*, 1976, p. 27.
2. S. Neale, *Genre*, British Film Institute, London, 1980, p. 28.
3. M. Eaton, 'Laughter in the Dark', *Screen Education*, 1981, p. 33.
4. Neale, *Genre*, p. 9.
5. Ibid., p. 27.
6. Ibid.
7. R. Galton and A. Simpson, *Hancock's Half Hour*, The Woburn Press, London, 1974, p. 100.
8. Ibid., p. 104.
9. Ibid., p. 124.
10. C. Hickman, *Agony*, Arrow Books, London, 1980.
11. S. Freud, *Jokes and their Relationship to the Unconscious*, Pelican, London, 1976, pp. 200–1.
12. Galton and Simpson, *Hancock's Half Hour*.
13. Freud, *Jokes*, pp. 282–3.
14. *Television Sitcom*, BFI Dossier no. 17, British Film Institute, London, 1982.
15. L. Lowenthal, *Literature, Popular Culture and Society*, Prentice-Hall, Englewood Cliffs, NJ, 1961, p. xiii.
16. B. Dixon, *Catching Them Young*, vol. 2: *Political Ideas in Children's Fiction*, Pluto Press, London, 1977, pp. 68–9.

17.   A. Dorfman and A. Mattelart, *How to Read Donald Duck: Imperialist Ideology in the Disney Comic*, International General, New York, 1975, p. 95.
18.   F. Pearce, 'How to be immoral and ill, pathetic and dangerous, all at the same time: mass media and the homosexual' in S. Cohen and J. Young (eds), *The Manufacture of News*, Constable, London, 1973, p. 284.
19.   Sheldon quoted in R. Dyer (ed.), *Gays and Films*, British Film Institute, London, 1977, p. 16.
20.   Klapp quoted in ibid., p. 29.
21.   Ibid., p. 30.
22.   S. Neale, 'Stereotypes', *Screen Education*, 1979, p. 35.
23.   A. Medhurst and L. Tuck, 'The Gender Game' in *British Film Institute Dossier, Television Sitcom*, p. 52.
24.   C. James, *The Observer*, 11 March 1972.
25.   S. Hall, C. Critcher, T. Jefferson, J. Clarke and B. Roberts, *Policing the Crisis: Mugging, the State and Law and Order*, Macmillan, London, 1978.
26.   Ibid., p. 220.
27.   K. Blake, *The Professionals 4: Hunter Hunted*, Sphere, London, 1978.
28.   J. Speight, *Till Death Us Do Part*, The Woburn Press, London, 1973, pp. 136–7.

Additional Sources

The extract from 'Strangers on a Train', 9 January 1973, by I. La Frenais and D. Clements from *Whatever Happened to the Likely Lads?*, BBC Television, is reproduced by permission of The William Morris Agency (UK) Ltd.; the extract from 'The Offer' by R. Galton and A. Simpson from *Steptoe and Son*, BBC Television, is reproduced by permission of RSO Management Ltd.

11

Alan Clarke

'This is not the boy scouts': Television police series and definitions of law and order

He's not the sort of copper you'd ask for directions, not Jack Regan. Not as his super-charged Ford slews to a halt spraying gravel and burning tyre rubber like he owns shares in Pirelli. He's not the sort of copper you'd ask to find your dog. Not as the car door bursts open and he leans over it pointing a Police .38, so big it needs two hands to hold it. He's not the sort of copper you'd even ask for a warrant. Not as he grinds his knee into the pit of the villain's back as an added refinement to a half-nelson, spitting out: 'The Sweeney! You're nicked! 'But isn't he lovely?'[1]

This cameo captures the essential character of Jack Regan and of the series which gave him life, *The Sweeney*. The police series as a genre can be reduced to a very simple story-line consisting of the basic components of crime, chase and arrest. *The Sweeney* worked this formula into a popular art form and changed the direction of police series in the mid-1970s. The particular inflection of the genre owed much to the work of American film and television staff who had produced a brand of films and television police series known as 'action series'. By making use of the full potential of film, police procedurals had been transformed from the slow-moving, quasi-documentary origins in the 1950s into a fast moving entertainment for the 1970s. Here I want to address the political significance of this transformation by looking at the pilot episode of *The Sweeney* and locating it within the context of the debates about law and order which were current in 1974. This material has to be presented within a discussion of the institutional changes which were taking place in the media at the same time since these affected the conditions of production surrounding any one series.

So this is entertainment: an American inheritance

American film and television are an integral part of the culture of the production of television series in studios in this country. The late 1960s saw a profound change in the presentation of crime in American television

219

programmes.[2] Three elements were introduced to the televsion frame that developed the genre. These were violence, action sequences and the increasingly prominent role accorded to music in the development of the narrative. Action sequences covered everything from the variants on the car chase to the choreography of the stunts in series like *Kojak* and *Starsky and Hutch*. Indeed, the title sequence of *Starsky and Hutch* is an excellent example of what 'action' means in the context. The two heroes are introduced squealing round cars and corners in a rapid car chase. Even when the two are on foot, they run, and in one memorable, bone-jarring leap jump off walls on to the roof of a car. There is no time to walk, no time to use the stairs. This sense of urgency is underpinned by a musical score which drives the action on at a relentless pace. This twinning of music and action was a distinctive feature of television shows during this period and is one demonstration of the relationship which exists between the film and television industries.[3]

The introduction of violence dramatically changed the nature of police series on television. This stemmed from the breakthrough made in the so-called 'spaghetti Westerns' which demonstrated the inadequacy of the bloodless bullet holes and the bruiseless punches of conventional Westerns.[4] By dwelling on the painful and bloody consequences of violence, the spaghetti Western showed in gruesome detail that even the good get hurt. With slow motion action revealing the progress of the bullet through the exploding flesh of its victim, it became difficult to accept the authenticity of filmic massacres without any blood. The contrast is between the 1930s gangster movies and Arthur Penn's 1967 film of *Bonnie and Clyde*. The standard depiction of a shooting had been to show the shooter while he is firing and to cut to the victim, if at all, only after he has been hit and is clutching the wound. After the Spaghetti Westerns, and the less well-known Samurai films of the early sixties, these conventions were changed to allow graphic portrayals of murder and mayhem.[5] The flood of police movies which came out of America in the late 1960s and early 1970s used this new convention to construct a view of policing in which violence was represented as a way of life for the police in modern cities. Much of the violence was completely gratuitous unless it was seen as the necessary background to the war against crime which the police were fighting. This more explicit portrayal had gained a symbolic value.

At the forefront of the transformation of the values of the police programme was a set of films made by Don Siegel and starring Clint Eastwood. In *Coogan's Bluff* (1968), Eastwood plays a cop from Arizona flown into New York to bring home a villain who has been arrested in the big city. He arrives attired in the full 'cowboy' gear, much to the amusement of the locals. All he lacks from his character in the spaghetti Westerns is his poncho as he keeps his hat, boots, and inscrutable expression. He loses his prisoner and tracks him using physical confrontations as the quickest way of gaining cooperation. By the time *Dirty Harry* (1971) appeared the character had become more refined and the Arizonian edges had been polished. The character had become dedicated to hunting villains and was often at odds with a legal system which set strict parameters on the methods he could use in the chase. He did not operate outside or above the law, merely bending it on occasion where a minor technical infringement speeded the course of the villains' arrests. *Magnum Force* (1973) clearly pointed to the difference between this attitude and that of a group of rogue cops who had set themselves up as executioners of the local villains. The hero cannot enter into this enterprise as it denies the validity of the entire legal system. This step towards anarchy is not what the character stands for but for a redrawing of the boundaries of acceptable behaviour in favour of the hard-pressed policeman. It is this tradition which Regan steps into, a British Eastwood without the hats.

'When do you ever have a small case, Jack?'

Jack Regan was a Detective Inspector in the 'Sweeney', which is cockney rhyming slang for the Flying Squad, an elite squad of detectives operating throughout the Metropolitan police area. The purpose of the squad is to track down major criminals and prevent, wherever possible, such crimes taking place. In this sense, the 'Sweeney' was ideal material for a fictional treatment, particularly within the action series format. The London-wide responsibility gave the production team ample scope for different locations and fast-moving sequences between scenes, especially as the series was shot on film. Equally, by concentrating solely on serious crime, The *Sweeney* again fell neatly within the requisites of the action series. It is also a logical development in terms of the internal history of the police series, for the 'Sweeney' were not the first squad to be featured in such series. The television archives are littered with attempts to dramatise the action of the specialised sections of the police force. Constant attempts to move the genre on had seen *Special Branch, Fraud Squad* and the BBC's chronicling of the move from divisional to regional criminal investigation in the shift from *Z Cars* to *Softly, Softly*. What the new series offered was a closed unit of characters who would appear regularly enough to develop into individual characters against a background of serious crime. It should be remembered that the concept of 'serious crime' had assumed particular connotations by the early 1970s: it referred to crimes involving large amounts of money and large amounts of violence and usually both. *The Sweeney* legitimated the transition to violence as part of the routine of police work by locating the fiction within the framework of that section of the police force most likely to deal with violence in the course of its work. The Flying Squad was an ideal vehicle for this fictional representation both in terms of the internal logistics of the genre and the concerns of the law and order debate outside of the series.

221

The Sweeney marked a distinct shift away from the earlier police series because of its attitude towards crime. One of the distinguishing features of the police series prior to the 1970s had been the sense of social conscience that the series had displayed. Quite often the crime which formed the subject matter for an evening's episode would be treated in complex ways, considering the underlying causes of the action, the criminal's individual problems as well as the police response which was deemed to be most appropriate. *Z Cars'* origins in a drama-documentary series on police interrogation techniques often revealed itself in the treatment given to problems such as shoplifters and the well-being of hoboes. *Dixon of Dock Green* is still remembered for George Dixon's opening and closing monologues about the morality behind that night's story, even though these were dropped from the later series. They spoke of a sense of community which informed the concern about crime, represented as a neighbourly interest in something which could affect each and every one of the audience. The policemen/heroes were friendly types, an image captured in the opening sequence of *The Blue Lamp* where a pedestrian is seen approaching a policeman and asking for directions. As Walker pointed out, Regan is not that sort of policeman. The spirit of cooperation and optimism which the shared values of *Dixon of Dock Green* suggest is replaced by a world weary cynicism in *The Sweeney*. Dixon was an integral part of his 'manor' and the patrol cars became an important landmark in *Z Cars'* Newtown. The London of the *Sweeney* is not like that and the policeman no longer enjoys the sense of belonging.

Regan's cynicism is summed up in a speech he made in an episode called 'Abduction' (transmitted 27 March 1975). Things do not always go smoothly for Regan and this particular day was no exception. He tells his driver:

> I sometimes hate this bastard place. It's a bloody holiday camp for thieves and weirdos . . . all the rubbish. You age prematurely trying to sort some of them out. Try and protect the public and all they do is call you 'fascist'. You nail a villain and some ponced-up, pinstriped, Hampstead barrister screws it up like an old fag packet on a point of procedure and then pops off for a game of squash and a glass of Madeira . . . . He's taking home thirty grand a year and we can just about afford ten days in Eastbourne and a second hand car . . . No, it is all bloody wrong my son.

Such sentiments would not have been thinkable within the structure of *Dixon of Dock Green* but flow 'naturally' from the construction of *The Sweeney*. Regan does his job to put villains away where they can do no more harm to society. His motivation is to stop the country being swamped by the crime wave. Unlike Dixon, he has no time for contemplation about the outcome of a particular case because there is another one to attend to, and then another and another.

This transformation is vitally important in understanding the new police series which followed *The Sweeney* in the mid-1970s. The crime series of the 1960s developed a set of concepts about crime which had been cast in the period of post-war reconstruction. Crime was thought, though important, to be only a passing problem which would disappear, or at least return to acceptable levels, as society returned to an orderly routine following the disruption of the war. Crime was to be tackled cooperatively, with the police as one party in this concerted effort.[6] In the late 1960s, these attitudes were attacked from many sides. The crime rate did not return to 'normal' and periodically, as they were constructed, new 'crime waves' swept the country, with the popular press fanning the flames of concern. One of the causes of concern was the so-called permissiveness of the 1960s and the threat that this posed to our way of life as it had been known for generations. The 'soft' options on crime and punishment were vigorously attacked and a lack of discipline throughout society was frequently bemoaned. Crime became not so much a problem for the community but was represented as threatening the very existence of that community. It was becoming a problem truly recognisable as one of 'law and order'. The question had become how could law be enforced and order maintained.

In the theatre of politics these issues were brought together in the 1970 General Election by the manifesto of the Conservative Party and their subsequent actions when they formed the new government. Heath followed Nixon's lead in claiming to speak for the silent majority of decent, law-abiding citizens and promised not to allow the dangers of American-style crime to infect the streets of this country. The Heath government took recourse to the law as a means of confronting a range of situations from student protest to industrial action. This extension of the role of the state led to what the authors of *Policing the Crisis* called the 'exceptional state'.[7] 'Exceptional' precisely because the power of the state which had remained so effectively concealed was being unmasked to shore up the position of the ruling bloc threatened from so many quarters it did not know what else to do. The old systems of policing were being challenged by the new role which the ever-increasing legislation was thrusting upon the police and new systems of policing were being developed to deal with this new emphasis. The importance of public cooperation was not denied but was made one part of the policing process as a bifurcation took place within the force. Ideas of 'community policing' gained favour to meet certain 'local difficulties' but alongside this work, more and more police were being trained in crowd and riot control. Counter-insurgency measures were openly discussed and joint operations between the police and the army were organised.

The Sweeney was a child of its time but this is not to say that the series simply reflected the public debates about crime and the changes in policing practice which were taking place. In no way should it be thought that the series even attempted to reflect these changes. The process, as Voloshinov correctly observed, is not one of reflection but of refraction.[8] It is not possible to understand the series without some understanding of the conditions of its production, but these conditions are not sufficient to explain the particular form of the series as it was broadcast. The problem of the relationship between the fictional and what it portrays is particularly acute in the police series, where the referent is so clearly present in the world outside the series. However, all too often the criteria of reality imposed to assess the fiction are based only a partial knowledge of that reality. Hence, with the police series, the authenticity of the series may actually be judged against the fictional presentation of the police in other series, the well publicised views of certain leading police officers and the news reports — themselves constructed — of police actions. Only a very small minority of the audience for *The Sweeney* will have any direct knowledge of the Flying Squad or that kind of police work. The image which is finally presented in the series takes some of the public knowledge about the police, carefully selected to deny the 'outrageous', and refracts this through the medium of the generic conventions, which are themselves subject to change.[9]

In this way, the 1970s could give rise to police series which, at one and the same time, eulogised the police for the effectiveness of their efforts in the war against crime and raised issues about police wrong-doing which, according to some right-wing critics, could have undermined public confidence in the police force. It is noticeable, however, that the police wrong-doing complained of consists mainly of bad language, the slightly over-zealous use of violence, searching premises without a proper warrant and so on. The more serious claims which were levelled against the police during the same period are excluded — no one deals with racism within the police force, no one deals with deaths in police custody. Generic conventions which sensationalise the presentation of police practices do not extend to the presentation of such damaging images. More time can be spent in high-speed chases than in writing up reports, more time can be spent on actual arrests than on the collection of evidence but the amount of critical material is severely limited. The good guys have borrowed from the tough guy's wardrobe but have left the bad guys' clothes on the peg.[10] What we witness is, in fact, an inflection of the moral domain of the hero rather than a shift in the moral basis of the series and the genre.

The human face of authoritarianism

Before looking at any material from *The Sweeney* in detail, it is important to consider the character of Jack Regan and to compare this with earlier characterisations of policemen. What the inflection of the moral domain produces is not a complete transformation of the character but rather a character with a difference, a harder edge than previously found. George Dixon is the archetype of the British television police character. Dixon was one of the earliest policemen to be seen on British television and the series ran for so long that the character had an influence on other series at least until 1976 when it went off the air. I suspect that the influence of *Dixon of Dock Green* has lasted longer than the series itself, as the Dixon character has become a part of the popular folklore. Indeed, the *Financial Times* headlined a review of policing methods after the Summer riots of 1981. 'We can't leave it to old George any more'.[11]

George Dixon gave a good impression of a classic boy scout, living up to Baden Powell's standards of civilised behaviour at all times. He occasionally sang in the police choir, and enjoyed a happy home life. He was a true local, knowing everyone and being on speaking terms with most of them. He had an overriding concern for his family and his colleagues and would be polite no matter how arduous the circumstances. He was always correctly attired, with his uniform spotless and properly pressed. Above all else, George Dixon was honest. Any thought of corruption was impossible where he was concerned. He was a man of integrity who would not have devalued himself or the force he was serving by bringing the possibility of dishonour to the uniform. He belonged to a generation that had lived through the war and thus recognised the need for discipline, both within himself and within the force. The world of Dock Green is profoundly ordered and orderly. A world where the police uniform itself deserved respect but where the individual bearer of that uniform could earn personal respect by living up to the ideals of public service. Throughout his career, Dixon did that and much more. In many respects he was too good to be true and as the series progressed it became increasingly clear that Dixon was a product of a world which was in the process of ceasing to exist. He personified the world which many people in the 1970s were complaining was being eroded by the tide of permissiveness which was sweeping the country. When Jack Warner, the actor who had played Dixon, died on 25 May 1981, the BBC repeated an episode of *Dixon of Dock Green* as a tribute to the actor. It was a particularly appropriate episode as it focused on the allegations of corruption against an ambitious young policeman. Dixon was always cast in a paternal role to the new recruits and championed PC Warren's innocence throughout the inquiry into his activities. At the end of the investigation it is found that the allegations were false, but although his name had been cleared Warren presented his resignation. George Dixon asked him for his reasons:

> *Warren* When I joined the force, my friends thought I was mad. But then there was all that stuff about a career in the police force and once I was on the beat I thought to myself, 'Yes, this is worth doing'. Not that I meant to pad the streets for long. Commissioner of Police one day, that was me.
>
> *Dixon* Could be. Though I happen to think any job in the force is worth doing.
>
> *Warren* Yes, I know. Oh I'd have settled in the end for whatever came my way.

Dixon Why quit now? You're a good copper. We can't afford to lose men like you.

Warren Because there are some things I just can't take.

Dixon Look, we're a disciplined force any raw recruit knows that. We've got to be.

Warren Does that include being put under suspicion on the strength of an anonymous letter? Does it include having your room searched and your private papers gone through without permission? Does it include being required to explain your personal bank account and being suspected of taking bribes if you don't? No, not me. I'll do my job as a policeman to the best of my ability but I'm still a human being in my own right. I joined because I wanted to. A fine uniform, and quarters or rent allowance in lieu doesn't turn me into a bonded slave. I've too much pride for that.

Dixon Well, as it happens, Len, I've got quite a bit of pride myself. All the years I've spent as a copper, I think every minute has been worth it. Oh, the police force isn't perfect. It can't be, it's manned by ordinary men. I know we talk about red tape and frustration when a villain goes free and the harm done by the occasional bent copper. But for all the criticism, the police are there to protect the public and that's what we do. We curb violence. We do our best to deal with villains who want to prey on society. I've been proud to have been a part of that, even a small part. It's been my life for a long time now and I don't regret any of it.

It was this ideal image and associated sentimentalism of character which many of the subsequent writers attempted to get away from in their scripts. Yet, underneath the hard-hitting veneer of the new characters, a substantial element of Dixon remained.

There is no time to list all the characters who attempted to challenge Dixon here. Some were more like Dixon — like Gideon of *Gideon's Way* and Lockhart of *No Hiding Place* — than others — most memorably Barlow. However, even when we look closely at the Regan character, we can see the 'Dixon tradition' is still present. Several of the peripheral characteristics have changed: Regan is divorced rather than happily married; he does not have any permanent home and lives in an untidy bedsit; he is not always polite to his superior officers. Within the narrative of the series these changes are explained and woven into the development of the action in such a way that they become naturalised. Once they become an accepted part of the narrative format they cease to challenge the central notions of the policeman's character. We know Regan is honest and incorruptible. We know Regan is firm and fair. We know, above all else, that he is working to protect the public from the villains who would prey on society. This continuity of core values can be seen to perform two functions as we analyse the police series. One is to link the police heroes across time and reinforce the trust placed in the police as the upholders of the law and the maintainers of order. The other is to establish a link between the series themselves, to maintain the parameters of the genre. Early studies of genre worked on the iconography of content, stressing the audience's recognition of the essential features of the type.[12] This led to work on the Western, the gangster movies, horror films and musicals which identified the disparate imagery of the movies. Subsequently this was refined to include the specific filmic conventions of each genre as well. However these definitions by content are tautologous and do not serve to take the analysis on beyond an initial classification. For instance, in looking at the gangster movies, McArthur devotes a great deal of time to the importance of the gun.[13] Kitses, looking at the Western, also spends time elaborating the importance of the gun.[14] The two are making slightly different points which cannot be supported simply by pointing to the fact that the two genres make use of different weapons in different physical locations. It is how the presence of the weapons is constructed within the narrative which is crucial to the development of the argument and the analysis of this setting requires that the focus of attention be shifted from the iconographic to the narrative. What this means for the practice of generic criticism is that more attention has to be given to the clustering of ideological elements within each genre, thus locating the difference between genres not at the level of inconographic content but at the deeper structural level of ideology. This is the view Neale elaborates in his monograph on *Genre*, with an argument which is premised on a notion of narrative as 'a process of transformation of the balance of elements that constitute its pretext'.[15] Neale construes narrative as a process through which an initial equilibrium is disturbed — dispersed in Neale's term — leading to an eventual resolution which sees a refiguration of the elements into a new equilibrium. Neale makes two important points about the basic model:

> The first is that the 'elements' in question, their equilibrium and disequilibrium, their order/disorder, are not simply reducible to the signified components of a given narrative situation, nor are they solely the product of the narrative considered as a single discourse or discursive structure. Rather they are signifiers articulated in a narrative process which is simultaneously that of the inscription of a number of discourses, and that of the modification, restructuration and transformation they each undergo as a result of their interaction. The second point, following from this, is that equilibrium and disequilibrium, order and disorder are essentially a function of the relations of coherence between the discourses involved, of the compatibilities and contradictions which exist between them.[16]

Genres are therefore to be read through the presentation of elements and the specific clustering of these elements. The relation of compatibility and contradiction which exists between the character of Dixon and the

227

character of Regan is an example of the development of a genre through the transformation of the constituent elements.

The elements which typify the police series in the 1970s become clear if we consider the structure of the pilot episode for *The Sweeney*. 'Regan' was first broadcast on 4 June 1974, as part of the *Armchair Theatre* programme. The story-line concerns the struggle between two gangs of criminals — one from north of the Thames and the other from south of the Thames — for dominance of the London underworld. When one of Regan's detective sergeants gets a hint of what is happening, it leads to his death. Regan's investigation owes as much to a sense of revenge as it does to any legalistic notion of justice. The narrative uncovers a cluster of four elements which define the parameters for the series.

The threat of crime

We are presented with a world of rival gangs commited to the ruthless eradication of any competition. As the story unwinds, we see that the situation is worse than we were led to suspect. The members of one gang actually murder their own leader because they have received a better offer from the rival gang leader. It is the threat to society which this attitude signifies that Regan and Carter act to protect us, the audience, from. This profession of violence legitimates the violence of *The Sweeney*. The sense of threat is heightened by the stark contrast between the stereotyped villains, who are violent solely in pursuit of their own immediate interests, and the human face of the heroes, who, even in the pilot episode, are presented as more rounded characters. Regan arrests Dale, the villain responsible for killing the policeman and his former boss, after a tense confrontation in a disused warehouse. Carter covers Dale with one gun as Dale's three thugs all hold their guns on Regan. By suggesting that the three can save themselves by not killing him, Regan persuades them to leave the building. Once they have gone, Regan tells Dale that he wants their full names and we know that they will be arrested later. In the process of asking the questions, Regan hits Dale several painful blows to the body. The last ends with Regan sprawled across the bonnet of Dale's limousine, where he sees the road fund disc on the windscreen. He tells Dale 'This stinking heap was licensed to March. It's April the 20th. I'll have you for that an' all.' This touch of humour defuses the tension and shows Regan to be more than the violent automatons that the villains represent.

The family

The human side of Regan is picked up again in the way the programme handles the presentation of the family. Regan has been married and has one daughter. This is made clear to the viewer when Regan receives a message to call on his ex-wife. The opening sequence of the scene where they meet puts their relationship into sharp focus:

Kate You're late. I kept Susie up to seven thirty. She was so excited. She thought she was going to see her dad. Poor kid fell asleep on the couch. I had to put her to bed. Why can't you ever be on time for us?

Jack I'm on an important case. There's a young copper . . .

Kate Look I'm not interested any more in your silly cases and your stupid criminals.

Jack What do you want to tell me?

Kate It would be a good idea if you ate regularly and drank less. Have you looked at yourself lately? You look terrible. You're 35 years old and you look 45.

Jack What do you want Kate?

Kate I'm thinking of getting married . . .

Regan never had any time for his wife or family, his work always had to come first. A point Regan makes to the recently married Carter who complains that his wife will nag him for working with Regan rather than in a routine job where he could keep reasonable hours. 'You're not a nine-to-five man. Over there sitting behind a desk, swigging tea all day and waiting to get home to the roses. You're like me, you're a copper.'

Regan has sacrificed his personal family for the greater good of us all. The same problem arises in any relationship he could have. In this episode, it is his latest girlfriend, Annie, who experiences this. She has done Jack's latest load of washing for him, and as he collects it she says:

Annie Well, if that's all that's wanted. . . .

Jack I haven't got time for anything else.

Annie Will I see you tonight?

Jack No.

Annie Tomorrow night?

Jack Definitely.

Annie One night in nine. Not bad: Who gets you the other eight?

Jack Oh, I'm sorry Annie, I've got a big job on.

Annie That right? Tell me, Jack, when do you ever have a small job on?

Jack Tomorrow night, I promise.

Annie Knock-out. I'll run home now, get into my negligee and wait by the window.

This attitudes towards Regan from women in the series signify the complete demarcation between the masculine world of work, as it is inscribed within *The Sweeney*, and the feminine obsession with the domestic — that which is not contained within the definition of 'work'.

Rule-breaking

Regan transgresses the moral code of society but within strictly contained limits. He is moderately permissive but heterosexual. He is a moderately heavy drinker but not an alcoholic. The same is true of his attitude towards

229

police work. His view is that the only good rule is one which allows him to catch criminals. When Carter asked him whether he thought breaking in to a club where they might find crucial evidence was a 'good idea', Regan replied: 'I think it is a good idea, yes. 'Cause if I don't sort this out in the next 12 hours before they get their Cowley inquiry organised, I'm out of the force for good. Now if you don't see it that way, then on your bike and out of my way.' He is against bureaucratic structures which would clip his freedom of action. The pilot episode makes this abundantly clear. As Regan tells Carter:

> You know what the latest is? Robbery squad, regional crime squad, all amalgamated into one sprawling mess. There'll be hundreds of little grey men all working on top of each other, pots of tea and committees. I'm one of the best D.I.s on the Squad, you know that, but they don't listen to me — they listen to committee men now.

The rule-bending covers minor indiscretions, like the breaking and entering of premises and using weapons without the proper authorisation. All of this is of no consequence in the quest for the villain. The final sequence of the programme has Carter saying to Regan: 'Got away with it again, didn't you?' Regan replies, 'Ah don't you start "got away with it". I got the bastard who did it:' This is the total and only explanation of his actions.

Individualism

This strand is inextricably linked with Regan's stance against bureaucratic restrictions. The contrast comes out in the sense of frustration that his superiors feel in dealing with him:

Haskins	He [Regan] is not listening to anyone . . . and contrary to my explicit instructions to go snooping around the Serious Crime Squad. Visit Tusser. Interview Mallory's girl friend. Now he's left orders for me to go and dig up some bloody farm!
Maynon	You mean disciplinary charges?
Haskins	Yes.
Maynon	It will not stop Regan. 20 years ago, he would have been a perfect cop in the days of the individualists. Now he's out on a limb. I sometimes wonder if these ideas are for the best.
Haskins	I think so, Sir.
Maynon	OK bring him in. Put him on suspension with full pay.
Haskins	Right, Sir.
Maynon	By the way I think he's right . . .

Regan's position is secured by his record of successful cases and of course he was right, but it is this individualism which sets him apart from the rest of the force. He could have gone through the correct procedures and arrrived at the same conclusion but, by cutting corners, he achieves the results more quickly.

The Sweeney does not offer a romantic notion of policing in the way that *Dixon of Dock Green* had done, but it still offers a powerful moral. The consensus no longer guarantees the police force the cooperation of the public but the police series underline repeatedly that any sensible person would help the police. Regan explains the situation to an ex-member of one of the gangs in this way:

> Detective Inspector Regan, Flying Squad. Now you work for Mallory so you know the score. I want to ask you some questions. You don't want to answer them. So, up front, I'll lay it on. This is a colleague of mine, he hits people. Isn't that right, colleague?

The questioning ends without a punch being thrown, as Regan says:

> Because you're smart. Now you stay smart. You think of all the things you'd tell us if you got very smart. We'll be back.

The answers are obtained, even if certain threats have to be made to elicit the information. We cannot expect the police to behave like perfect gentlemen because they are presented as the frontline soldiers in the war against crime and not as boy scouts.

The generic specificity of the police series in the 1970s owes much to the way that the attempt to confront contemporary situations was situated within a framework set by the earlier series. Overthrowing the stylistic conventions of the earlier series was not enough to free series like *The Sweeney* and *Target* from the moral certainties of the previous series. It is possible to see how these series help to construct the understanding of the law and order issue through portraying fictional resolutions to what become ever more familiar problems. Each episode poses the threat anew, each episode provides a restoration of the equilibrium within the established framework.

Attempts have been made to operate outside this framework, particularly in the serial format. Freed of the constraints of the series conventions both *Law and Order* and *Out* challenged the pattern of presentation by concentrating on the corruption of the police. These serials were condemned for overemphasising the extent and scope of corruption and the Metropolitan police withdrew all cooperation with series made by the BBC. Even within these serials, the power of the genre and the institutional practices which facilitate the production of series held the serials within their parameters. The police are still seen to restore the equilibrium by their positive intervention and even their corruption is portrayed as motivated by an underlying desire to stamp out crime.

The 1970s series have themselves been superseded by a return to a more orderly, gentler world of crime in series like *Juliet Bravo* and *The Gentle Touch*.[17] These series feature women in senior positions and use this device to present the world of crime from what is presented as a new perspective. The 'feminine' viewpoint allows the return of the social conscience into the series creating an angle of interest. In fact what is produced is the

Alan Clarke

recreation of an earlier presentation, previously seen in the late 1960s episodes of *Z Cars, No Hiding Place* and other such series. The use of women in key roles defuses the representation of violence by overlaying a caring dimension to the work of the police officer. In this change a transformation in the genre is accomplished, not in the change of character but through the reordering of the ideological elements.

The transformation of the genre is the product of the social forces of production shaping the clustering of the elements. The political forces of society cannot be disentangled from this configuration, the dramas are enacted within a structured ideological field.[18] The role in shaping the consensus, which is not a simple entity but a complex set of matrices, is important here. It is not that the police series are partisan in any straightforward sense but that they are contained within the mode of reality of the state. As such they constitute one site on which ideological struggle can take place. As this brief sketch has shown, the continuities which this generates are central to the understanding of each specific moment of ideological production.

Notes

1. F. Walker, 'It's The Sweeney', *Fiesta*, vol. 11, no. 6, 1977, p. 26.
2. See P. Kerr, 'Watching the Detectives', *Prime Time*, vol. 1, 1981.
3. See C. Wicking and T. Vahmagi, *The American Vein*, Talisman Books, London, 1979
4. See L. Staig and T. Williams, *Italian Western: the opera of violence*, Lorimar, London, 1975.
5. See I. Cameron, *Crime Films*, Hamlyn, London, 1975.
6. See A. Clarke, 'Holding the Blue Lamp', *Crime and Social Justice*, 19, 1983.
7. See S. Hall, C. Critcher, T. Jefferson, J. Clarke and B. Roberts, *Policing the Crisis. Mugging, the State and Law and Order*, Macmillan, London, 1978.
8. See V. Voloshinov, *Marxism and the Philosophy of Language*, Seminar Press, New York, 1973.
9. See R. Barthes, *Mythologies*, Paladin, St Albans, 1976.
10. See H.R.F. Keating (ed.), *Crimewriters*, BBC Publications, London, 1978.
11. *Financial Times*, 28 July 1981.
12. See T. Ryall, *BFI Teachers' Study Guide 2: Gangster Film*, British Film Institute London, 1978.
13. See C. McArthur, *Underworld USA*, Secker and Warburg, London, 1972.
14. See T. Kitses, *Horizons West*, Secker and Warburg, London, 1969.
15. S. Neale, *Genre*, British Film Institute, London, 1980, p. 20.
16. Ibid, p. 20.
17. See A. Clarke, 'An Interview with the Chinese Detective', *Marxism Today*, October, 1983.
18. See S. Hall, 'Culture, the media and the ideological effect', in J. Curran, M. Gurevitch and J. Woollacott (eds.), *Mass Communication and Society*, Edward Arnold, London, 1977.

Index

Abercrombie, Nicholas xix
Ack Ack Beer Beer 113
Addison, P. 116
Adorno, Theodor W. xi, 21, 157, 160–1, 168; on the culture industry 17; on popular music
Afro-American music 161, 164; influence of 165–7
Agony 202, 216
Albury, David 89
Alexander's Ragtime Band 166
Alexander, Sally 88, 90, 92
Allen, Tony 212
Althusser, Louis 213
Altick, R. 48
American Forces Network 111
Americanisation, attitudes to 11, 109–11, 142, 146, 150–1
Amis, Kingsley 186
Anderson, Benedict 13, 21, 181–3, 189, 194
Anderson, Perry 28, 143, 153
And Mother Makes Five 209
Armchair Theatre 228
Arnold, Mathew xi, 11, 51; on culture and the state 41; influence of 42–3
Arts Council 38
Aspinal, A. 49
At the Armstrongs 100, 113
Attwood, Thomas 79–80
audience studies 43, 53–4, 94, 97–8; see also *Listener Research Unit* under *British Broadcasting Corporation*
Avron, D. 172, 176
Award for Industry 102

Bakhtin, Mikhail 4, 14, 154, 194; on carnival 60, 147–8, 152; on the novel 190
Baldwin, Stanley 44
Ballad of You and Me and Poeneil, The 168
Balzac, Honoré de 177
Bamford, Jemima 77–8, 80, 89; at Peterloo 73–5
Bamford, Samuel 89–90; at Peterloo 73–5
Banks, Marjorie 102
Banks, Tony 6
Barrie, Sir James Mathew 124
Barthes, Roland 4, 51, 54, 68; 156–9, 175–6, 232; on pleasure 54–5, 169–73; on Charlie Chaplin 61–2
Beach Boys, the 166
Beatles, the 168, 173
Benjamin, Walter 67
Bennett, Tony xvii–xviii, 2–3, 20–1, 49, 60, 71–2, 116, 154
Benny, Jack 110
Bentham, Jeremy 51, 91; and panopticism 65
Berkely, Busby 67
Berlin, Irving 166
Berridge, V. 49
Beveridge, William 96
Beveridge Committee 45; Report 96, 106; BBC coverage of 107
Bevin, Ernest 95
Bhabha, Homi K. 134
Birmingham Brotherly Society 86, 91
Birmingham Journal, The 79
Birmingham Political Union 79

233